David Cronenberg:
Author or Film-maker?

Mark Browning

'The time of desperate stratagems was over, the car crashes and hallucinogens, the deviant sex ransacked like a library of extreme metaphors.'
(*The Kindness of Women*, J. G. Ballard)

David Cronenberg:
Author or Film-maker?

Mark Browning

intellect Bristol, UK / Chicago, USA

First Published in the UK in 2007 by
Intellect Books, PO Box 862, Bristol BS99 1DE, UK

First published in the USA in 2007 by
Intellect Books, The University of Chicago Press, 1427 E. 60th Street, Chicago,
IL 60637, USA

A catalogue record for this book is available from the British Library.

Cover Design: Gabriel Solomons
Copy Editor: Holly Spradling
Typesetting: Mac Style, Nafferton, E. Yorkshire

ISBN 978-1-84150-173-4

Printed and bound by Gutenberg Press, Malta

CONTENTS

INTRODUCTION:
'A LIBRARY OF EXTREME METAPHORS'[1]

'There are things you can do in fiction and in writing that you simply cannot do in cinema and vice versa. I don't think one supplants the other; ideally they enhance, reflect one another...I have great respect for the art of fiction, huge in fact'.[2]

In the 23-year period between *Videodrome* (1982) and *A History of Violence* (2005), Canadian director David Cronenberg has been repeatedly drawn to basing his films on the literary works of others. He has realized a series of adaptations from a number of sources, including *Naked Lunch* (1991) from William Burroughs' 1959 experimental novel, *Crash* (1996) from J. G. Ballard's 1973 cult text and *Spider* (2003) from Patrick McGrath's dark 1990 account of a mental patient's subjective universe. Even films not ostensibly adaptations draw on previous written material, for example, *Dead Ringers* (1988) derives directly from Jack Geasland and Bari Woods' novel *Twins* (1977). Almost in passing, Gaile McGregor, looking at Cronenberg from the perspective of Canadian culture, feels that 'literary parallels provide a key', but rather disappointingly provides few specific detailed examples.[3] This book will examine specific passages of literature that can be used to highlight previously neglected features of Cronenberg's cinema, endeavouring to avoid what Andrew Klevan sees as a lack of close reading in critical work on Cronenberg.[4]

In terms of critical analysis, the period upon which this book will focus is effectively 'book-ended' by the collection of essays *The Shape of Rage* (edited by Piers Handling, 1983) and *The Modern Fantastic: The Films of David Cronenberg* (edited by Michael Grant, 2000). Peter Morris' *A Delicate Balance* (1993) provides a sketchy outline of Cronenberg's work up to *Naked Lunch* (1991), and Chris Rodley's *Cronenberg on Cronenberg* (1992) and Serge Grünberg's *David Cronenberg* (2004), although very valuable, are both composed of a series of interviews with the director, rather than detailed commentaries on his films. Michael Grant's *Dead Ringers* (1997) and Iain Sinclair's *Crash* (1999) focus on individual films, but until William Beard's *The Artist as Monster* (2001), there was no single-authored book-length study of Cronenberg in English, analysing the central span of his career. Beard's text is largely a compilation of previously published material (much of which is referred to in this study) and focuses on binary oppositions rather than detailed comment on the literary works of figures like Vladimir Nabokov. This book will also refer to certain philosophical figures, such as Ludwig Wittgenstein and Jean-Paul Sartre, whose work Cronenberg readily discusses in interviews.[5] The distinction between fiction and philosophy can be fairly protean, and the work of some philosophers such as Jean Baudrillard reads more like novels at times, and writers like the Marquis de Sade and Sartre juxtapose dramatic events with more abstract musings.

There is a nexus of literary connections surrounding Cronenberg's films, ranging from trivial facts like Burroughs' personal acquaintance with Debbie Harry, star of *Videodrome*, to more concrete examples, such as Burroughs' authorship of the preface to the American edition of Ballard's *The Atrocity Exhibition* (1969).[6] Ballard, in turn, is a great admirer of Burroughs whose fiction, he believes, 'constitutes the first portrait of the inner landscape of the post-war world'.[7] All the main literary influences on Cronenberg discussed in this book, Nabokov, Burroughs, Ballard, Barker, even Brett Easton Ellis, use cinematic terms and allusions in their writing, all display a strong interest in film, and several have had some involvement with writing screenplays.[8] Cronenberg's literary awareness is present even in projects he never actually started, such as *Frankenstein*, those involving months of preparation, like *Total Recall*, based on Philip K. Dick's short story 'We Can Remember It For You Wholesale' (1966) and potential future projects, such as Martin Amis' 1989 novel *London Fields*.

Goals of the book

The primary goal of the book is to consider how comparisons between literary texts and Cronenberg's films can highlight features of his work that have remained relatively neglected by critics and take this a stage further to reveal fresh areas that have, hitherto, not been commented upon at all. The consideration of the relationship between Cronenberg and literature will focus on three main areas. Firstly, the book will examine direct adaptations from a literary source, for example, Ballard's *Crash* and Burroughs' *Naked Lunch*. A key feature of such discussions will be what Cronenberg has made of his source material, including what has been added or removed and how literary material has been visualized. Secondly, the study will look at texts that have influenced Cronenberg's films more tangentially, including literary sources cited directly in the films themselves, which may or may not be acknowledged by the director himself, e.g. Bari Wood and Jack Geasland's 1977 novel *Twins* (itself based on a real event – see chapter 2). Thirdly, texts that can be used as analogous material, will be discussed, e.g. links that could be made between *Videodrome* (1982) and Clive Barker's *Books of Blood* (1984, 1985) or Brett Easton Ellis' *American Psycho* (1991). In these latter cases, there will be no attempt to prove a causal link (indeed this is not possible where the text was produced after the film concerned). Notions of influence will therefore fall into three (often closely related) categories: overt translation, covert translation and analogy.

The importance of psychoanalysis to the horror genre and Cronenberg

Psychoanalysis has certainly been an important tool in the analysis of film, evolving through the 1970s, where the theories of Sigmund Freud and Jacques Lacan, particularly those concerning the unconscious and sexuality, castration anxiety, oedipalized narratives and hysteria, were used to explore the notion of the apparatus of cinema and relationships between spectator and film. However, in an article in *Screen*, Richard Rushton suggests that 'the engagement between psychoanalysis and cinema has, to a large degree, disappeared from the agenda of most film students and scholars'.[9] This may be true in some areas of film scholarship but in the study of horror (and directors most frequently associated with this genre) such frameworks endure. Indeed, in 1998, *Screen* carried a number of pieces about David Cronenberg's *Crash* (1996), including models of criticism that overtly draw upon psychoanalytical models. This introduction is not dismissing psychoanalysis wholesale as a legitimate approach to the study of film per se but suggests that there are significant problems with using most psychoanalytical frameworks to analyse Cronenberg's work. This has implications for other film-makers who may have stylistic and aesthetic similarities with Cronenberg and for the horror genre as a whole, which has historically been viewed through the distorting prism of Freudian notions of psychoanalysis.

According to Noel Carroll, the adoption of Freudian analysis has become 'more or less the *lingua franca* of the horror film and thus the privileged tool for discussing the genre.'[10] In *The Philosophy of Horror* (1990), Carroll accepts that psychoanalysis can provide some insights into particular aspects of the horror genre but that it cannot offer a comprehensive account. One example of such insight comes in Carroll's discussion of Ernest Jones' *On the Nightmare* (1936), which follows a Freudian-influenced notion of repression and sees dreams as unconscious wish-fulfilments. As critics like Vicky Lebeau have explored, there are interesting parallels between the evolution of psychoanalysis, especially in the career of Freud and the development of cinema, and to make generalized links between the dream-like state of viewing a film in a cinema and a discipline, which includes the interpretation of dreams, seems fair.[11] However, such a totalizing critical framework, which can apparently be applied to any film, can also seem indiscriminate and likely to yield repetitive outcomes. There are occasional dreams in Cronenberg's work, notably in *Dead Ringers* (discussed in chapter 2), but even Lacanian notions of a divided subject struggle to ascribe consistent motivation to characters when they are part of highly subjective narratives, such as we find in *Videodrome* (1982), *Naked Lunch* (1991), *eXistenZ* (1999) and *Spider* (2003).

James B. Twitchell locates the psychological purpose of the horror genre as cultural fortification against sexual taboos, especially masturbation and incest and social roles ('precisely whom to avoid as reproductive partners').[12] However, Cronenberg's films work in precisely the opposite direction, challenging rather than reinforcing notions of what constitutes taboo acts. Twitchell's stance is undermined by assumptions that audiences of horror films, whilst admitting there is no research base for his assertions, are predominantly adolescent and male and cater for sadistic pleasures, apparently denying viewing positions which encompass female, post-teen and masochistic identification and pleasure (as explored subsequently by theorists such as Carol J. Clover).[13]

For Freudian-influenced critics like Robin Wood, horror films articulate the return of certain ideas that individuals have tried, unsuccessfully, to repress but which only emerge in unexpected and displaced locations.[14] He proposes that psychoanalysis, in conjunction with feminism and gay liberation and Marxism, can help to question how patriarchal capitalist ideology is created and perpetuated. For him, the horror genre's monstrous 'Other' represents the attempted but unsuccessful repression of characteristics and entities, which a dominant capitalist, heterosexual ideology needs to exclude in order to maintain its centrality. However, Wood's notion that 'normality is threatened by the monster,' is not borne out in Cronenberg's case.[15] The narratives of almost all of the films after 1982 (*Videodrome*, *Dead Ringers*, *Naked Lunch*, *Crash*, *eXistenZ* and *Spider*), problematize exactly what constitutes 'normality'. Even accepting Wood's broad definition of 'normality' as 'conformity to the dominant social norms', Cronenberg's work conveys little sense of an equilibrium from which the entrance of a monstrous 'Other' forces the narrative to depart or to which it might return in some kind of 'happy ending'.[16]

Wood describes how 'in a society built on monogamy and family there will be an enormous amount of surplus energy that will have to be repressed, and that what is repressed must always strive to return.'[17] However, in Cronenberg's work, at least up to *A History of Violence* (2005), the narratives make no attempt to construct 'a society built on monogamy and family'. The mechanisms that dominate the protagonists' central relationships include open and promiscuous marriages in *Naked Lunch* and *Crash*, thinly veiled incestuous desire in *Dead Ringers* and sado-masochistic pornography in *Videodrome*. The underlying assumption of Wood's case is that horror films are 'our collective nightmares' and yet it is Cronenberg's intensely personal vision that is part of what distinguishes his work from mainstream horror.[18]

It could be said that part of the appeal of horror films is the vicarious pleasure they allow in rehearsing and thereby subduing subconscious fears, such as one's own death by watching a series of victims succumb to a monstrous attacker. Contemporary horror films often focus on the physical and metaphysical limits of the body, both of the (usually female) victim of a monster and the monster itself.

This has been an important focus for psychoanalytical work such as Julia Kristeva's *Powers of Horror: An Essay in Abjection* (1982) and Barbara Creed's work, based on it, especially *The Monstrous-Feminine: Film, Feminism, Psychoanalysis* (1993). Abjection, castration anxiety and the position of the abject can provide useful insights if there is a monstrous mother figure who terrifies with the threat of castration. However, the films of Cronenberg under discussion here do not feature such a character type. Furthermore, Cronenberg has shown little or no interest in classic horror subgenres like werewolf or vampire tales, stalk-and-slash narratives or supernatural horror. Standard horror tropes like the screaming victim, male or female, play little part in his aesthetic. Protagonists largely accept and indeed embrace monstrous change and death as part of a process of evolutionary, biological change.

Psychoanalysis can be helpful in making links between the subtext of a film and the culture of which it is a part or upon which it comments, as seen in the socio-historical aspect work of critics like Charles Derry (1977), Peter Biskind (1983), Andrew Tudor (1989) and Vera Dika (1990). However, if Robin Wood feels that the notion of the 'return of the repressed' only has validity when applied to a political context, then this is precisely what is missing here. Cronenberg takes great pains to remove from his work any suggestion of a sociological link. Directorial choices in each of the films discussed in this study make allegorical readings of his films difficult, such as the cutting of any references to parents from the adapted source of *Dead Ringers*, the removal of time markers from the narrative of *Crash*, and the basic structure of *Naked Lunch* showing a narrative in the process of being constructed. In *eXistenZ*, Cronenberg took the conscious decision to remove any technical or cultural references which would allow sociological readings of the film. So, there are no computers or TVs, no running shoes, no jewellery or patterns on the clothing. Cronenberg explains that 'it's my attempt to dislocate the audience without being really obvious about it.'[19] It could be said that this very absence draws the viewer's attention to underlying issues but this is 'political' with a small 'p'. Cronenberg focuses on existential dilemmas of what it is to be human, rather than how these conflicts are played out in wider society. Occasionally, the outside world intrudes, such as when the Mantle brothers' deviance in *Dead Ringers* can no longer be ignored (see chapter 2) but the environments in which Cronenberg's protagonists move are largely enclosed, private, and mostly highly subjective. In terms of character, they are often eccentric outsiders and not typical of a class, a gender or ethnicity; it is their *difference*, not their typicality, which makes them interesting and possibly also hard for audiences to relate to at times. Attempts to argue that his films constitute sociological statements, for example, Xavier Trudel's suggestions that *Crash* represents a warning about the dangers of cults, just seem contrived and unconvincing.[20] Indeed, Cronenberg has been criticized for overtly severing links where they existed in his source material, so that in relation to *Crash*, Iain Sinclair feels that Cronenberg's film 'depoliticises Ballard's frenzied satire.'[21]

In terms of surface content, Cronenberg's work includes topics that do feature in a range of psychological theories: repression (homosexuality in *Naked Lunch*), interpretation of dreams (*Dead Ringers*) and sexual activity that could be regarded as perverted and a compulsion towards death (*Crash*). However, once specific analysis starts, it soon breaks down. Marq Smith attempts to view *Crash* using Freudian notions of fore-pleasure, seen as a stage on the way to full consummation or end-pleasure. He accepts Freud's definition of perversions as 'sexual activities which...linger over the intermediate relations to the sexual object', but such definitions, including 'sexual activities which...extend, in an anatomical sense, beyond the regions of the body that are designed for sexual union',[22] are explicitly questioned in *Crash*. Cronenberg has been interested in re-siting sites of sexual interaction, ever since Forsythe's dream in *Shivers* (1976) where 'even old flesh is erotic flesh' and Rose's penile armpit growth in *Rabid* (1977), but this process finds further articulation with Gabrielle's vaginal-style scar in *Crash*. Notions of 'perversion' can only hold true if there is a consensual norm, from which characters are seen to 'deviate'. Significantly at *no* time in the film does any character express any doubts or qualms about any of the sexual activities undertaken, which raises the question of whether an action in a fictional world can be dubbed perverted if no one in that world sees it as such. The notion of what constitute 'perversions' is culturally determined and, therefore, will change over time, such as the increase in importance in the late twentieth century of active fore-pleasure in a sexually enlightened, and particularly post-AIDS, culture.

In 1972, as Ballard was putting the finishing touches to his novel *Crash*, Bernado Bertolucci was directing *The Last Tango in Paris*, featuring a sex scene where Maria Schneider, as Jeanne, suggests to Marlon Brando, as Paul, that they try to 'come without touching'. Bertolucci, an admirer of Cronenberg's *Crash*, also dramatizes the potential power of touch, *not* in the sense of end-pleasure as Freudian perversion but as a perfectly legitimate end in itself, including a transcendent capacity often associated with religious experience. Smith admits as much in referring to 'a different order of sexual contact' in *Crash* which 'takes the form of an offer of both explicit and discreet instances of touching between human and extrahuman bodies, bodily parts, things, and surfaces. Some of these instances confer a different manner of sexuality, others imply a nonsexual intimacy', such as the slow tracking shot used as Catherine lingeringly caresses James' injured leg.[23]

In analysing the overt sexual content of *Naked Lunch*, *Crash* or *Videodrome*, and the barely suppressed homoerotic impulses of *Dead Ringers* (1988), assumptions of normative relations between the sexes are not helpful. Developments in reproductive technology, gay and lesbian equality, greater economic female liberation and the open discussion of many topics so suppressed in Freud's era, that they were not even recognized, casts a Freudian model of the family based on married heterosexuality as largely redundant. Ideas that Freud took as psychological givens, like the manifestation and frequency of hysteria, are now seen to vary according to cultural shifts and Freud's psychoanalytical approach *'presumes* heterosexuality to such a degree that it often appears to *demand* it'.[24] In Cronenberg's work, sexual practices linked to masochism and sadism are not tied exclusively to heterosexual relationships and a range of sexual contexts, including extra-marital sex, sex with prostitutes, sex in public places and 'deviant' sexual practices, such as anal sex, sado-masochism and lesbianism, all take place with little apparent discrimination between them.

A critical standpoint that sees the portrayal of same-sex relationships or sadistic acts as necessarily implying disgust is going to struggle to accommodate Cronenberg's work. In relation to the car wash scene in *Crash*, Creed asserts that this scene is 'the only one in which sex involves vaginal entry and in which the woman is beaten' and, furthermore, feels that Catherine, 'contrary to her expectations is not aroused by Vaughan's violence.'[25] This ignores the likelihood that at least some of the rear-entry sex is vaginal, especially the earlier scene of Catherine sitting astride James in their flat (although it is an impossible distinction to prove either way) and also passes over Catherine's apparent acquiescence to being treated in this way. Creed feels that 'unlike the anal sex scenes (which almost always commence with the woman offering her breast to the man), and the episode of "wound" sex, this one is not only "disconnected", it is sadistic'.[26] However, Catherine *does* offer her breast as before, her lengthy staring at Vaughan in the car does indicate attraction and what Creed sees as a weakness, dismissing the scene as 'sadistic', is arguably a crucial point for Ballard and Cronenberg. For them, Creed's criticism, that 'the possibility of union between human and machine is displaced, in the main, on to the woman's body', represents a creative development in the range of human sexuality in which concepts of gender seem less important than a potential fusion with technology. [27]

Similarly, Creed describes the parrot cage scene in Cronenberg's *Naked Lunch* (1991) as 'horrific and sadistic', but this is attributing to the characters the emotions of this particular viewer.[28] Sadism can be pleasurable and it is ambiguous whether Kiki is either horrified or that he is being 'raped' as Creed asserts. Barker's *The Hellbound Heart* (1986), which he directed as *Hellraiser* (1987), contains an episode very similar to *Crash*'s post-car wash scene in which monstrous villain Frank seduces the heroine, Julia, and their coupling 'had, in every regard *but the matter of her acquiescence*, all the aggression and joylessness of rape', and 'the bruises were trophies of their passion'.[29] Like the rough rear-entry sex in *Basic Instinct* (Paul Verhoeven, 1992), between Nick (Michael Douglas) and Beth (Jeanne Tripplehorn) and what Cronenberg terms the 'gangster-sex' of Tom-as-Joey and Edie on the stairs in *A History of Violence* (2005), it contains the same key proviso of *consent*. Cronenberg's and Clive Barker's mutual distrust of simplistic and manipulative psychoanalysis is seen in the casting of Cronenberg as the deranged therapist Decker in *Nightbreed* (1989), based on Barker's own 1988 novel, *Cabal*.

A problem with Creed's notion of the 'monstrous-feminine', is that there are very few films that neatly fit her theoretical paradigm, and those that do, such as *Alien* (Ridley Scott, 1979), seem to constitute a self-fulfilling prophecy, i.e. she discovers in the film the model that she proposes, rather than deriving a model from the evidence in the film. Cronenberg's films clearly do feature notions of monstrosity but apart from *The Fly* (1986), in the last 20 years, there is a lack of what might be termed a clear-cut monster, even given Robin Wood's broad definition of what this term might constitute.[30] Furthermore, an underlying problem for psychoanalytical frameworks is that they cannot accommodate alternative ways of reading a text. Sequences cited as evidence of Creed's theories can be read in ways that do not support her argument, particularly connected with imposed moral judgements about sexual activities and pleasure.

Creed's position partly relies upon Kristevan theories, which themselves are problematic. Kristeva's notions of what is 'clean' and 'proper', are extremely subjective and protean concepts, dependent on cultural factors and given to change over time.[31] Furthermore, Kristeva's position attempts to illuminate ideas of sexuality in the context of Old Testament morality, thereby rather blurring the logical sequence of cause and effect, seeking to explain God-given law in psychological terms. Kristeva categorically states that '[a]n unshakeable adherence to Prohibition and Law is necesssary if that perverse interspace of abjection is to be hemmed in and thrust aside,' that 'he who denies morality is not abject' and that abjection is explicitly linked to acts that are 'immoral'.[32] However, notions of perversity are meaningless in the amoral universes of films like *Naked Lunch*, *Dead Ringers* and particularly *Crash*. For Kristeva, abjection manifests itself as a 'rite of defilement' and 'persists as exclusion or taboo'.[33] However, it is not feasible to draw on incest taboos in particular to explain character motivation, when no parental relationships are contained in the main films discussed here and when the only familial relationship is between the brothers in *Dead Ringers*. For all the discussion in Kristeva about narcissism, she has to admit that 'a narcissistic topology has no other underpinning in psychosomatic reality than the mother-child dyad,' a relationship axis which Cronenberg explicitly denies us between 1982 and 1999 and only uses in *Spider* (2003) as part of an unreliable, delusional memory.[34]

As the generic label suggests, horror tends to evoke visceral responses, particularly fear, by exposure to images, which audiences find repulsive or shocking. However, fear, both in the characters on screen, or engendered in the viewing audience by sudden movement or sound, does not play a significant part in Cronenberg's films after 1982. Indeed, images, which we might find shocking are usually approached by languid camera movement and held in shot for several seconds, such as the two-headed lizard in *eXistenZ*. This reflects Cronenberg's fascination with the notion of sentient existence as being in a state of flux, constantly evolving into alternative incarnations. These might be potentially horrific but there remains a strong sense of fascination, which we are encouraged to share by Cronenberg's insistence on opening up and showing aspects of bodies, at which we might otherwise choose not to look (see chapters 1 and 2) and by the persistent avoidance of a voice-over in all his work, which could provide a voice of consolation and comforting explanation for what we are seeing. If Kristeva believes that the individual suffering a state of abjection 'causes, along with loathing, one word to crop up – fear,' then it would seem irrelevant to films largely devoid of this.[35]

The scarcity of clear attempts by Cronenberg to evoke fear in his audience after 1982 is also one reason why Freud's notions of the uncanny, often central to psychoanalysis of horror films, are also not particularly helpful here. It could be argued that in a film such as *Dead Ringers*, the appearance of the phenomenon of the double, which is a central example of Freudian notions of the uncanny, should make reference to Freud illuminating. However, apart from the single scene where Clare sees both brothers together for the first time, the uncanny is not evoked. Unlike Clare, the cinematic viewer has seen both brothers from the beginning as children and by using real identical twins rather than computer-aided motion photography, Cronenberg acclimatizes us to this unusual sight. By the time we encounter the adult Mantles in medical school, we are not likely to be surprised by their appearance any more than any other characters within that scene, who show no reaction at all to working alongside identical twins. To use a Freudian approach to Cronenberg's work would have to ignore the aesthetic reality of his style.

Lacan and the question of 'flatness'

Lacanian notions that rely on a Saussurean linguistic model of a stable relation between signifier and signified in which phonetics and semantics can be straightforwardly mapped are problematic, as such concepts have been largely dismissed. The grammatical revolution that Noam Chomsky caused with *Syntactic Structures* (1957) moved the analytical focus from word to sentence and questioned how Saussurean structures cope with ambiguity, language change or how meaning is made from previously unheard sentences. Furthermore, Lacan problematically ascribes to linguistic features the status of psychological phenomena, equating a Saussurean signifier with the conscious and a signified with the unconscious. Despite Saussure's original attempt to avoid assumptions about how individuals think when they use certain words, this is how Lacan applies Saussurean theory and yet still keeps his analysis focused on the operation of language as if it were an entity independent of the speaker who uses it. Modern developments in cognitive science and neurology by figures like Oliver Sacks show language processing as more complex than the kinds of binary relationships adopted by Lacan.

The best way to show the shortcomings of psychoanalysis as a theoretical model in relation to Cronenberg is to consider closely the most detailed example of where this model has been tried. Parveen Adams' essay on *Crash*, 'Death Drive', represents the most detailed attempt to date to apply psychoanalysis (here of a Lacanian variety) to Cronenberg's work. Adams suggests that *Crash* 'puts you at the very limit of three-dimensional space', which she terms 'flatness', claiming that 'the film alters the psychical situation of the viewer by depriving us of all the usual parameters of depth.' Her position is based around notions of visible construction, the use of repetition and a lack of overt framing in filmic enunciation. However, Adams' argument about how Cronenberg constructs screen space can be refuted almost point for point. Certainly in *Dead Ringers*, the reverse tracking shots of the Mantle brothers firstly as boys and then as students, in which they do not walk in front of each other, emphasize a plane within and across the shot, not *through* the frame in order to create depth.[36] However, by contrast, in *Crash*, where Cronenberg does not have to consider the restraints of motion-controlled photography, the forward tracking shots in the opening scene, the love scene in the apartment and the pile-up sequence all create a sense of depth.

Adams compares *Crash* with Robert Bresson's *Lancelot du Lac* (1974) and asserts that Bresson 'sets a limit on flatness with a depth that constitutes itself through a series of flat but *nested* surfaces', which she calls '*formal depth.*'[37] Cronenberg is effectively following the advice of Carl Dreyer, who once suggested that to heighten audience involvement in the image, 'one could move away from the perspectivistic picture and pass on to pure surface effect. It is possible that by taking this direction we might obtain quite singular aesthetic effects.'[38] Dreyer's notion of reducing the third dimension, depth, and thereby relating the first two (the horizontal and vertical) to Time and Spirit, the fourth and fifth respectively, may partly explain why, for critics like Bertolucci, *Crash* seems 'a religious masterpiece'.[39] Adams does not discuss Cronenberg's car wash scene in detail, but here the forward motion of the car in combination with the electric roof and window creates an elaborate mosaic of screening devices moving vertically and horizontally, which obscure parts of the frame but also focus attention on the remaining parts, which reveal the interior of the car and the embracing lovers, effectively creating a high-tech version of the iris. Indeed, the screen is more than just segmented because as the glass is tinted, the focus of viewer attention is not completely closed off, so that this closing of the shell of the car also creates a sense of playing with varying planes of depth. This is also captured in the shifting vectors in the credit sequences of *M Butterfly* and *eXistenZ*, which give the illusion of different movements and speeds within three dimensions. Movement *across* the frame creates the illusion of depth *within* it.

For Adams, this 'flatness' is partly achieved by Cronenberg's camera placement that 'involves a limited, narrow direction of view where you remain in the same place even though you are moving, and where what you see does not vary.'[40] She does not provide specific details but this effect is present in James' taxi ride back from the hospital.[41] Adams cites Cronenberg describing how he 'put it (the camera) more *outboard* of the car body...' and elsewhere he has spoken about how, in an attempt to avoid cinematic clichés about sex and cars, he 'split the screen, the driver on the left half and the road, far down the road, on the right.'[42] However, this does not produce, as she claims, an effect in which 'what you see does not vary.'[43] The camera may be fixed but the car in question (James' taxi) is moving. This creates the effect of clinging onto the car with one's head pressed sideways against the door as if in an embrace – the pose adopted by Catherine at the close of the first scene in the aircraft hanger and later by Gabrielle in the car showroom. The effect of this is the sense that 'you hadn't seen this relationship of driver to car, or car to road, or car to car before,' so that both passenger and the length of the car and a portion of road can be viewed simultaneously.[44] In relation to cars, Cronenberg rarely uses conventional camera placement in this film, like a shot from the bonnet through the windscreen, undermining Adams' claims that 'in *Crash*, the film's construction remains in the background even as we experience the flatness.'[45] Indeed, for Sinclair, the drifting tracking shot of the opening scene, which is 'stately and voyeuristic in intent, announces the presence of the crew,' emphasizing that what we are witnessing 'is being staged for the benefit of an audience.'[46] Far from construction being hidden, it is highly foregrounded as reflected in one of Cronenberg's additions to Ballard's novel, the reconstruction of the James Dean crash as a spectacle (discussed at greater length in chapter 4).

Adams' analysis of what she sees as the flatness in *Crash* is dependent on a Lacanian notion of subject formation in relation to the Other, involving a sequence whereby there must be phases of seeing, comprehending and concluding before the subject can enter the three-dimensional space of the Other. However, time is precisely the dimension that Cronenberg denies the audience by placing them in a perpetual present. Notions such as memory and related narrative features like flashbacks (except in *Spider*, where it is problematized) play no part in Cronenberg's aesthetic in the films discussed here. The limitations of Freudian and Lacanian paradigms can be seen in Adams' designation of the accident between Helen and James, in which Helen's husband is killed, as 'a primal scene'.[47] Notions of primal scenes only make literal sense during discussions of childhood trauma and no children feature in any substantial way in this or indeed any other Cronenberg film in the period 1982–1999 (see chapter 6 for discussion of this in relation to *Spider*). *Dead Ringers* is the only minor exception to this and, after a very brief prologue, Cronenberg removes any mention of a family background which is present in the source material, thereby denying any attempt to read adult psychosis as the product of a childhood trauma. Even if taken metaphorically, and with a definition of 'primal' stretched to mean the first example of an adult trauma, the concept does not work in relation to *Crash*. The accident between Helen and James may be the first crash we see and the first involving James, but the scars on the dead man's hand, Helen's instinctive reaction in revealing her breast and her later familiarity with Seagrave and other crash devotees all suggest that this is not the first time that she has experienced a crash.

Adams asserts that '*Crash* swallows up space, producing the effect of flatness. If this is true, *Crash* cannot accommodate a space of voyeuristic desire.'[48] The problem is that Adams' premise is not true and the film can accommodate desire. For example, the car wash scene and the central love-making scene between James and Catherine are both very overtly voyeuristic. In particular in the latter scene, we experience a POV that slips into the room apparently unseen and gradually moves closer to the bed, cutting in on the axis, giving a privileged view of the sex act, using the standard porn trope of an unseen viewer. Whether desire is produced in the cinema audience is unprovable without detailed physiological research but within the confines of the film, characters take part in sex acts that, put bluntly, would not be possible without a modicum of desire. Adams' suggestion that the film 'describes the space in which death begins to appear as the object of a new desire, the desire not to desire', is rather undermined by the fact that Vaughan does die, apparently happy.[49] Although there is the suggestion of circularity (which chapter 5 will suggest is developmental rather than empty), there is also closure in the figure of Vaughan, who effectively consummates his relationship with death. His sex acts with an airport prostitute, Catherine and with James himself are steps on the way to his ultimate expression in the death crash.

Certainly, there is a scarcity of jouissance, particularly for female characters. In the third scene, the questions between James and Catherine only refer to female pleasure and parallel the exchange between Joan and Lee in *Naked Lunch*, where there is a verbal sharing of sexual infidelities between a married couple (albeit with the resignation of the husband rather than active involvement in contriving liaisons as in *Crash*). However, James can still perform sexually, and Vaughan in the car wash produces visual evidence of jouissance. Indeed, the sperm, which is held in shot on Catherine's hand, seems almost designed to verify its possibility in the world of the film. The film portrays an evolution in the language of desire, not a denial that it can take place at all. It may be soulless and require stage-managed repetition, but it endures, as does the relationship of James and Catherine.

The flatness that Adams ascribes to a lack of self-reflexive awareness in *Crash* is more precisely created by what Victor Sage refers to as 'extreme stylisation', involving Cronenberg's direction of acting style, which is traceable to literary origins.[50] Referring to Ballard's *Crash*, Stuart Laing suggests that 'the most common adjective is stylized' and Cronenberg translates that notion of stylization into the minimal gesture and facial reaction, and monotone, almost soporific delivery of his protagonists, particularly in his realization of the character of Catherine.[51] In the very opening scene, Deborah Ungar strikes a pose akin to a figurehead on a ship with arms outstretched and hair blowing back in a strong wind. Rather than psychoanalysis, it is intertextuality that is helpful here. Cronenberg is drawing, without acknowledgement, on a precise scene in J. G. Ballard's *The Kindness of Women* (1992). Blond-haired Sally Mumford approaches pilot David Hunter as he climbs from his Tiger Moth and 'she peeled away her silk scarf as if they were about to make love under its wing' and 'as she stood on tip-toe and kissed David, her crutch ruled the airfield.'[52] Ballard's description of Catherine, in particular 'the porcelain appearance of her face,' 'the perfect forgery of an Ingres' and her most attractive quality to James, 'her total acceptance of any situation', is realized by Cronenberg in Ungar's glacial demeanour.[53]

The logic of Adams' assertion that 'a desire without an object must be a wish not to wish' is also flawed.[54] A desire, like pleasure, cannot exist without an object and it does not follow that lack of an object creates a nihilistic drive towards death. Rather, it creates an impulse to search for a new object as we see in James and Catherine's infinite deferral ('Maybe the next one...') and reflects the fact that they choose to stay together through the course of the narrative. This search, one that Cronenberg shares with the early work of Clive Barker, does not elevate the characters beyond desire but involves them in the development of a new language with which to express it.

The parergonal logic of the frame

As Salman Rushdie notes in *The Ground Beneath Her Feet* (2000), '[t]he only people who see the whole picture are the ones who step out of the frame.'[55] If we need a theoretical explanation for the flatness in *Crash*, then a more helpful notion might be Jacques Derrida's notions of 'the parergon'. Derrida defines the parergonal logic of the frame as referring to a liminal space that is derived from material not solely within the filmic space, nor outside it, but in the relation between the two.[56] Although in *The Truth in Painting* (1987), as the title suggests, Derrida's primary context is painting, his concepts of the parergon can be usefully applied to film. Derrida's parergonal logic, largely a deconstruction of Immanuel Kant's *Critique of Aesthetic Judgement* (1790), describes a fluid concept, by which the spectator is positioned and repositioned in relation to the cinematic frame and also contains the excesses of a text, which might include features that we do not usually see in film. Derrida takes issue with Kant's notion of what features constitute an artwork and what should be considered mere 'ornamentation (parerga), i.e. what is only an adjunct and not an intrinsic constituent in the complete representation of the object.'[57] Kant's examples of drapes on statues and colonnades of palaces are also considered by Derrida, but it is the framing of pictures which is of primary significance here.

The concept of the parergon problematizes notions of what is 'inside' and what is 'outside' an artwork, a key concern of Cronenberg, particularly in relation to films like *Dead Ringers* (see chapter 2). More broadly, this idea also could be used to describe the interwoven textual connections between critical readings of the films themselves, the many interviews that Cronenberg has given over his career and biographical facts about his own background. It is tempting, like Kant, to try and exclude certain factors when making an aesthetic judgement about a work of art, but, as Derrida shows, it is far from simple to 'distinguish between the internal or proper sense and the circumstance of the object being talked about.'[58] Such a process is flawed when features that initially appear to be beyond the work are actually part of the totality of its meaning. The extra-textual material used in this book thus functions as a parergon, in that it is 'in addition to the ergon, the work done, the fact, the work, but it does not fall to one side, it touches and cooperates within the operation, from a certain outside.'[59]

A prime reason for the flatness of *Crash* is that significant scenes draw their meaning from a parergonal logic. Adams mentions Christian Metz's interest in the field of enunciation, particularly the operation of frames within frames and claims that they are 'singularly missing from *Crash*', although she does admit that 'I could not easily elaborate the argument' without recourse to a comparison with Bresson.[60] However, issues of framing are raised right from the opening of the film. In the credit sequence, there is the illusion of the text approaching the viewer by becoming larger and by appearing to pass over slight undulations, there is the creation of depth within the blank screen space. The text does not fade out or pass to the right or left of the frame as might be expected. Instead, it becomes blurred and almost seems to overwhelm the viewer before falling away, as if we were standing at the end of a conveyor belt with objects falling off in front of us. This suggests there is a space between the screen and the image, which is created by the presence of the spectator, with the image blur conveying the sense of an invaded focal distance.

The second scene appears to position the viewer from within a car looking out, but the 'screen' and its borders are both revealed as an illusion. The fascia of a dashboard is pushed away to reveal that what we had assumed was the frame of the cinematic screen was in fact only the frame of the windscreen. Such effects do not create a flatness as Adams suggests but rather create a depth that includes the viewer. The call for James to give his stamp of approval for a Steadicam shot also applies to us. We are, in effect, required to be present to complete the shot as we are part of the parergonal logic of the framing. This is not a psychological point in which 'the voyeur completes a space' such as Adams makes but a literal feature of Cronenberg's camera placement.[61] Adams' claim that there is a lack of framing devices is contradicted implicitly by the presence of James' anonymous sexual partner, the 'camera girl', responsible for framing and focusing and explicitly so in the following scene where James is clearly framed leaning against a doorway before moving across to Catherine who is visually defined by the concrete of the balcony and the roof of their apartment.

A further feature of the parergon, which contributes to the 'flatness' of *Crash*, is absence. As Derrida states, 'the parergon...is called in by the hollowing of a certain lacunary quality within the work.'[62] This is not the 'lack' of Lacanian theory. Derrida is referring here explicitly to what he sees, and what Kant admits, are flaws in *The Third Critique*. It is the gaps in Kant's thinking, particularly the lack of a theory of framing, which intrigues Derrida, and the point at which his own thoughts on the parergon come into play.[63] What critics like Botting and Wilson see as a critical deficiency is at the heart of Cronenberg's aesthetic here: absence is not a flaw, it is what *Crash* is about. Action can take place off-frame but still affect what we *do* see. In *Crash*, we do not see Vaughan's murder of a pedestrian by the airport or, indeed, his own death, but we do see its consequence as James becomes the new Vaughan, driving his battered Lincoln and tempting death by running Catherine off the road. It is not by depriving the viewer of depth cues as Adams suggests, but the blend of glacial acting and the movement around and through the parergon that provides access to the Lacanian Real.

The Real

Adams is more persuasive when she states that 'the film is indeed about the re-emergent failure to integrate some impossible kernel of the Real.'[64] According to Lacan, the Real is whatever is excluded or cannot be symbolized; it continually resurfaces, highlighting its own repression and a pursuit of the Real constitutes a seeking after impossibility.[65] Adams does recognize that the film 'bears closely on the Real' but chooses not to pursue this in detail.[66] For Lacan, it is only possible to discover one's true desire by experiencing demands that cannot be met, an impossibility, an experience in the Real. Vaughan's 'project', although explained in rather vague terms about 'benevolent psychopathology' (and later undercut in a dismissive comment), could be seen as a mission to discover the reality of his desire in such a way. He cannot be involved in a celebrity accident without contriving one (with Elizabeth Taylor in Ballard's novel) and, hence, is forever pursuing an unattainable ideal.

A problem with the psychoanalytical method represented by Adams' piece is that what is posited as a metaphor about internal thought processes, the notion of 'psychical space', for example, is then discussed as if it had an external, concrete reality. In discussing Cronenberg, there is no need to have recourse to some of Lacan's more bizarre notions like *the lamella*, an amoeba-like creature that 'is something extra-flat' that can 'run around'.[67] In attempting to apply the figure of the *lamella*, 'the libido as indestructible life' to the notion of the wound, Adams is led to overstate its importance, asserting that 'you can see how the attempt at the experience of sexuality in the Real relies upon the wound.'[68] However, there are no wounds in the first three scenes, Vaughan's encounter with an airport prostitute, James' first sexual exchange with Helen or the subsequent and parallel scene with Catherine. A perception of wounds can act as a catalyst and aphrodisiac to a sexual encounter within the Real, such as the verbal descriptions of Vaughan's scarred genitalia, but it is not the only means of access to the Real. Adams suggests that *Crash* inhabits 'the domain of the death drive, where the trauma repeats and something is lost over and over again.'[69] However, what this 'something' might be is not entirely clear, and the film features repetition that is incremental and progressive as new wounds are formed rather than old ones re-opened, i.e. the narrative operates within the Real but seeks to go beyond it.

One of the main proponents of the value of Lacan, Slavoj Žižek, is interested primarily in the ubiquity of the Real rather than Lacan's earlier structuralist work on the nature of the signifier. In his developments of Lacanian thinking, Žižek overcomes some of the problems associated with theories that can be traced back to Freudian-influenced notions of sexuality. Žižek enthusiastically draws on examples from popular culture, including film, in his refinements of how the Real might be accommodated. Particularly relevant for Cronenberg is Lacan's notion of *le sinthome*, an invisible fragment of the Real, present in every subject but resistant to symbolization. The main additions that Cronenberg makes to Ballard's novel (the reconstructed James Dean crash, the tattooing and the ending) could all be read as encounters with the Real. The crash reconstruction particularly recreates the space of an event from the past, where there were no witnesses and could be seen as a Lacanian *symptom*, a compromise with the Symbolic and the means by which the unconscious can repress acceptance of the terrifying nature of the Real.

Žižek draws on two literary examples to exemplify his notion of the eruption of the Real, which can be usefully compared to Cronenberg's *Crash*, as both involve a focus on borderline states represented by car windows. Žižek cites a Robert Heinlein short story, 'The Unpleasant Profession of Jonathan Hoag'(1942).[70] This narrative involves a protagonist called Randall, who becomes aware that his everyday world is actually constructed by otherworldly beings as a work of art. Occasionally, there are faults in the creation, which are assessed by disguised visitors. During one such visit, Randall is instructed to drive home but under no circumstances must he or his wife open any of the windows during the journey. The trauma of witnessing a car accident leads Randall to disobey this instruction and he has a momentary glimpse of a terrifying, formless void, which is usually masked by a more comforting vision of reality, projected onto the window. The pile-up sequence in the film of *Crash* also features a car carrying the protagonist and his wife, who are tempted to stop by curiosity at the sight of an accident. The way in which Vaughan, their passenger, cranes to get a clearer view of the carnage reflects how his project is centrally concerned with creating the circumstances when he could have a literal collision with the Real.

Žižek briefly mentions a second example of a car windowpane functioning as a metaphorical barrier/screen with the Real, drawing on a different J. G. Ballard text, *Empire of the Sun* (1984).[71] Here the young protagonist, Jim Ballard, on his way back from a night at the cinema, describes the excitement of watching lurid street life in Shanghai as seen through a windscreen. To his youthful imagination, it seems that 'the spectacle outside the theatre far exceeded anything shown on the screen.'[72] His wish that something would break into his cosy and safe world (which could be read as an intrusion of the Lacanian Real) comes true as his home and family are shattered when the Japanese attack the city and subsequent visions through car windows are tinged with a guilt as he blames himself for what he is witnessing. Both Žižek's examples are from inside a car looking out and feature the windows of the car becoming a screen onto which is projected a view of reality that is a symptom of the Real. By contrast, Cronenberg focuses on a viewing position from outside a car looking in, not only from a fixed position as in the taxi shot but also a more mobile, roving, voyeuristic view as in the car wash scene and the later pile-up sequence, where we are taken on a languorous tracking shot, allowing us to peer in at bodies in shock. Both locate the Real at an interface, but Cronenberg looks at the Real particularly in relation to what might constitute the borders of the human body (or a near analogous object in *Crash*, the car).

For Lacan, the Real is an unrepresentable kernel of meaning that resists the Symbolic coding of language and is manifested in the return of traumatic events. However, a key part of *Crash* is the *lack* of trauma experienced by those on screen. Adams uses the term 'trauma' in the sense of 'that which is traumatic, involves a violent shock and implies a wound', but *Crash* explores what can be represented by exploring the limits of the Symbolic.[73] Adams suggests that the film of *Crash* 'shows us what a world where trauma failed to operate would be like', but both novel and film insist on a 'presentness' precisely to convey that the 'death of affect' is not some futuristic phenomenon but is already an implicit part of urban modernity.[74] Lacan places language as the prime force shaping human identity and it also occupies a central position in Cronenberg's cinematic aesthetic, albeit not in the Lacanian sense of linguistic development. Psychoanalysis strives to move trauma into the arena of the Symbolic via talking about problems in therapy. However, Cronenberg is interested in the limits of language. In *Dead Ringers*, he dramatizes the inability of the Mantle brothers to sustain an existence in the Lacanian realm of the Symbolic. Beverly finds himself unable to speak; not initially to Elliot about his feelings for Claire or at the end to Claire about his feelings for Beverly. He cannot escape the Real, the impossible, but neither can he stay there. Death is the only other option open to the twins.

Adams' reading of *Crash*'s sexuality as 'textured like a wound, gaping, open, unsutured', can be taken further in relation to Žižek's notions of a Lacanian Real.[75] Adams' intuition, stated rather than argued, could be partly due to Cronenberg's use of techniques that Žižek identifies in the work of Krzysztof Kieślowski. For Žižek, the failure of an exchange of objective and subjective shots to produce a suturing effect, produces what he terms an 'interface', in which 'a part of drab reality all of a sudden starts to function as the "door of perception", the screen through which another, purely fantasmatic dimension becomes perceptible.'[76] In addition to the conventional suturing conventions such as shot/reverse-shot, Žižek describes how Kieślowski creates a shot in which 'we see a person in close up face-to-face and, behind him or her, on a glass partition...a larger-than-life reflection of the face of another person with whom the person we see directly is engaged in a conversation. By means of this simple procedure, the spectral dimension is rendered present in the middle of an utterly plain scene.'[77]

Particularly relevant for Cronenberg, Žižek talks about the 'meta-suturing effect of the interface', in which a shot contains its own counter shot, often by use of a reflected image.[78] This simplifies one of Žižek's earlier theories that 'the "horizon of meaning" is always linked, as if by a kind of umbilical cord, to a point within the field disclosed by it; the frame of our view is always already framed (re-marked) by a part of its content.'[79] This describes an effect very close to what we have in the taxi shot mentioned earlier. Cronenberg effectively creates a split screen effect, diagonally across the frame, thereby contrasting the flatness of the reflected image with the main image within the car, which has greater depth. The same effect is created later when we see the reflection in the television screen of Helen, James and Vaughan as they watch tapes of crash tests or in *Dead Ringers*, where a reflected image of a female patient about to be operated upon overlays a shot of Beverly being dressed in his priest-like gown.[80]

The final shots of *Spider*, show a further use of this meta-suturing feature. The adult protagonist, Dennis Cleg, known as Spider, is taken back to the institution where he has spent most of his adult life for the murder we now know that he committed. Sitting on the back seat, he is seen through a car window and superimposed over his face is the underlying reality of his situation: the specific place, designated by a house number, where he killed his mother. The car moves away with the camera placed, as in *Crash*, from a position that can accommodate car, occupant and road simultaneously *as well as* the reflected image. The final shot cuts to the same position but now with Spider as a boy looking fixedly ahead in the car as it moves, with rows of anonymous houses superimposed over his face. The measure of eye contact emphasizes how the child denies all knowledge of the crime, whereas the adult Spider can now accept partial responsibility, although he looks down at the spot where his mother lay on the pavement, still unable to look squarely at the house and the guilt that it represents. As in *Crash*, camera placement and picture composition convey an intrusion of the Real and a character's inability to fully grasp it.

Cronenberg is cited as stating that he wants to 'show the unshowable, speak the unspeakable' and, indeed, Cronenberg's films in the period 1982–2003 could be seen as a search for the impossible, to question the limits of articulation: of speech (*Dead Ringers*), of space (*Crash*), of suppressed desire (*Naked Lunch*), of an observable reality (*Videodrome* and *eXistenZ*) and of memory (*Spider*).[81] If psychoanalysis has a role in relation to Cronenberg, then it might be used to explore what could be seen as his interest in protagonists who are striving after the Real (and its implicit links with impossibility) as the arena where a new language of desire might be articulated.

The New Flesh

The paradigms of Freud (and those that follow his lead) are fatally weakened if sexual acts are culturally derived and protean. As Michel Foucault explores in *The

History of Sexuality (1978), the foci of sexual desire and the means by which this might be expressed have changed over time. The cornerstones of Freud's paradigms based on childhood (sexual) traumas are drawn from a late nineteenth, early twentieth century perspective and initially applied within a white, middle-class, Viennese cultural milieu. As Slavoj Žižek notes, the so-called erogenous zones 'are not biologically determined but result instead from the signifying parcelling of the body. Certain parts of the body's surface are erotically privileged not because of their anatomical position but because of the way the body is caught up in the symbolic network.'[82] Psychoanalytical models based on conventional human anatomy become contrived when applied to a view of the body as evolutionary, particularly concerning sexual acts, like the stomach slit in *Videodrome* (see discussion of Clive Barker in Chapter 1).

As will be seen in the following chapter, the phrase 'the New Flesh' is never overtly defined in Cronenberg's 1982 film *Videodrome*. However, there is something of a carnivalesque aesthetic in Cronenberg's celebration and revelling in what might be termed monstrous. Activities, which might be expected to lie at the margins of society and challenge conventions are brought to the centre and celebrated, such as pornography, drug culture, car crash culture and underground video games. Furthermore, there is a playful sense of subversion about the ludic quality in *eXistenZ*, a combining of Eros and Thanatos in *Crash* and a release from sexual norms in *Naked Lunch*. Rather than psychoanalysis, the writings of Mikhail Bakhtin and particularly his discussion of Rabelais, share with Cronenberg a delight in difference and plurality and a view of the material body as an evolving and grotesque phenomenon, liable to open up at will.

Robert Stam notes that 'for Bakhtin, the body is a festival of becoming, a plurality, not a closed system but a perpetual experiment...Bakhtin is fascinated by the unfinished body, the elastic, malleable body, the body that outgrows itself, that reaches beyond its own limits and conceives new bodies.'[83] This transgressive process continually violates boundary states and, like Cronenberg, Bakhtin is particularly interested in the metaphorical membranes that appear to encase separate existences but which can be joined or even burst through. Cronenberg's concept of the 'New Flesh' carries ambiguity with it, making gender roles and sexuality appear protean and contestable, nullifying psychological paradigms that are built around an assumption of the dominance of the nuclear family. Cronenberg shares with Bakhtin a liberating view of corporeal existence in an implicit rejection of psychoanalytical readings of the body based on notions of lack: 'Bakhtin sees orifices not as symbols of lack but as openings, channels of communication.'[84] The idea of treating desire as lack (a crux of Lacanian theory) seriously struggles to accommodate the actuality of Cronenberg's work.

Although this appears to occupy some of the same content as Kristeva's abject, the attitude of figures like Barker and Cronenberg to liminal states is completely different. Where Kristeva imposes a moral structure on physical actions with terms like 'clean' and 'proper', Cronenberg rejects the notion of such behaviour as contained, ritualistic and part of a developing self. For him, monstrosity is part of a positive development in human evolution that should be celebrated, not cast in terms of lack or guilt. Stam notes that '[r]ather than privilege sexual difference *between* bodies, with the phallus as ultimate signifier, Bakhtin discerns difference *within* the body', and focuses upon zones of the body, such as the anus, which are non-specific in terms of gender.[85] Like Bakhtin, Cronenberg implicitly suggests a renegotiation of zones of the body that might be deemed erogenous, that the inner body is as fascinating as external appearance and that the distinction between the two can be blurred, often via metaphors of liquidity. Bodies are sacrificed in an act of merging or fusion, which creates a new reality, greater than the sum of their parts and, which once produced, cannot be reversed, sometimes casting processes of metamorphosis in a tragic tone as in The *Fly*.

Adaptation Theory

The idea of using literary texts to illuminate film is not new. In 1969, Peter Wollen asserted that 'we need comparisons with authors in the other arts: Ford with Fenimore Cooper, for example or Hawks with Faulkner', and it could be argued that as Leonard Bernstein believed, 'the best way to "know" a thing is in the context of another discipline'.[86] However, there remains a stubborn Leavisite tendency in discussing film that implicitly values literary works as superior to film on the grounds of being the more established art form and drawing on assumptions that, although increasingly questioned, have not been fully removed, that film can only be visual, whilst literature is linguistic, and that film cannot emulate fiction's ability to convey the depth and profundity of human thought. As Deborah Cartmell and Imelda Whelehan state, '[t]here is still the preconception that the novelist produces a work of quality, of "high" art as it emerges from the solitary efforts of the individual to express their distinct vision, untrammelled by concerns about the commercial value of the product'.[87] As I hope to show, it is this novelistic status to which Cronenberg appears to aspire.

Theoretical discussion of adaptation has not really developed very far, partly due to the persisting assumption of the novel's cultural superiority and, what Brian McFarlane describes as, a tendency to be 'bedevilled by the fidelity issue'.[88] Notions of remaining faithful assume an essentialist position – that there is an irreducible core meaning to the original source text but narratives are read in different ways at different times by different audiences. It is not always obvious as to precisely what the film-maker should be faithful. Events in a plot may seem transparent but the method of their presentation is not. Erica Sheen talks about fidelity criticism as 'not so much as a loss of articulation as an articulation of loss', in the sense of a drift from an intellectual property that has been diluted.[89] McFarlane rejects both a reliance on subjective judgements between the relative merits of book and film or, that as a different medium, there can be no meaningful discussion of a relation to a source text. He concludes that 'fidelity...cannot profitably be used as an evaluative criterion; it can be no more than a descriptive term to designate loosely a certain kind of adaptation'.[90]

Linked to the fidelity issue as a critical stumbling block is the notion of what is actually going on in any process of adaptation. Referring to the film-maker, George Bluestone asserts that 'what he adapts is a kind of paraphrase of the novel – the novel viewed as raw material'.[91] Those who compare book and film unfavourably ignore that 'ultimately we are not comparing book with film, but rather one resymbolisation with another – inevitably expecting the movie projected on the screen to be a shadow reflection of the movie we ourselves have imagined'.[92] More precisely, and more constructively for the purposes of this study, as Neil Sinyard reminds us, 'adapting a literary text for the screen is essentially an act of literary criticism', which should serve to illuminate *both* source text and filmic version drawn from it.[93]

The kind of literature towards which Cronenberg seems drawn is best known in academic or cultish circles rather than populist best-sellers, and he has chosen to keep the titles from his source material where possible for his more overt adaptations (*Crash*, *Naked Lunch*, *M Butterfly*), so that a literary connection seems important to him. It is unclear what proportion of Cronenberg's audience will have read texts like *Naked Lunch* or even heard of *Crash*, so there is a sense in which the adoption of a literary title confers an air of academic prestige, which cannot be easily challenged. The distinction made by critics such as Pierre Bourdieu between popular best-sellers of the 'here today and gone tomorrow' variety and '*classics*, bestsellers in the long run, which owe their consecration, and therefore their widespread durable market to the educational system', also seems an important one to Cronenberg.[94] By drawing on literary texts that are by reputation infamous, unfilmable and experienced primarily on Higher Education courses, Cronenberg appears to be seeking cultural respectability after the generic labelling as the 'Baron of Blood' from his films of the late 1970s and the endorsement of the very cultural establishment from which he appears to rebel. Cronenberg cites Borges when he states that 'a phenomenon like Kafka actually creates his own precursors, linking together strings of writers not seen to be connected before...'.[95] This book will consider to what extent Cronenberg does create his own precursors and to what extent his work is truly free of influence from source texts.

'Film is film, literature is literature' (intertextuality in film and literature)[96]
The extensive generic possibilities and the range of other art forms upon which film draws overtly, such as drama, literature art and music, would suggest that the medium of film is highly transpositional. However, Wood's comments, cited above, reflect an enduring feeling that the media of film and literature remain distinct in some ways. It was, after all, the difficulty of visualizing the interior world of Brett Easton Ellis' novel *American Psycho* (1991) that finally persuaded Cronenberg to drop this text as a potential film project (see chapter 1). The title of Seymour

Chatman's 1978 essay, 'What Novels Can Do That Film Can't (and Vice Versa)', seems to offer a definitive analysis of how literature and film remain distinct media. However, the whole area is much more complex than Chatman suggests. It would only be possible to comprehend a film ostensibly based on a novel if different signifiers from different language systems were recognizable to a range of audiences as referring to related signifieds, i.e. narrative is not wholly medium-specific. Roland Barthes notes, using a parasitical image, how 'cultural codes...will emigrate to other texts; there is no lack of hosts.'[97] Increasingly, novels appear to be written with half an eye to the ease with which they can be visualized, reflecting the optioning of film rights, sometimes even before a book is written.

Studies on adaptation by Brian McFarlane (1996) and collections of articles edited by Tim Corrigan (1998), Ginette Vincendeau (1999) and James Naremore (2000) all share a concern to link media-specific concerns with case studies. However, they all tend to find themselves struggling with the same dilemma. As Vincendeau states, 'critics are still searching for a specific theoretical framework to understand the relationship between film and literature in general.'[98] Trends in adaptation theory have drawn on Roland Barthes' structuralist and poststructuralist poetics and David Bordwell and Kristen Thompson's neoformalism, but generally approaches oscillate between George Bluestone's comparison of formal systems of media-specific features which focuses on fidelity to the written text or an auteurist approach, which emphasizes stylistic differences. Writing on adaptations often features a relentless focus on case studies and as James Naremore notes, 'tends to be narrow in range, inherently respectful of the "precursor text," and constitutive of a series of binary oppositions that poststructuralist theory has taught us to deconstruct: literature versus cinema, high culture versus mass culture, original versus copy.'[99] Critics like Naremore and Robert Stam find more hope for optimism in notions of Bakhtinian dialogics and intertextuality. This study looks at one particular strand of intertextuality, the literary.

Chatman assumes that when passages of description appear in novels, 'events are stopped...and we look at the characters and the setting elements as though as at a *tableau vivant*.'[100] However, this is quite a narrow view of description and relegates it to the function of static prettification and obstructing narrative momentum. This raises the question of what kinds of narrative information can be conveyed by different devices. For example, the opening three explicit sex scenes in *Crash* are not a gratuitous and frustrating pause in the plot – they *are* the plot (see chapter 4).[101] Chatman's focus on single frames does not represent the audience conditions of viewing the film and imposes upon an image the static quality, which he seeks to ascribe to it.[102] The inherently kinetic quality of moving pictures is later acknowledged but only in terms of a slighting comparison between arts like painting and sculpture, which allow a viewer to dwell at leisure on the viewing time and film, where the duration of an image is beyond the viewer's control (assuming a theatrical, rather than a home-video context).[103]

Chatman also assumes a transparency in the medium of film in which 'details are not asserted as such by a narrator but simply presented,'[104] and asserts that although terms like 'pretty' are subjective, if an author tells you that a character in prose is so, then we will believe him or her. However, the fact that narrators in literature can be unreliable, whether by design or delusion, such as the eponymous hero in Jonathan Swift's *Gulliver's Travels* (1726), would imply that rather more meanings are capable of being generated and contested than he suggests. There is some slight common ground between Cronenberg and Chapman in their disdain for voice-over as 'then the film would be using its sound track in much the same way as fiction uses assertive syntax.'[105] The rejection of a voice-over for *Crash* (in disagreement with author of the source material, J. G. Ballard) and *Spider* (present throughout Patrick McGrath's initial script) reflects the sense that, in common with a typical modernist text, Cronenberg's works resist a single, privileged narrative voice, that might direct an audience's sympathies.

Theoretical possibilities and ways forward

Analysis of Cronenberg has been dominated by certain key articles, which have tended to entrench critical positions. Robin Wood's 1978 dismissal of *Shivers* as dominated by sexual disgust and reading its underlying ideology, particularly its denouement, as 'reactionary', draws on a blend of Marxist and Freudian theory.[106] Films like *Shivers* (1975), *Rabid* (1976) and *The Brood* (1979) have been usefully discussed with reference to the diseased body or the apparent Cartesian dichotomy between mind and body, but Cronenberg's work after 1982 can be seen as less overtly body-centred than his previous films.[107] Critics like Barbara Creed have placed Cronenberg's work in the specific psychoanalytical context of the monstrous feminine, male hysteria and castration anxiety but whilst some Cronenberg films like *Dead Ringers* can be illuminated to a degree by this approach, the attempt to extend this apparatus to *Naked Lunch* and, particularly, *Crash*, fails to see the potential of same-sex desire or sado-masochistic relations as anything other than repulsive.[108] Equally, critical approaches that might be called broadly 'feminist', including Julia Kristeva's notions of repression of feelings towards the abject mother articulated in borderline states or Melanie Klein's interpretation of infantile desires, can struggle to embrace notions of monstrosity in the same spirit as Cronenberg and writers like Clive Barker.[109] Approaching Cronenberg's work by striving to ascribe representational status to characters and actions that may not be 'politically correct' will not be as valuable as being sensitive to a film's own internal logic.

Ultimately, arguments based around medium-specific issues, i.e. whether either film or literature are innately effective at particular kinds of expression, is just reductive. A more productive approach to the question of adaptation, according to theorists like Robert Stam, would be to look more positively at the range of means by which film generates meaning and adopt 'a much broader intertextual dialogism.'[110] As Stam notes, 'although novels only have character, film adaptations have both character (actantial function) and performer, allowing for possibilities of interplay and contradiction denied a purely verbal medium.'[111] In film, a single actor can play more than one role, such as Jeremy Irons as twin brothers in *Dead Ringers* or Judy Davis as both Joan Lee and Joan Frost in *Naked Lunch*. Conversely, a single role can be played by more than one actor, for example, in *Spider* (2003) the eponymous protagonist is played as a boy and subsequently as a man, by Bradley Hall and Ralph Fiennes respectively.

Stam's approach is influenced by Bakhtin's theory that any utterance is inherently linked to 'the entire matrix of communicative utterances within which the artistic text is situated' that was later developed into the conceptual area known as 'intertextuality' by figures linked to the *Tel Quel* journal such as Kristeva.[112] Although Kristeva's notions of the abject can be seen as flawed, her work on intertextuality is more useful for this book. As she states in *Revolution in Poetic Language* (1984), 'if one grants that every signifying practice is a field of transpositions of various signifying systems (an inter-textuality), one then understands that its "place" of enunciation and its denoted "object" are never single, complete, and identical to themselves, but always plural, shattered, capable of being tabulated.'[113] She is not referring directly to film here but the analogous notion that the meaning of a film may not be contained solely within the confines of the screen, is an important one. This book will explore how the potential meanings of a text, cinematic or literary, can only be fully apprehended when considered by its interactions with other texts.

Gérard Genette's notions of narratology offer a more precise and positive way to consider the relationship between written text and film, particularly the term 'transtextuality', meaning 'all that which puts one text in relation, whether manifest or secret, with other texts.'[114] According to Genette, there are five types of transtextual situations: 'intertextuality', 'metatextuality', 'paratextuality', 'architextuality' and 'hypertextuality'. Intertextuality describes the simultaneous presence of at least two texts in terms of plagiarism, allusion or quotation, such as the 'talking asshole' speech in Cronenberg's *Naked Lunch*, drawn directly from Burroughs' novel. This could be extended slightly to include synecdochic structuring, involving a part of something coming to stand for a whole in which the intertextual links are by association rather than direct parallels in plot or sequence. For example, the involvement of an aircraft hanger, an anonymous pilot and a glamorous, but glacial, blond woman in the opening scene of Cronenberg's *Crash* draws upon a range of dominant motifs in Ballard's fiction (discussed in chapter 4).

Where intertextual references between the film text and any other work become knowing and self-aware, one might speak of metatextuality. Features in films that problematize narrative structure, such as *eXistenZ*'s questioning whether the protagonists are still in a computer game, force a viewer to reconsider the meaning systems in place not just in that particular film but look for similarities in other films, hence intratextual factors can also encourage intertextuality. In *The Role of the Reader* (1979), Umberto Eco's notion of 'extra coding' (akin to Todorov's notion of the fantastic) would suggest that when faced by an unfamiliar textual system, readers have only two choices. Either they can integrate the text with known systems of meaning or devise new ones that can accommodate it. A viewer of *eXistenZ* may well come to that particular text after seeing *Naked Lunch* and *Crash* and be prepared for Cronenberg's appropriation of literary material from a range of sources, particularly from the author of the named source. By this stage in his career, Cronenberg is able to indulge in the playful siting of overtly literary references for his *cognescenti* to spot, such as the 'Perky Pat' allusion to Philip K. Dick on the burger bag.

Paratextuality is used to mean all those factors, which affect the meaning of a film beyond the work itself, such as the director's comments on his own work. The relative status of such texts is problematic and discussed later in this introduction in a consideration of authorship and intent. Architextuality refers to the significance suggested by the titles of a text. All of Cronenberg's major adaptations retain their original literary title, suggesting that a literary link is important to him. Hypertextuality is used to describe the relationship between a core or 'hypertext' to a 'hypotext,' which modifies the earlier text in some way. The running time of most commercial features means that many words must be cut in translating a novel into a film. Stam suggests that the process of adaptation can be seen as 'a source novel hypotext's being transformed by a complex series of operations: selection, amplification, concretization, actualization, critique, extrapolation, analogization, popularisation, and reculturalization.'[115]

Potential factors that might be altered in an adaptation include location, for example, *Crash* moving from Ballard's London to Cronenberg's Toronto, largely for the relative ease of filming in the Canadian city using real streets. Characters might be added, such as the Frosts and Hank and Martin in *Naked Lunch*, as ciphers for literary figures of the time (see chapter 3). Character may be condensed or even removed, such as the figure of the secretary Renata in *Crash*, as a companion for Catherine, thereby focusing on James', rather than Catherine's sexual pleasure and emphasizing the Ballards as the dominant couple. Events might be changed slightly, for example, the explicit death crash that Vaughan seeks with Elizabeth Taylor is transferred to Katherine Mansfield (possibly to avoid litigation from a living star). There may be changes for ideological or commercial reasons, such as the removal of explicitly incestuous overtones in the relationship of the Mantle brothers in *Dead Ringers* and the cutting of family references inhibits a Freudian reading of the brothers' behaviour.

What can make a Genette-influenced analysis more complex is that several of his notions can apply at the same time. In *Dead Ringers*, although the initial plot premise is based on a series of real events (the paratextual), Cronenberg learned about them through the medium of written texts. He drew particularly on a specific 1974 article in *Esquire*, from whence the title comes (the architextual), and more substantially the novel *Twins* (1977) by Bari Wood and Jack Geasland (the intertextual).[116] His relationship with this latter text (the hypertextual) is discussed in chapter 3 and is categorized by unacknowledged borrowing and denial.

The theoretical approach of this book will be informed by Genette's terms but in a particular context. Derrida's logic of the parergon, and Žižek's particular development of Lacanian theory in relation to the meetings of surfaces both highlight the intertextual nature of Cronenberg's visual aesthetic, in which, as Stam suggests, 'every text forms an intersection of textual surfaces.'[117] Far from mere flatness, Cronenberg creates a visual aesthetic which approaches the screen as a kind of palimpsest, a flat surface upon which impressions can be made and re-made; a surface that has an element of depth but cannot be pierced.

The Brain is the Screen – Cronenberg and Deleuze

'The brain is unity. The brain is the screen. I don't believe that linguistics and psychoanalysis offer a great deal to the cinema.'[118]

This book is underpinned by David Bordwell's survey of contemporary film theory and his conclusion that 'you do not need a Big Theory of Everything to do enlightening work in a field of study'.[119] However, one figure with whom Bordwell openly admits his ignorance is Gilles Deleuze. Deleuze's work has spawned a mini explosion of interest in the last few years, particularly on the Net. Where Baudrillard seems tired and cynical, Deleuze in his companion pieces, *Cinema 1: The Movement Image* (1983) and *Cinema 2: The Time Image* (1985), seems fresh and hopeful, proposing ideas which appear to open doors rather than close them. With an intimate knowledge of French art film, Deleuze develops a fresh approach to classifying film, or, as he calls it in *Negotiations*, 'a natural history of cinema', by focusing on the senses. His attempt at a cinematic taxonomy draws its inspiration squarely from the films themselves and from practice, not existing outside the film itself. For Deleuze, the movement-image is epitomized by the 'classical' Hollywood film, driven by linear temporality and causal logic. The division between the two books is signalled by the end of the Second World War and particularly the Holocaust, after which Deleuze suggests no stable system of cinematic signs could function. The time-image represents a shift from action to a focus on time-in-itself and the power that Deleuze sees within it to open new pathways of perceiving, feeling and thinking. His work explores tensions between film and philosophy, two disciplines with which Cronenberg is closely acquainted, and of particular relevance here opens up fresh ways of considering notions of cinematic time and how we actually experience film.

In Cronenberg's short film *Camera* (2000), an unnamed actor (played by Les Carlson) delivers a monologue straight to camera, which contains a powerful statement about the ontological possibilities and limitations of the film medium. *Camera* was released as part of a 2004 Criterion DVD package alongside *Videodrome*, in which Carlson plays Barry Convex, head of Spectacular Optical. The juxtaposition of the same face almost twenty years apart, physically represents the central point of *Camera* – the passage of time. The actor recounts a dream he once had:

> I dreamt I was in the cinema, watching a movie with an audience. And suddenly I realised I was ageing, rapidly. Growing horribly old as I sat there. It was the movie that was doing it. I had caught some kind of disease from the movie and it was making me grow old, bringing me closer and closer to death. I woke up terrified. And look at me now.

Albeit within the frame of a dream, Carlson's character is articulating a notion of cinema and time in which he participates. The film that he talks about does not merely reflect the passing of time, it *affects* it too. As the actor states, 'When you record the moment, you record the death of the moment.' Time-passing and time-present are both contained within, and paradoxically affected by, the cinematic image and its consumption by the viewer. In a graphic realization of Deleuze's time-image, Carlson's dream creates time 'within himself', causing him to age. Time affects flesh by scarring it but this is still within an enduring presentness. As Deleuze notes, '[a] scar is not the sign of a past wound' but of 'the present fact of having been wounded.'[120]

A new generation of Deleuzian critics, such as Steven Shaviro and more recently Anna Powell, see the visceral immediacy of the viewing experience (especially when one has a personal passion for a particular genre) as contrary to discussions of lack and absence. As Powell states, 'we respond corporeally to sensory stimuli and dynamics of motion. Fantasy is an embodied event' and '[t]he body is not separate from the mind, but forms part of a perceptual continuum.'[121] In relation to a horror film, which sets out to evoke a visceral response, this can be convincing but it is highly debatable whether Cronenberg's films are designed to evoke such responses (going as far as to parody the notion of such effects in *Videodrome*) or indeed whether they fall into the genre of horror at all. His films certainly have elements which might be deemed horrific – one has only to think of the stomach slit scene in *Videodrome*, the parrot cage scene in *Naked Lunch* or the fish farm in *eXistenZ*. However these are only small elements in a much larger whole, often only held in shot briefly and or whose 'validity' in context are directly problematized as hallucinations, whether due to brain tumours, drugs or virtual reality computer games. Most common definitions of horror film would have to be distorted considerably to accommodate the main filmic foci of this book. Post-1982, there is no stalk-and-slash in Cronenberg's work, no phallic murder weapon, no 'final girl' – in short, few of the structural or semantic features that one would need to construct a psychological reading according to current theory. It would be hard to imagine a horror film fan choosing to view *Dead Ringers*, *Naked Lunch* or *Spider* in the hope of experiencing the thrill of fear.

What *is* useful here, though, for a consideration of Cronenberg is the notion of embodiment. As the title of Shaviro's key text, *The Cinematic Body* (1993), suggests, a Deleuzian approach accepts and, indeed, embraces an identification with and a visceral response to film in which thought is not separate from but a *key part of* the viewing experience. This is closer to more recent statements by Cronenberg himself, in looking back on his film career and acknowledging a new realization of his relation to the notions of the body: '[a]s a filmmaker, too, it's all body...So the body as the first fact of human existence is one of the underlying realities of my moviemaking, even though I couldn't have articulated it until a few years ago.'[122] Furthermore, he has shown a greater ability to articulate his 'belief that the mind and the body are the same – that they are inextricably entwined, but more than that, that they are actually one and the same in that one cannot exist without the other.'[123]

Conventional film theory struggles to accommodate how disturbing images can nevertheless be experienced as pleasurable. However, according to Deleuze, the gaze, in concert with the cinematic apparatus, acts as a machine that sets up a complex web of interconnecting lines of flight, which are not based around moral or gendered hierarchies. Deleuze approaches film as intrinsically an embodied event, connecting notions of film, audience and thought. Rather than totally supplanting existing theory, what this theory offers is a more flexible, open and less judgemental means to approach the study of film. Perhaps, most usefully, it is a way of considering how a particular film might work rather than offering a totalizing theory of the film medium. It can be helpful in the revelation of existing connections rather than an interpretative tool. For Cronenberg, conventional divisions around gendered gazes and notions of active and passive simply do not work. A key part of his aesthetic is the notion of evolutionary multiplicities in the area of sexuality (discussed further in chapter 1 in relation to Clive Barker and in chapter 3 in relation to Burroughs). Indeed, all the films covered in this book contain an element of exploration in terms of sexualities, whether with bioports in *eXistenZ* or using *Crash*'s use of impacts, scars and even tattoos to create the immediacy which appears lacking in affectless modernity.

In *Cinema II: The Time-Image*, Deleuze argues that movement is automatic in the film image and that this provokes the viewer to thought, awakening in us what he terms a 'spiritual automaton'. He defines this as the 'artistic essence of the image' realized once movement becomes automatic and 'producing a shock to thought, communicating vibrations to the cortex, touching the nervous and cerebral system directly.' He describes this as 'the shared power of what forces thinking and what thinks under a shock; a *nooshock*.'[124] The spiritual automaton does not refer to repressed images in our unconscious but refers to the experiences of the body, when 'the sensory shock raises us from the images to conscious thought' as if thought were independent.[125] This echoes Cronenberg's response to the frequently asked question of what he is trying to say in his films. He (perhaps knowingly) uses an image from *Scanners* (1980): '[i]magine you've drilled a hole in your forehead and that what you dream is projected directly onto a screen'.[126]

However, post-1982, the kind of response that the films discussed in this book demand can best be described as literary, not based around a shock to the senses. Camera movement is slow, acting styles are languorous, dialogue is often delivered with a ponderous deliberation and easily won emotions are avoided. We are forced to think and 'read' what we see, not experience the visceral thrill of a *Scanners*-style exploding head. His work does not appeal directly to the visceral nerve-endings of the audience but to their literary sensibilities. He creates a cinema that is concerned with embodiment, but the reaction which he provokes is measured, reserved and detached. It is to the literary cognoscenti that Cronenberg's aesthetic appeals and so, instead of special effects, there are literary titles, joint interviews and photo shoots alongside authors and in the films themselves long takes and forward tracking shots (especially opening sequences – think of *Crash*, *Spider* and *A History of Violence*) dominate over crowd-pleasing spectacle (reflected in the critical disappointment at *Crash*'s lack of kinetic drama). The special effects in a Cronenberg film, post-1982, are *acting qualities* – Jeremy Irons' performance in *Dead Ringers* as much as the motion-control photography or Ralph Fiennes' incoherent but meaningful mumbling in *Spider* as much as the bleeding potato and rat-in-the-bread hallucinations which were filmed but cut from the final version. The 'nooshock' is *in* the film, not *from* the film directly. We participate in the pain of a character's thinking, not reacting to a gross-out act of violence. It is still an embodied event, but unlike gut reactions, which also start in the brain, our reaction is not directly linked to the emission of an abject substance (vomit, faeces, semen).

Cronenberg does not favour ostentatious jumpcuts or obvious breaches of classical Hollywood editing style, but, nonetheless, he is implicitly involved in practices which are quietly revolutionary. His avowed intent to 'show the unshowable and speak the unspeakable'[127] has connotations beyond his desire to explore transgressive states, which inevitably bring him into conflict at times with censorious bodies (notably over *Videodrome* and *Crash*). It also reflects an abiding interest in literature which is deemed 'unfilmable' and an ongoing fascination with notions of impossibility (see chap 6). For him, the 'unshowable' includes portraying the present to denote the past and the 'unspeakable' to denote communication. Cronenberg is interested in thinking as a creative act and there is a restless search in his films to isolate the exact point at which creation takes place. The object of creation extends from pornography (*Videodrome*), to new life (*The Fly*, *Dead Ringers* and the aborted *Frankenstein* project), to reconstructed car crashes (*Crash*), to computer games (*eXistenZ*), to new identities (*A History of Violence*) but is focused most precisely on the act of writing (*Naked Lunch* and *Spider*).

Deleuze is also interested in pinpointing the moment of creation and highlights the potential of the affection-image, particularly in the close-up, to induce a reaction in the viewer far greater than the more obvious visceral appeal of the action-image. When 'the spiritual automaton' is in operation, according to Deleuze, the mental state of the individual becomes no longer that of a 'doer', one who can act on his or her environment but that of a 'seer, who sees better and further than he can react, that is, think'.[128] This is relevant for Cronenberg because what we see, literally, in every Cronenberg film discussed in this book is a male protagonist, shown in close-up, *thinking*. Such close-ups, held in shot slightly longer than we might expect and a refusal to cut directly to what might be looked at, creates an effect in which the viewer has to search the face for meaning. It may be one reason that the lead roles in such films are often felt to be career-enhancing, or even career-defining (Jeremy Irons paying tribute to Cronenberg on receiving his Oscar for *Reversal of Fortune*). James Woods in *Videodrome*, Christopher Walken in *The Dead Zone*, Jeff Goldblum in *The Fly* and Ralph Fiennes in *Spider* are all forced to draw on abilities to show, by facial expression alone, interior states that other films rarely require. The transformative power of thought, whether as telepathic scanner (*Scanners*), existentialist gynaecologists remapping the female anatomy (*Dead Ringers*) or bemused schizophrenic (*Spider*), is a central part of the Cronenberg protagonist (discussed further in chapter 6). The potential impact of an image, for Deleuze (drawing from Bergson), lies in the 'zone of indeterminacy' or 'gap' it creates between perception and action.[129] This pause provides the space from which acts of thinking and creation arise.

In *A History of Violence*, Cronenberg portrays the gradual emergence of a suppressed identity as Joey the killer erupts through the façade of Tom, the mild family man. This is not achieved by special effects, dubious doubles, shadows or heavy-handed symbolism but by Mortensen's face. In the scenes where Tom expertly unloads the shotgun, the rough sex with Edie on the stairs and particularly where he negotiates the exchange of his son with Fogarty, Joey's face, a harder, more cruel face, starts to come through. In particular, this is apparent in the parallel scenes where Tom first shoots the killers who attack his diner and later when his son rescues him by blasting the mobster Fogarty with a shotgun as he is about to execute Tom. In both cases, a close-up of a bewildered Tom is juxtaposed with a gun and in both cases his hand is cropped from the frame so that the face turns to look at the weapon and, by implication, the hands that wield them, as if they are acting on their own volition. This same trope of bewildered fascination at the unconscious synergy of mind and body is present in *eXistenZ* (see chapter 5). In many of these close-ups, it is the coming-to-terms with change that is the central feature. As Tom approaches his son who has just saved his life, neither character is what the other thought. The father is not a hero but a killer and the son is not a weak victim but capable of violent action in a crisis. Most strikingly, in the final shot, a close-up of Viggo Mortensen's tear-streaked face manages to convey the contradictory elements of suffering, despair and, as Josh Olson's script suggests, 'hope'. When Joey confronts his alter ego, Richie, the two indulge in a strange head-bumping/rubbing ritual as if they are physically joined and like the Mantle brothers, separation inevitably means death for one, and one left scarred, possibly terminally. Echoing *Scanners*, a fight to the death between brothers has led to a fusion of identities, a loss, a bodily change (complete with accent shift) and an ambivalent hero, broken but alive. The face of a Cronenberg protagonist, especially as realized by Christopher Walken, Jeremy Irons and Viggo Mortenson, acts as a focal point for the experience of emotional pain and shifting identities in a continual flux.

In *Cinema 2*, Deleuze also uses the image of a crystal to describes his notion of a flat depth in which past and present combine, creating a perpetual present: '[t]hus the image has to be present and past, still present and already past, at once and the same time...If it was not already past at the same time as the present, the present would never pass on. The past does not follow the present that it is no longer, it coexists with the present it was.'[130] In exploring issues of embodiment, Cronenberg's films work in a similar way. Prior to *Spider*, Cronenberg's characters do not have pasts, they only have a continuous present (discussed in chapter 5). Without a past, there is no method of unearthing a previous trauma that could be seen as causing current anxiety. In the case of *Spider*, Cronenberg does provide us with access to a past but only in order to question its validity. In this context, theories of childhood seduction, whether actual or only fantasies, become irrelevant. Indeed, more than rejecting a sense of the past, from Max Renn's 'New Flesh' in *Videodrome* to Bill Lee's Interzone adventures in *Naked Lunch* to Vaughan's 'project' in *Crash*, Cronenberg's films are centrally concerned with embracing a future, which is in the hands of the individual. In an echo of the plot line of one of Cronenberg's abandoned projects, *Total Recall*, methods of retrieving incest-survivor narratives have also come under increasing critical scrutiny, suggesting that true and false memories cannot always be reliably distinguished.[131] In the case of *Spider*, Cronenberg uses flashback for the first time in his film career in order to dramatize this precise problem of 'infected memory' as the hero, Dennis Cleg, projects guilt for the murder of his mother onto his demonized father.

At first, *A History of Violence* would appear to provide us with a past for the main character. However, the focus of the narrative is very much the present. The presence on screen twice of a large town clock is symbolic. It appears to emphasize the passage of time but, on both occasions, the time displayed is the same: 1.15. Paradoxically, the narrative takes place within an extended frozen moment. It concerns the past but principally how this co-exists with the present *at the same time and within the same person* – Viggo Mortensen's character. We have no flashback structure (as in John Wagner and Vincent Locke's graphic novel), very little direct reference to what has happened twenty years before and in the final section of the film, Tom Stall now transformed into Joey Cusack, confronts his brother Richie via a sudden shift of setting from Indiana to Philadelphia, not by a chronological shift. The past doesn't meet the present – the two have always co-existed. Tom Stall's split between his past as a killer and his present as a loving father and small-town businessman is based on a division entirely of his own making, not due to a past psychological trauma, and one which he consciously exorcizes by killing his brother and then returning to his family.

What we are really presented with is a largely unexplained present, which, like Tom Stall, we must simply 'deal with'. We do this by creating and moulding the present, not by looking backwards for answers in the past. One could even say that the relationship between Edie and Tom, whilst appearing to look back by Edie's initiation of sexual role play as a cheerleader because 'We never got to be teenagers together', is still based on creating a fiction in the present. Indeed, it is debatable at what point an invented reality becomes true so that when confronted in the diner Tom's denial that he knows Fogarty is so complete, he appears to even believe it himself. The film problematizes the past and for all the suggestions of portentous events in Tom's previous life, we never really know which elements of it are true.

Cronenberg's focus on a perpetual present is reflected in his choice to leave a fairly gaping plot-hole unplugged. In the graphic novel, the mobster who comes looking for Stall having recognized him from local media reports has his suspicions confirmed about Stall's identity by a close encounter with Stall's son.[132] The idea that you would not recognize someone from twenty years ago, when their own son of about the same age is standing right next to them, is a wilful evasion on the part of Cronenberg who seems reluctant to suggest inherited characteristics. The character of the son does change and does so in reaction to the father's violent action but this takes place in the present, not the past, so that the question that the son asks is not 'Who were you ?' but 'Who *are* you ?' Cronenberg's conception of chronology is akin to a truism of set design that, irrespective of the era in which a narrative is set, in order to seem real it must contain a mixture of features from 'different pasts', which all occur within the present moment. In a sense, his actor's bodies are his set design, carrying the pasts of their characters with them. Having demonstrated his killing ability in despatching Fogarty's henchmen, Tom's past as Joey rises to the surface and Mortensen undergoes a bodily change, seen in his hunched shoulders and wearied gait as he returns to the house, a process that gains momentum in the final phase of the film as he subtly shifts from an Indiana to a Philadelphian accent.

Notions of authorship

The level of personal and artistic identification that Cronenberg expresses in relation to Burroughs in particular (see chapter three) is reminiscent of the protagonist in Jorges Luis Borges' short story 'Pierre Menard, Author of the *Quixote*', who attempts not to copy Cervantes' epic novel as such but to actually rewrite it word for word by immersing himself in all the influences that might have had an impact on the original author. Cronenberg is in some ways a paradoxical, Menard-like figure. Both claim to read an original literary text, discard it and then create one of their own; both seek a *fusion* with a source text; and yet both accept that what they are doing is inherently impossible. Moreover, in a strange way, like Menard's *Quixote*, some of Cronenberg`s adaptations are more meaningful than the works upon which they are based because they are created *despite*, not because of them. More particularly, as Borges notes, 'it is permissible to see in this "final" *Quixote* a kind of palimpsest, through which the traces – tenuous but not indecipherable – of our "previous" friend's writing should be translucently visible.'[133]

Cronenberg is fairly scathing about Sydney Pollack's methods of dealing with scriptwriters, involving months of meetings and socialising. Cronenberg concludes that 'this is a guy who really wishes he could write the script himself, but he can't write it, so he's trying to fuse with the other guy, so it's almost like the other guy is him writing'.[134] Although he calls this 'perverse', it is virtually identical to his comments about Burroughs, *Naked Lunch*, and himself (only one page later) and his statements elsewhere on Ballard and *Crash*.[135] This gives the strong impression that it is *he* who wished he had written the books from which he works, but adapting them for the screen is the nearest he can get: 'Burroughs and I get into the telepod together and we come out fused...Half the time I don't know whether I invented this, or it's part Burroughs and part me, or it's all Burroughs...it also felt like Burroughs could have written this. Maybe Burroughs did write this. Maybe I just memorised it, and I couldn't even tell anymore'.[136] This constitutes a rather unpleasant sense of basking in reflected literary glory: 'it's nothing that I would have done on my own. And it's nothing that Burroughs could have done on his own. It took the two of us'.[137] Although Cronenberg claims to be free of influences, this expression is very similar to comments by André Bazin (a figure to whom Cronenberg has referred with some familiarity in interviews) talking about Renoir's *A Day in the Country* (1936): 'this is the refraction of one work in another creator's consciousness...It took somebody like Maupassant, but also someone like Renoir [both of them, Jean and Auguste], to achieve it.'[138] Certainly, Cronenberg is very precise when it is *his* authorship that is in question, as seen in his swift clarification of a co-writing credit for *Fast Company* (1979).[139]

As Deleuze notes, 'the flattest of images is almost imperceptibly inflected, layered, with varying depths that force you to travel within it.'[140] From Professor Brian O'Blivion in *Videodrome*, who only exists as an image on television, through *Dead Ringers'* use of reflected images in the operating theatre scenes to *Crash*'s bravura camera positioning in the credit sequence, opening triptych and particularly car wash scene, where the cinema screen is redefined in terms of a car windscreen, Cronenberg has shown an enduring interest in the intersection of planes and of screens-within-screens. Cronenberg likes to assert that his films are fresh and creative departures from their source texts, but what we tend to find is that there is a kind of Turin-shroud effect with previous images bleeding through and affecting what we see. The oft-noted 'flatness' of Cronenberg's work is partly explained by this concept of film as a palimpsest. Where Cronenberg keenly accepts a link with a source text, such as with *Naked Lunch*, he often asserts there is complete creative overlay. This book will consider to what extent that process is as perfect as he claims, what happens when he claims to be working with an entirely fresh canvas and how overlaying apparently extraneous texts can illuminate aspects of his film-making aesthetic.

To reject the legitimacy of a study such as this one due to its focus on one particular director would cast doubts on much Film Studies scholarship past and present and would mean that no study of a film-maker's work could proceed without sketching out the full history of the auteur debate and constantly rehearsing the positions of figures like André Bazin, François Truffaut, Stephen Heath and Peter Wollen. It is not necessary, or indeed practical, to do so. However, this book does not ascribe 'authorship' uncritically to Cronenberg in relation to any of the films discussed here. It is important to acknowledge the tensions that exist in such concepts, whilst also accepting their enduring uses. As a potent marketing tool, studios and their publicity departments still encourage the public perception of a named director as having some sense of ownership of a film, thereby bestowing connotations of value on their product. The notion of the auteur remains an enduring part of most Film Studies degree courses, reflected in the continuing use of texts like the 1981 collection of essays edited by John Caughie, *Theories of Authorship*, Seán Burke's *The Death and Return of the Author* (1992) and more recent collections, Virginia Wrexman Wright's *Film and Authorship* (2002) and David A. Gerstner and Janet Staiger's *Authorship and Film* (2003). It would seem that it is a problematic concept whose demise has been announced frequently but also slightly prematurely. Even apparent attempts to remove director-status, such as the Dogma 95 manifesto, paradoxically required a certificate signed by its creators, effectively 'authoring' the text at one remove.

However, the mantra that even low-budget films cannot get made without large investment of capital and the huge numbers of people involved in creating a commercially viable film mean that lonely acts of creation are not possible, no longer rings quite so true. Lengthy credit sequences remain but so too do dedicated sequences of DVD extras showcasing previously unheard voices, e.g. screenwriters, producers and special effects teams, effectively reinforcing notions of auteurism. Indeed, in terms of volume, both number and length, the extras packages can seem to overwhelm the films themselves. Furthermore, the content of many of these extras focuses on a 'human element', such as out-takes, interviews, and behind-the-scenes explanations of special effects. Developments in digital technology, including blogging, captured video and webcams, have brought the possibility of exchanging images and text to a wider public, introducing new forms of authorship and as in the music industry, sampling and file sharing are continually undermining attempts to maintain clear ownership, not destroying the notion of authorship but making it more problematic. With the rapid development of services such as YouTube, where users can tag videos with keywords and initiate exchanges of video clips in a constantly changing interactive flux, shifting day by day and sometimes even hour by hour, notions of authorship are made more multiple and hybrid. To use a viral metaphor, which Cronenberg himself has explored in a number of his films, electronic material once released, spreads and mutates, independent of its source.

In the tension between modern and postmodern views of auteurism, it would seem clear initially that Cronenberg has positioned himself in the latter camp. All the literature he has adapted is drawn from the latter part of the twentieth century – *Naked Lunch* (1959), *Crash* (1973), *Spider* (1990) and *A History of Violence* (1997) and, certainly, according to Frederic Jameson's definition in *The Cultural Logic of Late Capitalism* (1991), Cronenberg's work includes features that might mark a text out as postmodern. These include divisions between high and low culture, stylistic flatness, a lack of history, an interest in schizophrenia (breaking the signifying chain, especially relating to chronology), a fragmentation of the subject, a focus on visual culture and a sense of multiple reality through electronic media. Key terms such as multiplicity, plurality, hybridity and impossibility recur in discussions of his work. *Videodrome*, as Beard notes, has proven 'irresistibly attractive to postmodern cultural theorists', appearing to almost have something for everyone of a postmodern persuasion: for followers of McLuhan, there is the literal extension of the self via the influence of visual media; for disciples of Baudrillard, there is the tension between simulacrum and original; and for readers of Debord, visual spectacle replaces lived experience.'[141]

However, other key features of his work, such as a continued focus on the written word and the figure of the writer, are more modernist in tone. Bluestone insists that adaptations should be assessed as autonomous works on their own terms and describes a view of cinematic authorship, that Cronenberg seems happy to perpetuate: 'the filmist becomes not a translator for an established author, but a new author in his own right.'[142] The image of the isolated, starving artist, only appreciated fully after their death, does seem quite appealing to Cronenberg.[143] He certainly talks about films in Romantic terms, ascribing to them a quality of personal vision, and he compares the censorship of the closing scenes of *Videodrome* to one of his children having a limb forcibly amputated.[144] Cronenberg repeatedly asserts that his films express literary connections but not influences and that he ruthlessly focuses on what is important to him alone – 'I insist on being very tightly bound to what is interesting to me and focus very intensely on that. It's kind of a simplification – perhaps that's some kind of a modernist, as opposed to a post-modernist, approach to movie-making.'[145]

Jameson identifies postmodernism as a break from existentialism and yet Cronenberg is a self-confessed 'card-carrying existentialist'. Similarly, it might initially seem as though his films challenge a high-low cultural divide but all his adaptation choices also betray an allegiance to cult fiction, which could be seen as differently elitist in its innaccessible non-conformity. Although *Videodrome* is often hailed as a postmodern classic, the correct poetic source of 'Love comes in at the eye' (wrongly attributed in the film) belongs to a modernist, W. B. Yeats and effectively he uses literary allusions to brand a film as Cronenbergian in ways which Bordwell associates with the art film (see chapter 5). Whilst there are references to *Videodrome* in postmodern novels by writers like Thomas Pynchon and William Gibson, Cronenberg himself in interviews frequently mentions modernists like T. S. Eliot or Beckett.[146] It is as if Cronenberg is playing postmodern games but for modernist ends and that ultimately he cannot bring himself to believe fully in the postmodern project. He is ultimately caught between asserting that his work is independent of an original (a form of simulacra) and yet sharing in the cultural capital of the original text (closer to a copy).

Historically, Deleuze traces the period when the simulacrum became fully visible to Italian neo-realism and the French New Wave, the latter marking the beginning of Cronenberg's film-making career. Perhaps if it is possible to place Cronenberg's work historically at all, it is in the sense of the history of theory. By the time of 'late Cronenberg' as in advanced capitalist society, linear causalities have broken down to be replaced by more complex but potentially more creative connections and new 'lines of flight'. In this context, Cronenberg's 'New Flesh' is ultimately a kind of literary hybrid, not a copy, typified by exhaustion but ultimately an affirmative, opening up of new possibilities. In such a process, the relationship between text and adaptation is not, and perhaps has never been, a matter of original and copy but copy and simulacrum in an ongoing process of reflection, simulation and enhanced *creativity*.

Peter Morris rather portentously declaims that at the start of Cronenberg's cinematic career, 'film would liberate him from his literary possession by Nabokov and Burroughs. He could find his own voice', and this book will examine to what extent he can be said to have broken away completely from these influences.[147] The notion of 'producing a film that is really a book' is present from the beginning of his film career when the funding for *Stereo* (1969) was obtained from the Canada Council under the auspices of writing 'a Nabokov-style novel'.[148] Sheen notes that 'the emergence of the author-function...also marks the emergence of that defining position of Western European privilege, the *intellectual*', and Cronenberg seems drawn to casting himself in this image, craving for film (and by extension, for himself as a film-maker) the same academic prestige traditionally accorded to literature.[149]

He claims that his predilection for European art cinema was 'just the same as being interested in obscure novels', and describes, in a rather contrived conceit, the directing process as akin to 'having to learn the form of the novel or the sonnet, and understand its history, and understand where we are now, its history, for your novel to actually make sense and be relevant', concluding 'at bottom, it's the same act'.[150]

Whilst he is aware of auteur theory, his views on directors like Truffaut, Alain Renais and Federico Fellini suggest that he himself appears untroubled by debates concerning authorship: '[y]ou entered a world of their own creation...when you went to see their films. That world was consistent from film to film. There was a tone, a feeling and dynamics that were consistently at work'.[151] In an uncritical acceptance of the basic tenets of auteur theory, Cronenberg asserts that 'the most accurate thing to say about my scripts is that they're the product of a personal vision', that 'I think thematic consistency is there', and he talks about certain readings of his films as being 'correct' or not.[152]

Linked to the problematic notion of authorship is the idea of intent. For McFarlane, 'it does seem important in evaluating the film version of a novel to try to assess the kind of adaptation the film tries to be. Such an assessment would at least preclude the critical reflex that takes a film to task for not being something it does not aim to be'.[153] Such comments seem fair until one raises the question of *whose* intention and whether notions of intent, like authorship, derive their fullest meaning from an interrelation with the audience, i.e. there may not be one single intention for every viewer. As stated by René Wellek and Austin Warren, 'the meaning of a work of art is not exhausted by, or even equivalent to, its intention. As a system of values, it leads an independent life.'[154] McFarlane implies a lack of contested meaning, which is the kind of approach that would parallel Foucault's concerns about potential ideological restrictions surrounding the authorship question.

In *Must We Mean What We Say* (1969), Stanley Cavell sees a consideration of intention in understanding works of art as unavoidable. He suggests that

> We follow the progress of a piece the way we follow what someone is saying or doing. Not, however, to see how it will come out, nor to learn something specific, but to see what *it* says, to see what someone has been able to make out of these materials. A work of art does not express some particular intention (as statements do), nor achieve particular goals (the way technological skill and moral action do), but, one may say, celebrates the fact that men can intend their lives at all.[155]

Critics like Monroe Beardsley and W. K. Wimsatt take the position that to come to a view about artistic intention, it may be necessary to look outside the work itself.[156] However, as Cavell points out, this approach is laden with assumptions about intention being a conscious act and fails to question where evidence of intention is to be found, such as overt statements. By contrast, he argues that 'the correct sense of the question "Why?" directs you further *into* the work.'[157] This book will be underpinned by the belief, shared by Cavell, that we do not illuminate a work by asking an author what their intention is, rather we discover the intention through interrogating the work.

Apart from the auteur-related difficulty in ascribing a clear 'intent' to a film, Cronenberg's pronouncements on his own films also remain problematic. Even if a film could be ascribed to a single creative force, whether the author is the person best placed to understand or articulate what the meaning of a text might be, is debatable. During the course of this book, I will refer to remarks made by Cronenberg about his own work. In any serious scholarly endeavour, it would seem presumptuous to ignore completely records of what an artist has said about his or her work, and Cronenberg has taken part in a large number of interviews about his films. Indeed, the whole premise of publications like the Faber series of which Chris Rodley's *Cronenberg on Cronenberg* (1992) is a part would suggest that the views of a director have value.

However, as Jill McGreal notes, the number of interviews and the repetitive nature of questioning means that 'Cronenberg handles most questions with alarming dexterity...his answers are charmingly standard and it's difficult to assess what's really important to him'.[158] Cronenberg appears equally at ease in interviews with both academic and mainstream journals, talking seriously about philosophy, literature and film as art. Such interviews exemplify Timothy Corrigan's idea of 'the writing and explaining of a film through the promotion of a certain intentional self; it is frequently the commercial dramatisation of self as the motivating agency of textuality'.[159] Cronenberg is very aware of the mechanics and the consequences of such a process, for example, in response to a question about how he would alter the human body, he replies, 'I can't really answer it spontaneously. Anything I say in the context of an interview has huge implications'.[160]

Cronenberg is very knowing about the impression that his films and interviews might make: 'I re-invent myself by that which I want to show'.[161] Corrigan's account of an interview with Francis Ford Coppola, with carefully rehearsed responses and even an interest in the recording equipment being used, closely parallels descriptions of Cronenberg in similar situations.[162] In an interview with Linda Kauffman, Cronenberg repeats within a matter of seconds an almost verbatim thematic summary of *Crash* ('it's a meditation on love, sex and mortality'), which sounds suspiciously like a compulsion to repeat a tag line for marketing purposes.[163] Elsewhere, Cronenberg claims that 'I did not really feel that I had any conscious influences in film', asserting 'that I had seen everybody who is normally considered a huge influence: Fellini, Bergman, Antonioni, I suppose I was just consuming them, rather than studying them'.[164] His expression here from 1992 is an almost verbatim repetition from an interview nearly ten years earlier, creating the sense of regurgitating rehearsed positions.[165] Cronenberg appears to exemplify the Barthesian notion of a figure who could be designated as author but whose 'life is no longer the origin of his fictions but a fiction contributing to his work.'[166] To use another Barthesian concept, it seems he aspires to produce a writerly text, which contains self-conscious rhetorical elements that call attention to themselves as artifice and in which the reader is the key factor in producing meaning. However, he cannot erase himself from the picture so that readerly traits, those tending to support a fixed pre-determined meaning, remain.

Michel Foucault links the development of notions of authorship with the emergence of 'individualisation', in which what he terms the 'author-function', rather than opening up semantic possibilities, actually functions as an ideological restraint on the range of a text's possible meanings.[167] To try and avoid this, where direct citations do appear from Cronenberg about his work, their inclusion will be intended to provide additional insight or information, rather than due to the fact that it is the director who utters them. Neither looking to a single viewpoint for definitive statements of meaning and intent or completely rejecting any link between a work of art and an individual, whether described by terms like author or artist or not, are wholly satisfactory. As Derrida points out, there is a paradoxical circularity of interdependent relationships in operation, which should make severing, or overemphasizing links, impossible:

> The work of art stems from the artist, so they say. But what is an artist? The one who produces works of art. The origin of the artist is the work of art, the origin of the work of art is the artist.[168]

Cavell's notion of intention and Derrida's parergonal logic, although deriving from different standpoints, both ultimately emphasize a need to focus on the work itself: in Cavell's case as evidence of authorial intention and in Derrida's as part of a more encompassing notion of what might constitute a work of art, including material that might traditionally be thought of as extraneous. The approach of this book will be primarily informed by such notions. Cronenberg's statements constitute, in Genette's terms, a paratextual source, which needs to be weighed up against other transtextual evidence, producing a multiplicity of, possibly contested, meanings, not presented as a definitive judgement on any given issue. If Deleuze has a role to play in this study, it is a similar opening-up to the possibility of meaning being created from a range of sources. In order to account for images which are pleasurable and yet disturbing, the 'extreme metaphors' of the title of this introduction, we may need to follow Barbara Kennedy's suggestion that we should seek 'to explain the cinematic as a "material capture", not as a text with a meaning, but as a body which performs, as...an assemblage, as an abstract machine,' and to understand Cronenberg more fully, the prime material to be 'captured' is literary.[169]

Literary influences
In a metaphor of literary abundance, Cronenberg describes his home in Toronto as being constructed with 'walls of books' and the name of the magazine for which his father wrote, *Reader's Digest*, accurately describes the young Cronenberg's consumption of literary influences.[170] Cronenberg himself is described as 'bookish', admitting that he 'read very widely, especially novels',[171] and at sixteen, he

submitted a short story to *The Magazine of Fantasy and Science Fiction*. As a student at the University of Toronto, he cultivated the appearance of 'a flamboyant, Byronic hero', and he switched from Science to what he describes as 'a very beautifully constructed English-philosophy-history course', eventually being awarded the Gertrude Lawler Scholarship for finishing first at University College.[172] In interviews, his literary references range from Kafka to *Moby Dick* to Catherine Mackinnon's feminist stance against pornography.[173] Kauffman describes Cronenberg as 'by far the most literate of contemporary filmmakers', and according to Morris, 'his understanding of literature and literary criticism is prodigious'.[174]

Cronenberg rejects psychoanalytical or feminist ideological systems as 'the right set of critical and surgical tools through which to make a very meaningful anatomical inspection of film'.[175] It is French critics of the *Cahiers* group, such as Serge Grünberg, who Cronenberg himself feels are most in tune with his work (and with whom he is much less guarded in interview), partly because 'the spectrum of their analysis is also very broad' and more particularly 'they also employ *literary* references as well as cinematic ones'.[176] Few directors would be able to allude with some precision, as Cronenberg does, during a discussion of de Sade with Grünberg, to a critical work on William Burroughs (Eric Mottram's 1977 *Algebra of Desire*).[177]

This book explores Cronenberg's interest in fictional structures and his clearest inspiration for that: literature that enjoys playing with its own limits. In the case of Burroughs (via his cut-up experiments), Nabokov (with game-playing motifs) and Ballard (proposing confrontational psychopathologies), we have authors who play very consciously on the relationship with readers. For someone like Cronenberg who describes himself as 'a card-carrying existentialist' (discussed later in chapter 5), in using literary comparisons, it makes sense to look at material which features protagonists who shape their own reality, a notable feature of all the main source texts in this book.[178]

Cronenberg is interested in the act of writing, both as a metaphor and a literal activity, connected with creating and ordering one's own reality (the subject of his version of *Naked Lunch*). If at some stage in his life he was not able to make films, he has stated that 'it would be very natural for me to write' and, whilst in Tourettes-sur-Loup, he claims to have written a novel, all drafts of which were apparently destroyed.[179] His literary aspirations appear to be displaced into his screenwriting: his script for *Crash* (1996), for example, uses detailed prose in its descriptions of setting and action. When asked about his lack of camera instructions in scripts, he replies with the air of a frustrated novelist that 'I want it to read more like fiction than something else', and Cronenberg's interview with Salman Rushdie in hiding in 1995 reflects the director's literary ambitions and the belief that 'I always thought that I would be a novelist'.[180] During the interview itself, Cronenberg reveals a strong sympathy with Ingmar Bergman who 'felt that he wasn't really an artist because he should have been a novelist' and describes how, when Bergman published his screenplays, 'he kind of rewrote them to novelize them, really to legitimise them. He admitted that he felt this kind of inferiority complex, that the novel was high art but film wasn't. I must admit that sometimes I still feel the presence of that hierarchy myself'.[181]

Where relevant, this study will also draw upon novelizations drawn from Cronenberg's films. Jean-Paul Sartre talks of readers who come to original novels after having seen the film version, and hence view the book 'as a more or less faithful commentary' on the film.[182] Ironically, a similar effect is produced by novelizations, works of literature, which had no existence before the film. Sartre describes a subjective impression, produced by ignorance of the literature, and novelizations literalize this impression but can also add to one's understanding of a film. To produce such a work, a writer must watch a film several times frame by frame and then produce a prose 'reading' or interpretation of that film. The product, in effect, becomes the literary work upon which the film could have been based. With front covers now routinely reprinted to feature shots from the film as a mutually reinforcing marketing strategy, Judith Halberstam refers to symptoms of a troubled cultural circulation, creating a sense of 'films that precede novelisations'.[183]

Structure
The following book is generally structured so as to focus on one film and one author at any one time, but the pervasive influence of certain literary influences, particularly Burroughs, Nabokov and Ballard, mean that it is necessary to keep returning to these 'mother lodes' of influence. I am not attempting to trace a simple causal connection between specific literary works and Cronenberg's films but suggest that understanding specific passages of certain writers will illuminate features of Cronenberg's literary aesthetic. Therefore, although J. G. Ballard's *The Kindness of Women* was not published until 1992, it is *how* Ballard's prose works rather than *when* it was written that is important here. As the focus of the book is on literary connections, the notion of the writer will prove particularly important, and my analysis will predominantly consider those films with which Cronenberg had a substantial part to play in the scriptwriting process.

Chapter 1 deals with *Videodrome* (1982) in relation to Brett Easton Ellis' novel *American Psycho* (1991), media prophet Marshall McLuhan, and the short stories of horror writer and film-maker Clive Barker, particularly from his *Books of Blood* (1984, 1985). Cronenberg's film is discussed within a Deleuzian-influenced notion of masochism and with reference to the fiction of Sacher-Masoch, particularly *Venus in Furs* (1870), against a background of Jean Baudrillard's concepts of surplus televisual mediation and Guy Debord's ideas of spectacle. Masochism and sadism (see chapter 4) have been traditionally viewed through the distorting lens of psychoanalysis but surprisingly little critical use has been made of the literary works that gave the practices their name. Sacher-Masoch and de Sade may not have invented the impulses they describe but they gave them powerful written expression.

Chapter 2 discusses *Dead Ringers* (1988). The significance of dream sequences, the 'evacuation' of language into silence and the talismanic significance of the gynaecological tools and Mantle Retractor are explored in relation to the source novel, *Twins* (1977), and a range of other texts featuring 'doubles'. These include Dostoevsky's short story 'The Double' (1846) and more modern novels including Bruce Chatwin's *On the Black Hill* (1983), Rose Tremain's *Restoration* (1989) and a consideration of the film as exposing patriarchal power structures in the medical profession linked to Margaret Atwood's *The Handmaid's Tale* (1987).

Chapter 3 focuses on Cronenberg's *Naked Lunch* (1991). The centrality of the creative act of writing, the importance of language for both Burroughs and Cronenberg, the levels of subjectivity in Lee's narrative, accusations of misogyny and the notion of homosexual disavowal are explored not just in connection with Burroughs' main source text but also other biographical elements from the earlier novels *Queer* (1986), *Junky* (1977) and *Exterminator!* (1979), as well as Ted Morgan's *Literary Outlaw: The Life and Times of William S. Burroughs* (1988), from which Cronenberg appropriates material for the film.

Chapter 4 covers Cronenberg's *Crash* (1996) and, like the preceding chapter, draws initially upon the overt source (J. G. Ballard's 1973 novel *Crash*) but also draws on a range of other texts by the same author, particularly *The Atrocity Exhibition* (1969) and Ballard's extensive body of short stories. This chapter considers to what extent both Ballard's novel and Cronenberg's film might be seen as pornographic, the relevance of de Sade, particularly concerning repetition and also connects the narrative organization of the film with structures favoured by Vladimir Nabokov.

Chapter 5 discusses *eXistenZ* (1999) in relation to the work of Nabokov in more detail, against a background of Sartrean notions of existentialism. A number of stylistic tropes are examined, including the artist as hero, motifs of game-playing, the use of *mise-en-abîme*, the significance of naming, self-consuming narrative structures and the markers of authorial intrusion in relation to a wide range of Nabokovian texts, particularly *Bend Sinister* (1960) and *Invitation to a Beheading* (1960).

Chapter 6 considers *Spider* (2003) in relation to developments in Cronenberg's thinking about a sense of how past and present interact and particularly the location of such interactions in borderline and threshold states within the frame. Links with Ian McEwan's novel *A Child in Time* (1987) focus on consideration of the realization of one particular flashback scene in Cronenberg's film. This chapter also discusses Cronenberg's conception of the derelict hero, whose literary antecedents can be found in the work of Fyodor Dostoevsky.

This book suggests that such a process of projection is highly coloured by literary influences, particularly when the director in question is so self-aware. When

Cronenberg states '[y]ou have to be outrageous. You have to turn it inside-out and make it physical and exterior', he is not making de-contextualized statements about sexual politics but referring to overlaying a physical body with another anatomical metaphor: the body *as text*.[184] What is being turned inside-out in films like *Naked Lunch*, is not just a physical body but what George Bluestone terms the 'mutational processes' involved in literary adaptation.[185]

Notes

1. J. G. Ballard, *The Kindness of Women* (London: Grafton Press, 1991), p. 347.
2. 'David Cronenberg and J. G. Ballard: Set for Collision', (http://www.indexon censorship.org/issue397/cronenberg.htm), p. 3.
3. Gaile McGregor, 'Grounding the Countertext: David Cronenberg and the Ethnospecificity of Horror', *Canadian Journal of Film Studies* 2:1 (1992), p. 56.
4. Andrew Klevan, 'The mysterious disappearance of style: some critical notes about the writing on *Dead Ringers*', in Michael Grant, (ed.) *The Modern Fantastic: The Films of David Cronenberg* (Trowbridge: Flicks Books, 2000), pp. 148–167.
5. See Xavier Mendik, 'Logic, creativity and (critical) misinterpretation: an interview with David Cronenberg', in Michael Grant, (ed.), op. cit., p. 172; Gavin Smith, 'Cronenberg: Mind Over Matter', *Film Comment* 33:2 (March-April 1997), p. 20; and 'The Interview', an interview with David Cronenberg conducted by William Beard and Piers Handling in Piers Handling, (ed.), *The Shape of Rage: The Films of David Cronenberg* (Toronto: Academy of Canadian Cinema, 1983; New York: New York Zoetrope Inc., 1983), p. 185.
6. See Victor Bockris, *With William Burroughs: A Report from the Bunker* (New York: Seaver Books, 1981), p. 86.
7. J. G. Ballard, *A User's Guide to the Millennium* (London: Harper Collins Publishers, 1996), p. 126.
8. See Brett Easton Ellis, *American Psycho* (London: Picador, 1991), 'panning down', p. 5, 'a slow dissolve', p. 7; Nabokov penned a screenplay for *Lolita*, although it was mostly ignored by Kubrick; Burroughs had discussions about *Naked Lunch* and did write *The Last Words of Dutch Schultz* (1970); J. G. Ballard admits, 'I am a great cinéphile' in 'Interview with J. G. Ballard' by Serge Grünberg, *Cahiers du Cinéma* 504 (July-August, 1996), pp. 31-32.
9. Richard Rushton, 'Cinema's double: some reflections on Metz', *Screen*, vol. 43, no. 2 (2002), p. 107.
10. Noel Carroll, 'Nightmare and the Horror Film: The Symbolic Biology of Fantastic Beings', *Film Quarterly*, vol. 34, no. 3 (1981), p. 17.
11. See Vicky Lebeau, *Lost Angels: Psychoanalysis and Cinema* (London and New York: Routledge, 1995) and *Psychoanalysis and Cinema: The Play of Shadows* (London and New York: Wallflower, 2001).
12. See James B. Twitchell, *Dreadful Pleasures: An Anatomy of Modern Horror* (New York; Oxford: Oxford University Press, 1985), p. 127 and p. 203.
13. Ibid., p. 245, n.3.
14. See Robin Wood, 'An Introduction to the American Horror Film', in Andrew Britton, Richard Lippe, Tony Williams and Robin Wood (eds.), *The American Nightmare: Essays on the Horror Film* (Toronto: Festival of Festivals, 1979), p. 7.
15. Ibid., p. 14.
16. Ibid.
17. Ibid., p. 15.
18. Ibid., p. 13.

19. Interview with Alan E. Rapp, 'You can never read too much into it', (http:77www.salon.com/ent/movies/int/1999/04=29/cronenberg/index.html), p. 5.
20. See Xavier Trudel, 'Signe des temps modernes ?', *émulsion*, (http:www.horschamp.qc.ca/Emulsions/crash2.hmtl), pp. 1–5.
21. Iain Sinclair, *Crash: David Cronenberg's Post-mortem on J. G. Ballard's 'Trajectory of Fate'* (London: BFI Modern Classics, 1999), p. 122.
22. Sigmund Freud, *Three Essays on the Theory of Sexuality*, translated and edited by James Strachey (London: Hogarth Press, 1962), p. 62.
23. Marq Smith, 'Wound envy: touching Cronenberg's *Crash*', *Screen* 40:2 (summer 1999), p. 200.
24. Bad Object-Choices (eds.), *How Do I Look? Queer Film and Video* (Seattle: Bay Press, 1991), p. 20.
25. Barbara Creed, 'The *Crash* Debate: Anal Wounds, Metallic Kisses' in Jackie Stacey (ed.), 'Special Debate: *Crash*', *Screen*, vol. 39, no. 2 (summer 1998), p. 178.
26. Ibid.
27. Ibid.
28. Barbara Creed, 'The naked crunch: Cronenberg's homoerotic bodies', in Michael Grant (ed.), *The Modern Fantastic: The Films of David Cronenberg* (Trowbridge: Flicks Books, 2000), pp. 96-97.
29. Clive Barker, *The Hellbound Heart* (London: Fontana, 1991), p. 28.
30. See Robin Wood, op. cit., pp. 9–11.
31. Julia Kristeva, *Powers of Horror: An Essay in Abjection*, (New York: Columbia University Press, 1982), p. 2.
32. Ibid., p. 16 and p. 4.
33. Ibid., p. 17.
34. Ibid., p. 62.
35. Ibid., p. 6.
36. Parveen Adams, 'Death Drive' in Michael Grant (ed.), op. cit., p. 102 and p. 108.
37. Ibid., p. 117.
38. Carl Dreyer, *Dreyer in Double Reflection*, translation of Carl Theodor Dreyer's writings *About the Film (Om Filmen)*, edited and with accompanying commentary and essays by Donald Skoller (New York: E. P. Dutton & Co. Inc., 1973) p. 185.
39. Bernardo Bertolucci, cited in 'Interview with Cronenberg', (http://www.flf.com/crash/cmp/cronenberg-interview.htm), p. 4 and Andrew Hultkrans, 'Body Work: Andrew Hultkrans talks with J. G. Ballard and David Cronenberg', *Artforum*, (March 1997), p. 81.
40. Adams, op. cit., p. 113.
41. See Sinclair, op. cit., p. 67.
42. David Cronenberg, cited in Adams, op. cit., p. 113 and David Cronenberg, cited in Gavin Smith, 'Cronenberg: Mind Over Matter', *Film Comment*, vol. 33, no. 2 (March/April 1997), p. 27.
43. Adams, op. cit., p. 113.
44. See Gavin Smith, op. cit., pp. 27-28.
45. Adams, op. cit., p. 115.
46. Sinclair, op. cit., p. 46.
47. Adams, op. cit., p. 106.
48. Ibid., pp. 102-103.
49. Ibid., p. 104.
50. Victor Sage, 'The Gothic, the Body, and the Failed Homeopathy Argument', in Xavier Men dik and Graeme Harper (eds.), *Unruly Pleasures: The Cult Film and its Critics* (Guildford: FAB Press, 2000), p. 152.

51. Stuart Laing, 'The Fiction is Already There: Writing and Film in Blair's Britain' in Jonathan Bignell (ed.), *Writing and Cinema* (Harlow: Longman, 1999), p. 144.
52. J. G. Ballard, *The Kindness of Women* (London: Grafton, 1992), p. 216.
53. J. G. Ballard, *Crash* (London: Vintage, 1995), p. 112.
54. Ibid.
55. Salman Rushdie, *The Ground Beneath Her Feet* (London: Vintage, 2000), p. 203.
56. See Jacques Derrida, *The Truth in Painting*, trans. G. Bennington and I. McLeod (Chicago: University of Chicago Press, 1987), pp. 9–12.
57. Immanuel Kant, *Critique of Aesthetic Judgement*, trans. Werner S. Pluhar (Indianapolis, IN: Hacket, 1987), para. 14.
58. Derrida, op. cit., p. 45.
59. Ibid., p. 54.
60. Adams, op. cit., p. 114.
61. Ibid., p. 102.
62. Derrida, op. cit., p. 128.
63. Ibid., pp. 42-43.
64. Adams, op. cit., p. 110.
65. See Jacques Lacan, *The Four Fundamental Concepts of Psycho-analysis*, [Seminar XI, 1963-64], edited by Jacques-Alain Miller, trans. Alan Sheridan (Harmondsworth: Penguin Books, 1979), p. 167.
66. Adams, op. cit., p. 107.
67. Lacan, op. cit., p. 197.
68. Adams, op. cit., p. 108 and p. 109.
69. Ibid., p. 108.
70. See Slavoj Žižek, *Looking Awry* (Cambridge, Mass.: MIT Press, 1991), pp. 13–15.
71. Ibid. p. 29.
72. J. G. Ballard, *Empire of the Sun* (London: Flamingo, 1994), p. 37.
73. Adams, op. cit., pp. 107-8.
74. Ibid., p. 111.
75. Ibid., p. 104.
76. Slavoj Žižek, *The Fright of Real Tears: Krzysztof Kieślowski Between Theory and Post-Theory* (London: BFI Publishing, 2001), p. 39.
77. Ibid., p. 20.
78. Ibid., p. 53.
79. Slavoj Žižek, *Enjoy Your Symptom: Jacques Lacan in Hollywood and Out* (New York and London: Routledge, 1992), p. 15.
80. See Mary Russo, 'Twins and Mutant Women: David Cronenberg's *Dead Ringers*', in *The Female Grotesque: Risk, Excess and Modernity* (New York; London: Routledge, 1994), p. 113.
81. David Cronenberg cited in Chris Rodley (ed.), *Cronenberg on Cronenberg*, (London; Boston: Faber and Faber, 1992), p. 159.
82. Slavoj Žižek, *Looking Awry* (Cambridge, Mass.: MIT Press, 1991), p. 21.
83. Robert Stam, *Subversive Pleasures- Bakhtin, Cultural Criticism and Film* (Baltimore; London: Johns Hopkins University Press, 1989), p. 157.
84. Ibid., p. 163.
85. Ibid., p. 162.
86. See Peter Wollen, *Signs and Meanings in the Cinema* (London: Thames & Hudson, 1969), p. 115 and Leonard Bernstein, *The Unanswered Question* (Cambridge, Massachusetts; London: Harvard University Press, 1976), p. 3.
87. Deborah Cartmell and Imelda Whelehan (eds.), 'Introduction', *Adaptations: From Text to Screen; Screen to Text* (New York; London: Routledge, 1999), p. 6.

88. Brian McFarlane, *Novel to Film: An Introduction to the Theory of Adaptation* (Oxford: Oxford University Press, 1996), p. 8.
89. Erica Sheen, 'Introduction', in Robert Giddings and Erica Sheen (eds.), *The Classic Novel: From Page to Screen*, (Manchester: Manchester University Press, 2000), p. 3.
90. McFarlane, op. cit., p. 166.
91. George Bluestone, *Novels into Film* (Berkeley: University of California Press, 1968), p. 62.
92. Joy Gould Boyum, *Double Exposure: Fiction Into Film* (Mentor-N.A.L., 1985), p. 60.
93. Neil Sinyard, 'Introduction', *Filming Literature: The Art of Screen Adaptation* (Beckenham, Kent: Croom Helm, 1986), p. *x*.
94. Pierre Bourdieu, cited in Sheen, op. cit., p. 8.
95. David Cronenberg, 'Appendix: Festival of Festivals' 1983 Science Fiction Retrospective', in Wayne Drew (ed.), op. cit., p. 57. See Jorge Luis Borges, 'Kafka and His Precursors', in *Labyrinths: Selected Stories and Other Writings* (New York: New Direction, 1964): 'In the critics' vocabulary, the word 'precursor' is indispensable, but it should be cleaned of all connotation of polemics or rivalry. The fact is that every writer *creates* his own precursors. His work modifies our conception of the past, as it will modify the future', (p. 201).
96. Robin Wood, cited in Ginette Vincendeau (ed.), 'Introduction', *Film/Literature/Heritage* (London: British Film Institute, 2001), p. 7.
97. Roland Barthes, *S/Z*, trans. Richard Miller (New York: Hill and Wang, 1974), p. 205.
98. Ibid., p. *xii*.
99. James Naremore, *Film Adaptation* (London: Athlone, 2000), p. 2.
100. Seymour Chatman, 'What Novels Can Do That Film Can't (and Vice Versa)' in W. J. T. Mitchell (ed.), *On Narrative* (Chicago and London: The University of Chicago Press, 1981), p. 119.
101. See Chris Rodley, *'Crash'*, *Sight and Sound* 6:6 (June 1996), pp. 6–11.
102. Chatman, op. cit., p. 121.
103. Ibid., p. 122.
104. Ibid., p. 121.
105. Ibid., p. 126.
106. See Robin Wood, op. cit, pp. 7–28.
107. See Pete Boss, 'Vile Bodies and Bad Medicine', *Screen* 27:1 (1986), pp. 14–24 and William Beard, 'The Visceral Mind: The Major Films of David Cronenberg', in Piers Handling, (ed.), op. cit., pp. 1–79.
108. See Barbara Creed, 'Phallic Panic: Male Hysteria and *Dead Ringers'*, *Screen* 32:2 (summer 1990), pp. 125–146 and *The Monstrous-Feminine: Film, Feminism, Psychoanalysis* (New York; London: Routledge, 1993); 'The naked crunch: Cronenberg's homoerotic bodies', in Michael Grant (ed.), op. cit., pp. 84–101; and 'The *Crash* Debate: Anal Wounds, Metallic Kisses', in Jackie Stacey (ed.), op. cit., pp. 175–179.
109. See Julia Kristeva, *Powers of Horror: An Essay in Abjection* (New York: Columbia University Press, 1982) and Melanie Klein et al., Joan Riviere (ed.), *Developments in Psychoanalysis* (London: Hogarth Press, 1952).
110. Robert Stam, cited in Naremore, op. cit., p. 60. Ibid., p. 64.
111. Ibid., p. 64.
112. Mikhail Bakhtin, cited in Naremore, op. cit., p. 64.
113. Julia Kristeva, *Revolution in Poetic Language,* trans. Margaret Waller (New York; Guildford: Columbia University Press, 1984), p. 60.

114. Gérard Genette cited in Naremore, op. cit., p. 65.
115. Robert Stam, cited in ibid., p. 68.
116. See Chris Rodley (ed.), *Cronenberg on Cronenberg* (London: Faber, 1992), p. 135.
117. Robert Stam cited in Naremore, op. cit., p. 64.
118. Gregory Flaxman (ed.), *The Brain Is The Screen: Deleuze and the Philosophy of Cinema*. (Minneapolis: University of Minneapolis Press, 2000), p. 366.
119. David Bordwell, 'Film Studies and Grand Theory', in David Bordwell and Noel Carroll (eds.), op. cit., p. 29.
120. Gilles Deleuze, *Difference and Repetition*, trans. Paul Patton (New York: Columbia UP, 1994), p. 77.
121. Anna Powell, *Deleuze and Horror Film*, (Edinburgh: Edinburgh University Press, 2005), p. 205 and p. 22.
122. David Cronenberg on *Spider*: Reality Is What you Make Of It', interview with Anthony Kaufman, (http://www.indiewire.com/people/people), p.2.
123. 'From Flies to Spiders', interview with Walter Chaw, (http://www.filmfreak central.net/notes/dcronenberginterview.htm), p. 3.
124. Gilles Deleuze, *Cinema 2: The Time Image*, trans. by Hugh Tomlinson and Robert Galeta (Minneapolis: University of Minnesota Press, 1989), p.157.
125. Ibid., p. 161.
126. David Cronenberg cited in Chris Rodley, op. cit., p. 152.
127. Rodley, op. cit., p. 43.
128. Deleuze, op. cit., p. 170.
129. Ibid., p. 54.
130. Gilles Deleuze, *Cinema 2: The Time Image*, trans. by Hugh Tomlinson and Robert Galeta (Minneapolis: University of Minnesota Press, 1989), p. 79.
131. See Frederick Crews et al., *The Memory Wars* (London: Granta Books, 1997), Malcolm Macmillan, *Freud Evaluated: The Completed Arc* (Cambridge, Massachusetts: MIT Press, 1991) and Adolf Grünbaum, *The Foundations of Psychoanalysis: A Philosophical Critique* (Berkeley; London: University of California Press, 1984).
132. John Wagner and Vince Locke, *A History of Violence* (New York: Paradox Press, 1997), p. 72.
133. See Jorges Luis Borges, 'Pierre Menard, Author of the *Quixote*', in *Labyrinths: Selected Stories and Other Writings* (New York: New Directions, 1964, pp. 62–71.
134. Ibid., p. 259.
135. 'Crash', an interview with Chris Rodley, *Sight and Sound* 6:6 (June 1996): 'I think this is a lovely fusion of me and Ballard. We're so amazingly in synch. We completely understand what we're both doing'. p. 8.
136. Breskin, op. cit., p. 260.
137. Ibid., p. 261.
138. See George Hickenlooper, 'The Primal Energies of the Horror Film: an Interview with David Cronenberg', *Cineaste* 17:2 (1989), p. 7 and André Bazin, cited in James Naremore, op. cit., p. 20.
139. David Cronenberg cited in McGreal, op. cit., p. 7.
140. Gilles Deleuze, 'Letter to Serge Daney,' in *Negotiations: 1972–1990* (New York; Chichester: Columbia University Press, 1990), p. 79.
141. Beard, op. cit., p. 124.
142. George Bluestone, op. cit., p. 62.
143. See Cronenberg in Chris Rodley, op. cit., p. 103.

144. Ibid., p. 103 and p. 105.
145. Interview with Alan E. Rapp, 'You can never read too much into it', (http:77www.salon.com/ent/movies/int/1999/04=29/cronenberg/index.html), p. 5.
146. The Reverend Fallon in William Gibson's *Virtual Light* (1993) and Dr Deeply in Thomas Pynchon's *Vineland* (1990) both allude directly to *Videodrome*, via a character who is using video technology as part of a process of spiritual exploitation.
147. Peter Morris, *A Delicate Balance* (Toronto: ECW Press, 1993), p. 33.
148. Ibid., p. 44.
149. Erica Sheen, 'Introduction', in Robert Giddings and Erica Sheen (eds.), op. cit., p. 7.
150. David Cronenberg cited in Jill McGreal, 'Interview with David Cronenberg', in Wayne Drew (ed.), op. cit., p. 12 and David Cronenberg cited in David Breskin, *Inner Views: Filmmakers in Conversation* (London; Boston: Faber & Faber, 1992), p. 227.
151. Morris, op. cit., p. 31.
152. David Cronenberg cited in Jill McGreal, 'Interview with David Cronenberg', in Wayne Drew (ed.), op. cit., p. 7 and David Cronenberg cited in Breskin, op. cit., p. 212.
153. Brian McFarlane, op. cit., p. 22.
154. René Wellek and Austin Warren, *Theory of Literature* (New York: Harcourt, Brace & Co., 1949), p. 42.
155. Stanley Cavell, *Must We Mean What We Say?: A Book of Essays* (Cambridge; London; New York: Cambridge University Press, 1969), p. 198.
156. See W. K. Wimsatt Jr and Monroe C. Beardsley, 'The Intentional Fallacy,' *Sewanée Review* 54:3 (1946), pp. 468–88.
157. Cavell, op. cit., p. 227.
158. McGreal, op. cit., p. 3.
159. Timothy Corrigan, *A Cinema Without Walls* (London: Rutgers University Press, 1991), p. 108.
160. David Cronenberg cited in Breskin, op. cit., p. 241.
161. David Cronenberg cited in Iannis Katsahnias, 'La beauté intérieure', *Cahiers du Cinéma* 416 (February 1989), p. 6.
162. See Corrigan, op. cit., p. 111 and 'And Then I Woke Up: an Interview with David Cronenberg', by Sean Axmaker, (http//www.nitrateonline.com/1999/fexistenz.htm), (23 April 1999), pp. 1–11.
163. Linda S. Kauffman, op. cit., p. 190, 191.
164. David Cronenberg cited in Piers Handling (ed.), op. cit., p. 164 and David Cronenberg cited in Chris Rodley (ed.), op. cit., p. 153.
165. David Cronenberg cited in Piers Handling (ed.), op. cit., p. 164.
166. Roland Barthes, 'From Work to Text', in *Image-Music-Text* (London: Fontana, 1977), p. 161.
167. See Michel Foucault, 'What is an Author?', in Michel Foucault, *Language, Counter-Memory Practice: Selected Essays and Interviews*, ed. Donald Bouchard, trans. Donald Bouchard and Sherry Simon (Ithaca, New York: Cornell University Press, 1977), pp. 113–138.
168. Derrida, op. cit., pp. 31-32.
169. Barbara M. Kennedy, *Deleuze and Cinema: The Aesthetics of Sensation* (Edinburgh: Edinburgh University Press, 2000) p. 5.
170. David Cronenberg cited in Breskin, op. cit., p. 205.
171. See Geoff Pevere, 'Cronenberg Tackles Dominant Videology', in Piers Handling (ed.), op. cit., p. 143 and David Cronenberg cited in Piers Handling (ed.), op. cit., p. 159.
172. See Morris, op. cit., p. 26 and David Cronenberg cited in Chris Rodley, op. cit., p. 8.
173. See Breskin, op. cit., p. 229 and p. 232 and see Kauffman, op. cit., p. 189.

174. Kauffman, op. cit., p. 188 and Morris, op. cit., p. 17.
175. Mendik, op. cit, p. 170.
176. Ibid., p. 171.
177. See Serge Grünberg, op. cit., p. 28.
178. Chris Rodley, 'Game Boy', *Sight and Sound* 9:4 (April 1999), p. 10.
179. David Cronenberg cited in Breskin, op. cit., p. 240.
180. David Cronenberg cited in Breskin, op. cit., p. 245 and see 'Interview with David Cronenberg', *Shift Magazine* 3:4 (June-July 1995), (http://www.cronenberg. freeserve.co.uk/cr_rushd.html), p. 5.
181. Ibid., p. 4.
182. Jean-Paul Sartre, *What is Literature?* trans. Bernard Frechman (London : Methuen, 1950), p. 245.
183. Judith Halberstam and Ira Livingston (eds.), *Posthuman Bodies* (Bloomington: Indiana University Press, 1995), p. 4.
184. David Cronenberg cited in ibid., p. 165.
185. Bluestone, op. cit., p. 5.

CHAPTER ONE

VIDEODROME: 'NOT A LOVE STORY – A FILM ABOUT PORNOGRAPHY'[1]

'My greatest ambition is to turn into a TV programme'.[2]

The focus of this chapter is *Videodrome* (1982). This is not an example of a text being 'translated' from a literary entity into a cinematic one but the analytical focus here will be on potential links between Cronenberg's work and a range of analgous texts including the work of media prophet Marshall McLuhan, some of the early short stories of Clive Barker and J. G. Ballard and Brett Easton Ellis' novel *American Psycho* (1991). The relationship of *Videodrome* to the generic area of pornography will be also discussed, particularly in connection with the writings of Leopold von Sacher-Masoch.

For Stephen King, '[t]he only director I can think of who has explored this grey land between art and porno-exhibitionism successfully – even brilliantly – again and again with never a misstep is the Canadian filmmaker David Cronenberg'.[3] However, on considering *Videodrome* specifically, critics seem to find it strangely puzzling and usually view it as an ambitious failure. Some commentators, like Julian Petley, 'find it profoundly uninteresting, deeply unattractive and generally quite underwhelming'.[4] Bearing in mind Cronenberg's last-minute re-writing, the censorship that the film received in its various versions and Cronenberg's own dissatisfaction with the project, *Videodrome* is perhaps best viewed as a partially successful experiment, with more ideas than space to breathe, a luxury that Cronenberg could afford in later years with the commercial success of *The Fly* (1986) behind him.

'Everybody's going to be starring in their own porno films...'
Pornography and Cronenberg[5]
In Ballard's *High-Rise* (1975), there is mention of 'a continuity girl' working in pornographic films, who 'has to note the precise sexual position between takes', a difficulty Cronenberg has mentioned in connection with his direction of the apartment scene in *Crash* (1996).[6] On being complimented on his direction of this scene, Cronenberg claims not to have seen Andrew Blake-directed pornography but admits 'I've done sex scenes before, you know, like in video'.[7] He does not expand upon what these were but the casting of porn star Marilyn Chambers in the lead role in *Rabid* (1976), although admittedly not his first choice for the part, and his own role as the 'disembodied, wide-eyed porno freak', Tom Cramer in *Blue* (Don McKellar, 1992), does seem to indicate at least a passing knowledge of the genre.[8]

Cronenberg has shown interest in the structures and stylistic tropes of pornography over many years. Referring to the opening of *Shivers* (1976), Victor Sage notes that 'we have at least two narrative codes being played with: the promo film and the porn film'.[9] A middle-aged man struggling with a woman dressed as a schoolgirl (a porn cliché itself) is intercut with a couple being shown around the building. The name of the clients, the Swedens, like the group watching Volvo crash videos in *Crash*, alludes to the stereotypical association of Scandinavia with the porn industry. As Mark Kermode notes, Cronenberg's breakthrough into mainstream cinema was achieved 'through the taboo orifices of the horror and soft-core porn genres' due to 'having failed an audition as a porno director for Canadian skin-flicks company Cinepix'.[10] In an interview with Cronenberg, Susie Bright jokes that 'maybe in your dotage we could corral you into making just an unabashed cock and cunt porn film', to which he answers in a manner which makes it unclear whether he is being serious or not: 'well, I like watching those myself...'[11]

However, it is simplistic to see Cronenberg's use of displaced genitals, such as Max's slit, as pornographic in itself. Marty Roth's notion that 'the border between horror film and pornography is a blurred one', is useful here.[12] Both genres share an inability to achieve complete narrative closure and Steven Shaviro notes that 'horror fans know that the dead always walk again, even as consumers of pornography know that no orgasm is ever the last'.[13] He also observes that '[v]iolent and pornographic films literally anchor desire and perception in the agitated and fragmented body'.[14] Both horror and pornography are about arousal, more specifically provoking fear and a sexual response respectively, and are the two prime genres that speak about and through the body. Ian Conrich underlines the 'relationship between the opened bodies of pornography and splatter-obsessed hard core horror' that Richard Gehr calls 'carnography', which suggests that a text like *Videodrome*, featuring as it does bodies that are tortured, with a protagonist whose stomach opens without apparent reason and an antagonist who, upon death, bursts open with cancerous tumours, could be deemed pornographic.[15] However, Cronenberg's 'new flesh' redefines how this might manifest itself.

Is *Videodrome* pornographic?

We see how the porn industry works in Max's first meeting of the day with Hiroshima Video, whose name reflects the poverty of taste in the environment in which he moves but also the sense of an over-stimulated environment to which Nicki refers later. The meeting itself is portrayed like a drug deal. The merchandise is kept in a suitcase and the deal revolves around price and the purity of the product, which is validated by a test of a key batch, the last one, talismanic number 13. The request seems strange as it takes the tapes out of order but reflects the serial nature of pornography and that the order of episodes is unimportant. The product is discussed in terms of mass production and of regular supply ('thirteen with the possibility of another six'), expressing Debord's notion that 'the real consumer becomes a consumer of illusions...and the spectacle is its general manifestation', so that 'the spectacle is the developed modern complement of money...'[16]

Later, Harlan asks Max after being exposed to the Videodrome programme, 'Are you in some kind of drug warp?' Certainly, William Burroughs' descriptions of drug withdrawal accurately evoke Max's altered perceptions of video technology: 'sense impressions are sharpened to the point of hallucination. Familiar objects seem to stir with a writhing furtive life. The addict is subject to a barrage of sensations, external and visceral'.[17] Max's explanation of Civic TV's status on *The Rena King Show* continues the sense of pornography, rather than Burroughs' preferred metaphor of drugs, as a prime paradigm of capitalist economics: 'It's a matter of economics. We're small and in order to survive we have to give people something they can't get anywhere else'.

The viewing of 'Samurai Dreams' acts as a bridge between the hotel deal and the Civic TV management as we track back from the screen to see Max and his associates around a table. Street level operations interconnect with corporate business. Max muses whether they will 'get away with it', as if cheating their audience with a product that is in some way inferior or diluted. Max's listless dismissal of 'Samurai Dreams' expresses on behalf of his consumers (and possibly himself) a level of sexual ennui that is later articulated in *Crash*. There appears to be little pleasure in fooling his audience as he asks rhetorically, 'Do you *want* to get away with it?' On repeated viewings, it is possible to recognize the girl as the subject of one of the photos in Max's kitchen earlier, implying possibly that the woman is a known star or alluding to a sense of precognition on his part (i.e. that the product has become predictable).

The Head of Production at Universal Studios, Bob Rehme, demanded cuts to the 'Samurai Dreams' sequence, when a doll is lifted to reveal a dildo beneath. Ironically, in a film about the potential effects of the media, such an image of female self-pleasure might have helped Cronenberg's reputation with critics like Robin Wood. The cuts to the scene for the version shown on BBC2 mean the actions of the girl are incomplete but guessable, making the effect of the scene even more coy and Max's frustration with its 'softness', even more appropriate. For Roth, 'Videodrome is all about pornography, about the difference between hard and soft pornography, the pornography of the present as opposed to that of the future'.[18]

Roth is only partly right here. Max and his two colleagues express different views on the film, which represent an historical perspective on pornography. One expects that it will get them an audience they never had before (the present), another rejects it as 'not tacky enough...to turn me on' and moralizes that 'too much class is bad for sex' (the past). These represent the traditional positions of white middle-class/aged males, whose tastes have historically dominated the US porn industry. Whilst Max is looking for 'something that will break through....something...tough' (the future), a film poster behind him shows a variation on Raglan's book cover for 'The Shape of Rage' in *The Brood* (1979), with an upturned hand and 'Something' in large print. Literally, the 'something' which he seeks in the remainder of the film is already indicated behind him: a bodily need to interact with filmic spectacle. This contrast is underlined later with the stylistic differences between Masha's 'Apollo and Dionysius', (representing 1970s-style porn), the 'Samurai Dreams' extract (which reflects a yearning after some kind of oriental novelty, but is fundamentally conventional and even coyly romantic) and the Videodrome programme (which, for Max, seems to be 'what's next'). Max rejects Masha's mythic or biblically motivated scenarios, as he is looking for something a lot more 'contemporary'.

Ballard has stated that 'I believe that organic sex...is becoming no longer possible simply because if anything is to have any meaning for us, it must take place in terms of the values and experiences of the media landscape...'[19] Ballard's *The Kindness of Women* (1992) mediates ideas of death and pornography through the image of television. The final project of television presenter Dick Sutherland is a series of programmes filming his own death. As Ballard states 'in 1979 the idea of an explicit filmed record of the last weeks running up to one's death seemed virtually pornographic'.[20] In effect, this is what we have of O'Blivion. We do not know the correct chronological order of the tapes we see of him or when they were made but the final one shown depicts his death (assuming it is not faked or Max's hallucination). Dick accepts 'that the electronic image of himself was the real one' in contrast to Ballard himself who has 'always been reluctant to appear on television'.[21] A friend of Dick, Cleo Churchill, exclaims in disgust 'he's actually going to make a snuff movie...he's staging a sex-death in which he's raped out of existence by the whipped-up emotions of those peak-time viewers'.[22] Sutherland's project anticipates AIDS narratives like David Wojnarowicz's *Close to the Knives: A Memoir of Disintegration* (1991), where a terminally ill individual is taped in his dying weeks to perpetuate his image after death.[23]

When Masha tries to warn Max that Videodrome is dangerous because it has a 'philosophy', he asks, 'Whose?' Eventually, she provides him with O'Blivion's name but the programme does not really express *his* philosophy. He can only comment upon it and ultimately claim to be 'Videodrome's first victim', garrotted by a masked assassin, revealed as Nicki now with red hair (evoking the sensuality of the red dress she wore in the chat show). This 'philosophy' may appear at first to refer to de Sade's *Philosophy in the Bedroom* (1795) but what we actually have is a narrative blend that is both Sadean and masochistic.

Masochism

Continuing the blend of sadism and masochism of some of Cronenberg's television work, such as 'The Lie Chair' and 'The Victim', the Videodrome programme is set in a torture chamber. Harlan's description of the Videodrome signal as plotless and containing nothing but 'torture, murder, mutilation...it's a real sicko, for perverts only', is ironically juxtaposed with Max's evident pleasure ('Absolutely brilliant...No production costs...You can't take your eyes off it'). In her historical analysis of torture, Elaine Scarry describes how 'the contents of the room, its furnishings are converted into weapons', which is exemplified by Videodrome's electrified walls and bars where victims can be tied.[24] In order to convert pain into power, the torturer must make pain visible 'in the multiple and elaborate processes that evolve in producing it', such as the whip in Videodrome.[25]

In Masoch's most famous text, *Venus in Furs* (1870), the protagonist, Severin, is emotionally humiliated by an aloof but beautiful woman called Wanda. Their relationship is always based on the key notion of consent, manifested in a written *contract* and although there are interludes of consensual physical punishment, involving whipping, these are relatively few in number and brief in duration.[26] However, to employ gender roles narrowly and to regard masochism as feminine and sadism as masculine is too simplistic as both categories contain elements of one another. Masoch's heroines are surrounded by images of cold, for example, in *Venus in Furs*, Wanda's body and pallor are described as 'marble', and yet in *Crash*, a predominantly Sadean text (see chapter 4), Catherine's demeanour could also be described as glacial.[27] Similarly, in *Videodrome*, an exploration of masochism, Nikki inflicts pain on herself by burning (or, as her name suggests, branding), she wears warm colours, and her hair changes colour to red when she appears on the Videodrome tape.

In *Videodrome*, the notion of consent is ambiguous. It seems unlikely that the women seen being tortured on the Videodrome programme are volunteers, but Nicki is certainly keen to be involved. Her claim 'I was made for that show' to which Max replies, 'No one on earth was made for that show', creates the sense that she has literally been 'made' as a non-human device of Spectacular Optical, which ties in with the contrived plot twists of her as an enemy 'agent'. Moreover, by using the 'life as a game show' metaphor, Cronenberg raises an existential question within the framework of a televisual 'contract' with the viewer, both in the general sense of the cliché of providing an entertainment product but also specifically here in the game show subgenre when Max jokes about no one coming back the following week. In Masoch's narrative, Wanda and Severin make a contract in which he agrees to be her slave indefinitely and forfeit his life if she wants it, constituting a virtual suicide note. Severin's masochistic ideal is expressed in the Biblical allusion of Samson and Delilah, in which the man is betrayed and ultimately killed by the woman.[28] At the end of *Videodrome*, Max follows Bianca's orders to kill Convex and his own associates before ending his own life (an instruction given through the mediated image of Nicki).

Theodore Reik describes four key features of masochism: the 'special significance of fantasy', the 'suspense factor', the 'demonstrative' way in which the masochist shows his or her suffering and the 'provocative fear', how the masochist commands to be punished.[29] All of these features appear in *Videodrome*. The narrative of *Venus in Furs* begins with a fantasy of a beautiful woman that is not signalled as a dream until the narrator is woken by a servant. In the second chapter, we see a painting with the title 'Venus in Furs' that depicts the woman from the dream and his friend, Severin, from several years before. The narrator concludes that 'it appears my dream was prompted by your picture'.[30] *Videodrome* begins with a sequence that could be construed as a dream and Max's hallucinations could stem from the pictures of porn actresses that adorn his kitchen and dominate his professional life. Before encountering his ideal woman, Severin finds his fantasy in a photograph entitled 'Venus with the Mirror'.[31] Although Max meets Nicki on the set of a chat show, we first see her through the mediated image of a television monitor. Severin admits that Wanda has 'brought my dearest fantasies to life', as Nicki awakens and validates Max's sado-masochistic tendencies.[32] Linda Ruth Williams asserts that Nicki's primary function is not to be looked at (Debbie Harry's extra filmic role as lead singer of *Blondie*) but to be 'masochistic seer' in the senses of initiator, voyeur and prophet.[33] However, unlike *Videodrome*, Masoch ends his narrative by having the hero break out of his state of willed subjugation and closes the frame story with a salutary lesson about manipulative women: '[i]t was as though I were awakening from a long dream'.[34]

The retention of certain scenes, ultimately cut by Cronenberg, could have maintained the fragility of Max's fantasy more effectively. Ian Hill details three alternative scenes in the Cathode Ray Mission, where Max whips back a curtain on one of the cubicles to reveal either Nicki, Bianca or Masha on screen and an earlier concept of Bianca's character that showed her fusing with Nicki, indicated by Nicki adopting more conservative suits and Bianca in a red dress. According to Hill, a scene cut from the MCA-TV version, originally featured Max stopping on the street to light a cigarette, looking at his reflection in a shop window and seeing that he is still wearing Convex's hallucination helmet.[35] Max's shocked 'double take' would have underlined the subjectivity of the narrative and brought it closer in structure to *Venus in Furs*.

Reik's 'suspense factor' refers primarily to the masochist's deliberate deferral of pain in actions like the raised whip hand. Shaviro notes how 'the masochist seeks not to reach a final consummation but to hold it off, to prolong the frenzy, for as long as possible', prefiguring *Crash*'s mantra, 'Maybe the next one…'[36] In *Videodrome*, masochistic suspense is alluded to in the medium that carries the images of sexual pleasure. By watching his 'porno' on tape, Max can freeze the action at a particular moment, replay it again and again and thereby interrupt a narrative or hasten its progress. Masochistic deferral and Sadean repetition are achieved by technology. The sexual scenarios of the Videodrome programme itself are predominantly masochistic (with the admitted proviso of an ambiguous consensual position), featuring a woman bound and hanging from a wall or a post and being whipped. Dramatic suspense is used sparingly but appears more often as Max's hallucinations take hold. A horrified Max wakes up next to the corpse of Masha, which we see, so we can empathize with his panic. This allows the creation of suspense before Harlan comes in, and the bed is revealed as empty.

Reik's 'demonstrative' way in which the masochist shows their suffering would have been clearly seen in one rejected ending of *Videodrome*, which featured a sweeping tracking shot past the whole cast in the torture chamber, all chanting, 'Long Live the New Flesh!' and stopping on a close-up of a victim's handprint on the clay wall, in an echo of Hollywood's 'Walk of Fame'.[37] Even without this, Nicki demonstrates the pleasures of pain to Max by piercing her ears, whilst the light from a television screen is 'flickering like a crackling fire'.[38] In *Venus in Furs*, the narrator dreams of a beautiful woman sitting before 'a crackling fire'.[39] Nicki consciously wears an off-the-shoulder top, displaying the scarred site of previous self- or consensually inflicted wounds and, later, instructs Max to watch as she burns herself. He calls, 'don't' but too late and winces as she stubs a cigarette on her breast. She gives him the cigarette back and offers her shoulder to cut. There is both an element of blackmail here (he must hurt her or she will do it to herself anyway) and the possibility that he finds this action arousing (and Nicki too in seeing his revulsion overcome). Reik's 'provocative fear' appears in Nicki's command: 'Take your Swiss army knife and cut me here', and Max is so disturbed by Nicki's request to cut her, he asks her for clarification three times.

So Who Owns Death TV?[40]
McLuhan, Burroughs and the impact of mass exposure to television

Mark Czarnecki sees *Videodrome* as 'a Burroughsian interpretation of Marshall McCluhan's influential book, *Understanding Media: The Extensions of Man*'.[41] In this 1967 text, McLuhan proposes that '[w]e have extended our central nervous system itself in a global embrace…rapidly, we approach the final phase of the extensions of man – the technological simulation of consciousness'.[42] It is a relatively small step between Max's hallucinations as a result of exposure to the signals from Videodrome and the potential for influence and coercion by the media as expressed by figures like Burroughs: 'there are sound tracks that bring you down, ugly sounds that can be concentrated and directed and put out where you want the damage done'.[43] Admittedly, Max's tapes also have a visual element and he has to go searching for the signal rather than it being generally available but as it transpires later, he has been deliberately targeted by Spectacular Optical.

Cronenberg refers easily and knowledgably to McLuhan as a fellow Canadian who could bring to bear a slightly detached critical perspective on the US-dominated global media, observing that 'we come from the same town and the same university...I did read everything he wrote'.[44] Max dramatizes a number of McLuhan's sententious statements, such as '[m]ental breakdown is the very common result of uprooting and inundation with new information'.[45] Although McLuhan is a little alarmist about the impact of television in its fledgling era, Cronenberg explores the possible effects of exposure to a particular kind of audio-visual signal. *Halloween III* (Tommy Wallace, 1983), produced at the same time as *Videodrome*, with very similar surface features like low-tech television jingles, dramatizes McLuhan's warnings not to sit too close to the screen by literally turning brains to mush, in a *Scanners*-like global conspiracy plot.

For Sharrett, '[w]hile Cronenberg has professed an interest in McLuhan's theories, it is difficult to ignore the criticism he (Cronenberg) offers of the media and the soft-headed utopianism of his McLuhan figure'.[46] When Bianca points out to Max that he 'said some very superficial things' on *The Rena King Show*, he does not deny this and it is debatable whether O'Blivion's preference for monologue as 'the preferred mode of discourse' is any less simplistic. When Max asks Bianca about the role of the Mission, he is ironically missing the significance of the very medium in which he works, perpetuating the same intellectual snobbery that sees television as of minor cultural consequence compared to film or literature. O'Blivion's sententious warning that the lesson for Max beginning 'The battle for the mind of North America will be fought in the video arena', is packed with great repetition of 'therefore', conveying the appearance of logic, where really none exists. Bianca's later explanation that her father saw Videodrome 'as the next phase in the evolution of man as a technological animal', and his subsequent betrayal and death at the hands of his partners implicitly attributes to O'Blivion a certain naivety and pomposity that by implication is also linked to McLuhan.

For Badley, 'David Cronenberg's concept of the "video Word made Flesh" in his 1982 film *Videodrome* owes much to Foucault's *Panopticon* in *Discipline and Punish* (1979)', but she does not clarify exactly how.[47] Michel Foucault analyses anti-plague measures taken in the seventeenth century and links this to Benthamite notions of a *Panopticon*, the architectural model of prison, hospital and even school institutions in following centuries. The Cathode Ray Mission, a blend of prison, madhouse and hospital, could be seen to function as a kind of *Panopticon*. Upstairs, the old mansion style of bookcases, heavy wooden furniture, stained glass, sculpture and chess set in foreground clearly surprises Max, who looks around in curious bewilderment. Sharrett asserts that O'Blivion's office is 'supposedly modelled on McLuhan's home', covered with 'images of Moses, Christ and iconography from various stages of civilisation's evolution. O'Blivion sees the earlier saints and prophets as mediators; like those figures, he is a lawgiver, synthesising older language forms to create new vision'.[48] All the cubicles can be viewed from O'Blivion's office above, immediately noted sarcastically by Max: 'I love the view' and 'I think it's a style that's coming back' to which Bianca replies that it is 'not a style, it's a disease…' The Kafkaesque cubicles, evoke Bunuel's reversal of toilet and dining room in *Discreet Charm of the Bourgeoisie* (1972) but here the nourishment of a soup kitchen/treatment room is electronic.

Baudrillard and spectacle

For Shaviro, '[t]he brutally hilarious strategy of *Videodrome* is to take media theorists such as Marshall McLuhan and Jean Baudrillard completely at their word, to overliteralise their claims for the ubiquitous mediatization of the real'.[49] However, *Videodrome* is not so much a Baudrillardian 'requiem for the media', as an exploration of its existential possibilities.[50] Baudrillard posits a disappearance of the real into a world of simulacra but *Videodrome* suggests a process of reinscription in, and transfiguration of, the body as a site where new meanings might be explored. Using the resources of the media itself to combat a global media conspiracy had been an abiding concern of Burroughs who 'assumed that all reality, sight, taste, smell, sound and touch was some form of hallucination' and 'that whoever was doing the conditioning was running the universe like an engineer running a cinema sound stage with tape machines and films'.[51]

Cronenberg realizes the excess of mediation by a ubiquity of screens. Brian O'Blivion only exists as pre-recorded tape and Max later becomes a machine, programmed first by Convex and later by Bianca O'Blivion. Max often sees Nicki through a screen. Although his first meeting is face-to-face on a television chat show, the representation of this event is conveyed by elaborate picture composition with Renn in the studio and Nicki on the camera monitor. Later, when he visits her at the radio station, he sees her through the glass of a studio on her agony show and later still she appears on television, apparently in a hallucination.

As Guy Debord in *Society of the Spectacle* (1967) suggests, 'all of life presents itself as an immense accumulation of *spectacles*. Everything that was directly lived has moved away into a representation'.[52] Unlike the Panopticon model of power that is 'visible and unverifiable', *Videodrome* is less about being looked at than the experience of watching.[53] When Max asks Masha about Videodrome, he explains the term by language games: 'you know, like video-*circus*, video-*arena*'. Both these compound neologisms convey a sense of visual, and traditionally death-defying, *spectacle*. Barry Convex describes Spectacular Optical as 'a global corporate system', but their visionary apparatus veils a darker purpose, betrayed by his admission that they 'manufacture cheap eye-glasses for Third World countries and missile-guidance systems for NATO'.

However, although Linda Kauffman describes *Videodrome* as 'the vision of a world seamlessly enveloped in spectacle', this is not the case.[54] Cronenberg's film problematizes identification with what viewing pleasure is being offered to Max (and by extension the viewer), such as the hollow theatricality of the Spectacular Optical product launch, the only example of musical spectacle in Cronenberg's entire cinematic output. Like the political assassination in *The Dead Zone* (1983), this overtly commercial spectacle provokes a lone hero to take violent action against a body, which is uncaring and duplicitous. The incongruity of the song and dance routine in *Videodrome* reflects the public face of the corporation, whose real intentions are best represented by the torture and murder of the Videodrome signal. The misappropriation of poetry for commercial ends as slogans and the wrongly attributed source of these words (see chapter 5) focus on the eye and what we see, not that we are being watched. In political terms, if we are looking, we are not acting and there is the sense during the musical number that a proletariat is being exploited in order to be better controlled. Even Max's attempted blow against the system occurs *on stage*, constituting a more exciting cabaret. The death of Convex allows Cronenberg to indulge his (and our) taste for spectacle with a lengthy close-up on Rick Baker's special effects (see further discussion in chapter 5).

'Long Live the New Flesh'
(Clive Barker's *Books of Blood* and J. G. Ballard's shorter fiction)

In *Posthuman Bodies* (1995), Eric White analyses four evolutionist films involving human transformation into, or linkage with, other non-human species. In discussing Roger Corman's *Attack of the Crab Monsters* (1957), White stresses how those humans who fall victim to the radioactive crabs appear to be synthesized into a greater whole. As one character, Jules, explains 'something remarkable has happened to me' and another victim, Carson, also subsumed within the same mutant body, claims, 'it's almost exhilarating'. Like Cronenberg's Brundle in *The Fly* (1986), revelling in his new powers, White identifies an 'aura of mingled hilarity, exhilaration, and erotic excitement', which surround the scenes where characters are in the process of becoming monstrous.[55] In *Attack of the Mushroom People* (Inoshiro Honda and Eiji Tsuburaya, 1963) a group of shipwrecked sailors eat 'Matango', a magic mushroom that causes those who eat it to become a funghi-like creature. For White, 'the film suggests that this destiny can in fact be understood as equivalent to a multiplication and an enhancement of life's possibilities'.[56] White suggests that becoming crustacean or insect (*Five Million Years to Earth*, directed by Roy Ward Baker, 1967), rodent (*My Uncle in America*, directed by Alain Renais, 1980) or funghi 'entails entering a realm of imaginative and libidinal excess',[57] that often seems more attractive than human nature and by implication we should be responsive to what he terms 'the *menagerie within*'.[58]

In *The Wild Boys* (1970), Burroughs asserts that in the 'space age...sex movies must express the longing to escape from flesh through sex. The way out is the way through'.[59] Nicki, in her admission that she lives in a perpetual state of overstimulation, is seeking something beyond the flesh but needs to explore that to its extremity, to 'break through'. It is the verbal echoes of 'penetration', a term firmly associated with sexual acts, which appear to hold the key to a higher plane of perception. The end of *Videodrome*, rather than an expression of pure nihilism, includes Nicki's statement on the tape provided by Bianca that 'I've learned that death is not the end', which is a fairly categorical statement of transcendence. Nicki claims that 'To become the New Flesh, you must first destroy the Old Flesh' and offers, 'Watch. I'll show you how'. There is rehearsal before action. We see a forward tracking shot of Max, the gun being raised to his head, the mantra spoken and the shot fired, at which the screen explodes outwards. The sequence is then replayed as practised, except with a final cut to black. Therefore, in a sense, the New Flesh is the explosion of the simulated visual image outwards, a metaphor which Barker dramatizes in his short story 'Son of Celluloid'.

Clive Barker, illustrator, playwright and novelist is a director with whom Cronenberg has had an interesting symbiotic professional relationship. Apart from starring in Barker's *Nightbreed* (1990), based on the novel *Cabal* (1988), their visualizations of what 'the new flesh' might be closely inform one another. Barker has described 'a kind of "celebration of perversity" in his short story collections *The Books of Blood*, placing monstrosity at their centre, as symbolic of difference that should be embraced, not excluded.[60] Both Barker and Cronenberg see fantastic transformations as potentially beautiful if viewed on their own terms. For them, those undergoing such changes, whilst suffering pain, seem to be the more interesting and fulfilled for it, such as Barker's Cenobites in 'The Hellbound Heart'. Cronenberg's hero in *The Fly*, Seth Brundle, initially seems quirky but is also fairly dull (reflected in his wardrobe of identical garments) and becomes more engaging as his transformation progresses.

For Badley, Barker's short story 'Son of Celluloid' is 'like *Videodrome* in its attacks against the same visual pleasure that it exploits: the male gaze whose projection represents an elision of the female body'.[61] However, there is an underlying misreading of both texts here: neither attack the medium they show, they problematize it. For both Barker and Cronenberg, the fantastical mutations they portray are liberating possibilities. To see them as attacking the televisual culture in which they revel is to make the same mistake as Robin Wood, who labelled *Shivers* 'reactionary', partly due to what he saw as the 'achievement of total negation' and the assumed misogyny in Cronenberg's portrayal of female sexuality.[62] Likewise, Geoff Pevere asserts that 'Cronenberg's work also bears the stamp of an unpopular Orwellian conservatism, which views the onward march of science and technology as signalling a corresponding decline of all that is natural, romantic, and, in a word, human'.[63] As mutation, metamorphosis and final suicide appear so frequently in Cronenberg's films and as in interviews he comments on them as positive events, we should resist the temptation to reject what we may feel is physically or morally repulsive. Barker stresses this misreading in discussing

Cronenberg: 'there is an argument that he's being repulsed by the flesh he's writing about, whereas I tend to be having a good time with it. "Long Live the New Flesh" would be a cry that would come from both our lips'.[64]

In the view of Ramsay Campbell, Barker's 'Son of Celluloid' 'goes straight for a biological taboo with a directness worthy of the films of David Cronenberg'.[65] We see *the logic of spectacle* take material shape, i.e. the metaphysical effects of the gaze upon what is viewed explored through the example of a mutating body. Barberio, an escaped and wounded convict, holes up in the detritus of an abandoned cinema car lot. Unknown to him, the pain in his stomach is the beginning of cancer. The wall against which he is leaning starts to give way and he discovers a ventilation shaft that allows him to enter the back of the cinema. On the other side of the screen, Fellini's *Satyricon* (1969) is being shown (an image of libidinal release) as Barberio dies of his wounds. The cinema had been a Mission Hall and, like *Videodrome*'s Cathode Ray Mission, is now used for a media experience. Barker privileges the space behind the screen: '[l]ike a reservoir, it had received the electric stares of thousands of eyes...Half a century of movie-goers had lived vicariously through the screen of the Movie Palace, pressing their sympathies and their passions onto the flickering illusion...Sooner or later, it must discharge itself. All it lacked was a catalyst'.[66]

The following slasher narrative is fairly predictable in matters of form but not its metaphorical import. A creature develops who feeds on the energy of the cinema audience, reflecting the stifling dominance of Hollywood, the mesmerizing (and possibly corrupting) power of film and the need for stories, the implicit sense that a drive for narrativization is part of what makes us human. Trapped in a cinema foyer after a late-night show, the female protagonist, Birdy, implicitly satirizes the typical characteristics of the stereotypical heroine of horror by representing the emergent 'final girl' of the 1980s. She is not physically perfect (deprecating her fat arms), she has been left by her date and, most importantly, she is also 'very bright' and observant. She thinks in cinematic terms of her position with an injured boyfriend: '[w]oman in Peril: standard stuff. The darkened room, the stalking beast', but 'instead of walking bang into that cliché, she was going to do what she silently exhorted heroines to do time and again: defy her curiosity and call the cops'.[67]

The entity addresses her directly and explains that he is Barberio's cancer: 'I'm the piece of him which did aspire, that did long to be more than a humble cell. I am a dreaming disease'.[68] Barker is, in effect, creating an inverted existentialist fiction, in which the fictions define themselves through the audience. Birdy's boyfriend, Ricky, has a vision of Marilyn Monroe and she seduces him despite his seeing the grotesque sight of eyes of a previous victim in her vagina: 'the image was so engrossing, so pristine, it all but cancelled out the horror in his belly. Perversely, his disgust fed his lust instead of killing it'.[69] In a literalized metaphor of the male pornographic gaze turned back upon itself, (like Max's stomach slit) Ricky's vision of Marilyn 'was defining herself through him. I am a function of you; made for you out of you. The perfect fantasy'.[70]

In 'Son of Celluloid', Barker parodies the representation of women in horror and pornography. Birdy survives because of the cultural appropriation of the film title 'Dumbo' as a term of abuse, which prevents her from being seduced by the celluloid images all around her. Comically, Birdy allows the creature to crawl onto her and then rolls over and, turning a social disadvantage of being overweight into a means of survival, squashes it. Birdy reclaims her own body image in flattening the cancerous creature but also dispensing with the bimbo-stereotype Lindi Lee, who acts as a host for the monster. After disposing of her, like the infected inhabitants of the Starliner building in *Shivers*, Birdy 'steps out into the street, confident in her planning to live long after the credits for this particular comedy had rolled'.[71]

In her pro-active narrative role and her knowledge of gender roles in visual media, Birdy reflects Cronenberg's Nicki Brand. Nicki represents a modern example of a woman who is driven by what Melanie Klein calls 'epistemophilia' or a compulsive drive for knowledge. Nicki not only is instantly attracted to 'Videodrome' the programme, she wants to find out all about it and very shortly after that wants to be a contestant on the show. Viewing to participating becomes a very short step. Similarly, Rose in *Rabid* locks herself in an apartment with one of her own victims to see if she is responsible for spreading the plague. Knowledge in both cases is only gained through sacrificing the self. When Nicki asks what is the content of the Videodrome cassette, Max answers 'torture, murder' to which she replies 'sounds great'. Nicki acts as a teacher to Max, demanding the specific sexual acts that she desires and demonstrating them by her own hand.

Echoing Barker and Cronenberg, Ballard asserts that '[r]ather than fearing alienation, people should *embrace* it. It may be the doorway to something more interesting...We need to explore total alienation and find out what lies beyond'.[72] Cronenberg locates this quest firmly amongst the nexus of flesh, mutation and sex. According to Halberstam, 'cultural and technological changes have helped to separate the apparently symbiotic partnership of fucking and reproduction', so that 'the point where they converge is no longer an adequate anchoring point for a meaningful or workable system'.[73] This leads to a question explored by the penile extension in *Rabid*, the 'sex blob' in *Naked Lunch*, Gabrielle's scar in *Crash* and Max putting his head into the television screen in *Videodrome*: '[w]hat is allowed to be fucking?'[74] Max apologizes to Nicki about Videodrome: 'Well, it ain't exactly sex' to which she replies, 'Says who?'

In Steven Soderbergh's *Sex, Lies and Videotape* (1989), which also explores the evolutionary relationship between human sexuality and video technology, when asked what is on the tapes that he mysteriously collects, the enigmatic hero, Graham, replies in terms very similar to the exchange between Max and Nicki: 'Not sex exactly'. His documenting of women's sexual history, whilst overtly motivated within the narrative as a means to overcome his impotence, is also a useful parallel for Cronenberg's work. *Dead Ringers*, *Crash* and *Videodrome* all explore Michael Foucault's notion of sexuality, not as an immutable fact but a socially derived phenomena, dramatizing potential 'implantation of perversions', which then become 'institutionalised by discourses of medicine, psychiatry, prostitution...and pornography'.[75] This is consistent with statements Cronenberg has made on a number of occasions about the importance of C. S. Lewis' *The Allegory of Love* (1936), which made him question for the first time the notion of romantic love as a purely cultural construction.[76]

In another short story, 'The Age of Desire', Barker creates the Cronenbergesque Hume Research Laboratories, where experiments to develop a libido-enhancing drug go wrong, leading to murder and a break-out of an infected volunteer called Jerome. Like Brundle's exhilaration after teleportation in *The Fly*, desire is repeatedly described in imagery of intense fire: 'his every fibre seemed alive to the flux and flow of the world around him'.[77] While part of Brundle's new life force expresses itself sexually in his renewed appetite with Veronica and later picking up a girl in a bar, Jerome is positively consumed by his fiery appetite. Evoking James' use of Gabrielle's scar in *Crash*, 'aroused beyond control, he turned to the wall he had been leaning against...the bricks smelt ambrosial. He laid kisses on their gritty faces, his hands exploring every nook and cranny. Murmuring sweet nothings, he unzipped himself, found an accommodating niche, and filled it'.[78] In Ballard's *The Atrocity Exhibition*, Nathan muses 'in what way is intercourse per vagina more stimulating than with this ashtray, say, or with the angle between two walls? Sex is now a conceptual act, it's probably only in terms of the perversions that we can make contact with each other at all...We need to invent a series of imaginary sexual perversions just to keep the activity alive...'[79]

In 'The Age of Desire', Jerome's mind is described as 'running with liquid pictures: mingled anatomies, male and female in one undistinguishable congress'.[80] An early draft of *Videodrome* featured a kiss between Nicki and Max in which their faces melt, 'dribbling down and across the floor, and up the leg of an onlooker, melting him', sounding a little like James Cameron's morphing of liquid metal in *Terminator II* (1991).[81] Cronenberg's scene featured an orgiastic fusion of Bianca, Nicki and Max who all have abdominal slits, from which emerge mutated sex organs but he cancelled this, claiming that he did not want to repeat what he felt were the unconvincing 'liquid, alien sex scenes' in Nic Roeg's *The Man Who Fell to Earth* (1976).[82] This seems to constitute the kind of self-censorship which he frequently rails against and the end result is that 'The New Flesh' is alluded to at a number of points in the finished film but not explicitly shown, creating some narrative confusion for some audiences but also ironically possibly producing a better film.[83]

In a bizarre anticipation of the Viagra phenomenon, in 'The Age of Desire', Barker dramatizes an aphrodisiac that works, perhaps too well. Police scientist Johannson calls the discovery 'sex without end, without compromise or apology...imagine it. The dream of Casanova'.[84] As Jerome is hunted down, he plunges into a busy marketplace: 'but what was his body now? Just a plinth for that singular monument, his prick. Head was *nothing*; mind was *nothing*...He pictured himself as a walking erection, the world gaping on every side: flesh, brick, steel, he didn't care: he would ravish it all'.[85] Max in *Videodrome*, Seth Brundle in *The Fly* and Jerome here all suffer the consequences of breaking libidinal boundaries. However, whereas Cronenberg grants his protagonists a measure of self-awareness, for Jerome 'not once did it occur to his spinning, eroticised brain that this new kind of life would, in time demand a new kind of death'.[86] Eventually, Jerome dies 'of terminal joy', not so much in the sense of dying into life, rather a literalization of the Victorian notion of *le petit mort* or Ridley Scott's Roy Batty in *Blade Runner* (1982), who has to learn that 'the light that burns twice as bright, lasts half as long'.[87]

On several occasions, Cronenberg has mentioned an interest in 'the possibility that human beings would be able to physically mutate at will'.[88] In Barker's 'Jacqueline Ess: Her Will and Testament', by power of will alone, dissatisfied wife Jacqueline develops the ability to change the reality of those around her. Infuriated by her husband's overbearing and patronizing manner, she wishes him to be a woman and so he is transformed: 'she willed his manly chest into making breasts of itself and it began to swell most fetchingly, until the skin burst and his sternum flew apart. His pelvis, teased to breaking point, fractured at its centre...'[89] If we accept Peter Michelson's definition of pornography as 'the imaginative record of man's sexual will', then in texts like this, that parallel Max's feminization in his vaginal fissure, Barker shares a willingness with *Videodrome* and *Crash* to explore how that 'will' might develop.[90]

Jacqueline pursues a series of relationships, learning about power from Titus Pettifer, a millionaire businessman but when his cruelty becomes provocative beyond endurance, she transforms him into a beast, 'his hands knotted into paws, his legs scooped up around his back, knees broken so he had the look of a four-legged crab, his brain exposed, his eyes lidless...ears torn off, spine snapped, humanity bewitched into another state', like one of John Carpenter's creatures in *The Thing* (1982).[91] Titus' transformation is similar to Brundle's gene-splicing in *The Fly* as 'she was unlocking the plates of his skull and reorganising him'.[92] Some of Titus' guards eventually break into the room to see him 'waddle' out of his hiding place beneath a desk. Instinctively they open fire as he comes towards them. Titus' demise is similar to Brundlefly's: a transformation of a human has resulted in a piteous but revolting monster that staggers forward and is shot: 'Titus stumbled two steps back on his bloody paws, shook himself as if to dislodge the death in him, and failing, died'.[93] The tale ends with a unification of Jacqueline and Vassi, a suitor who has pursued her through the narrative, in a scene very similar to the one

Cronenberg ultimately cut from the end of *Videodrome*, where liquid imagery and polymorphous perversity create a process that exceeds matters of sex and gender: 'thinking they were together, her will was made flesh. Under her lips, his features dissolved, becoming the red sea he'd dreamt of, and washing up over his face, that was itself dissolving: common waters made of thought and bone...'[94]

American Psycho
(an unreliable narrator, sadistic video violence and parallel plot lines)
Linda Kauffman is probably one of the few critics to have written on both Cronenberg and Brett Easton Ellis' 1991 novel, *American Psycho*, but she misses the potential to make direct connections between them.[95] These might include the role of (sado-masochistic) pornography, an unstable first-person narrative that bleeds into the main narrative and the notion that both works are satirizing the genres they portray. Ellis' hero, Patrick Bateman, is a regular consumer of porn and has seen Brian de Palma's *Body Double* (1984) 37 times. This would appear to act as inspiration for him, although the extent of his repeated viewing, apart from vicarious fascination at on-screen violence, could also convey an inability to secure a pleasurable experience completely. In a video store, Bateman is scared that he might be seen buying porn and so settles for a Woody Allen movie: 'but I'm still not satisfied. I *want* something *else*', echoing Max's frustrated search for 'something *tough*'.[96]

Videodrome explores what would happen 'if what the censors were saying would happen, did happen,' by linking violent imagery to violent behaviour.[97] Bateman is clearly aroused by viewing films of sadistic violence against women. Both Nicki, explicitly ('it turns me on'), and Max, begrudgingly, find the Videodrome torture programme sexually exciting. Bateman plans to rent *Body Double* again so that he can 'masturbate over the scene where the woman is getting drilled to death by a power drill', although there is no sense of that he explicitly models his acts on video images; rather that his choice (*Bloodhungry*) reflects his underlying psychopathology.[98] Bateman's systematic, repeated and extremely sadistic violence towards women, using Mace and nail guns, stabbing and dismembering his victims and even indulging in acts of cannibalism, appears to be distant from Max and Nicki, in that at least their acts are wholly consensual, although they do seem to derive pleasure viewing violent acts that appear non-consensual (and are only performed on women).

There are some overt, plot-based echoes of *Videodrome*: Bateman decides 'this emptiness...could just as easily have something to do with the tracking device on my VCR'.[99] Like the slogan of Civic TV ('The one you take to bed with you'), which equates pornography with a sexual partner, Bateman is 'beginning to think that pornography is so much less complicated than actual sex, and because of this lack of complication, so much more pleasurable'.[100] In one of the many anonymous restaurant scenes, in amongst small-talk, Bateman imagines the girl he is with,

Daisy, 'naked, murdered, maggots burrowing, feasting on her stomach, tits blackened by cigarette burns', evoking Nicki's burns and Convex's death.[101] Cronenberg himself 'was amazed at how good the book was. I felt it was an existential epic...You invent a world where clothes and money and brand names are the value system...and the murders, the hideousness, are an attempt to break out of that, to try and shatter it and to connect with something real'.[102] He met Ellis to discuss the possibility of directing the film but the key difficulty was trying to find a way to translate the interior nature of Bateman's commodified universe.[103]

Like the experience of viewing *eXistenZ*, 'Renn's "hallucinations" are not presented as formal breaks in the film's narrative structure, but as determinants of that structure'.[104] Similarly in *American Psycho*, fantasy bleeds into the main narrative. Sometimes this is underlined explicitly. After mistaking a student for a beggar (he gives money only because she is pretty and well-nourished), Bateman tells us that he hallucinates 'the buildings into mountains, into volcanoes, the streets become jungles...'[105] Elsewhere, his psychopathic tendencies are buried in amongst all the other narrative detail with no sense of emphasis or moral judgement and given to us piecemeal so it may only gradually become apparent that we are inhabiting the point of view of a real psychopath. He says (or is described as saying) that his job is 'murders and executions', which his date for the evening hears as 'mergers and acquisitions' (perhaps the commercial equivalent of more deep-seated aggressive impulses).[106]

Even if in *Videodrome* we do not have a truly subjective narrative, we do have one, which is 'infected' by fantasy. The techno-geek Harlan speaks in the language of an adolescent fantasist. He dramatizes events so that his ability to track the source of signals becomes his own battle of wits, in which he casts Max and himself as part of a joint adventure ('I was pretty insulted when it just shrugged *us* off in less than a minute'). In addressing Max as 'Patrone' and answering 'si' to his questions, Harlan sees himself as the self-styled 'Prince of Pirates', the sign above the door describing the attic room as 'home of the buccaneers', sadly literalizing the notion of video piracy.

In *American Psycho*, dialogue is expressed in speech marks but either remains unheard or is actually unspoken, so that when Evelyn describes him as 'the boy next door', to which he answers, 'No, I'm not...I'm a fucking evil psychopath', this elicits no reaction from her.[107] Supposed victims, like Paul Owen, appear alive later, raising the possibility that if the murders are only Bateman's fantasy, then so might be the sexually explicit episodes. If he is finding arousal difficult in 'real life', (he is unsuccessful in trying to have sex with Evelyn and later Courtney) the notion of importing into his fantasy life the ability to repeatedly satisfy fantasy women from escort agencies might make sense. Towards the close of Ellis' narrative, first- and third-person expression collapse. In talking to Jean, he warns that she 'shouldn't fawn over him' pausing before correcting himself, 'I mean...*me*'.[108]

Bateman claims that he films his acts of torture and murder, in effect his own personalized Videodrome programme, '[a]s usual, in an attempt to understand these girls, I'm filming their deaths'.[109] However, this is only a very small, understated part of the process and it is unclear to what extent this constitutes his real motivation or, indeed, whether like his dialogue and sexual exploits, much remains at the level of fantasy. The fact that his cleaner seems to note nothing amiss in an apartment that he describes to us as being littered with dismembered corpses makes him a highly unreliable narrator. In *The Kindness of Women* (1992), Ballard describes Sutherland's career in sexual research, involving the production of many hours of film. When challenged that this material is 'indistinguishable from pornography', he agrees but adds that 'except for one thing – our aim is to analyse, not arouse'.[110] According to this logic, pornography is only defined as such by the intention of producer and the motivation of the consumer.

The relationship that Bateman has with his secretary, Jean, is similar to that of Max and Bridey in *Videodrome*. Both appear very loyal and attracted to their boss, although, in *Videodrome*, there is a little flirtation but nothing more. Ellis develops the delusion of his hero to the extent where Bateman describes Jean as 'my secretary, who is in love with me'.[111] He goes out for dinner with her and when she kisses him, Bateman feels odd: 'I am so used to imagining everything happening the way it occurs in movies, visualising things falling somehow into the shape of events on a screen... the seventy-millimetre image of her lips and the subsequent murmur of "*I want you*" in Dolby sound', evoking Max's vision of Nicki's lips reaching out from the television screen in *Videodrome* and reciting the mantra 'Come to Nicki'.[112]

Bateman is introduced to a girl called Alison, whom he met before and with whom he had had sado-masochistic sex. He had intended to let her bleed to death, but throughout her torture she never wept and 'maybe that was what saved her'.[113] Sadistic pleasure appears to be based not just in inflicting pain but in *seeing* clear evidence of pain, i.e. making it visible (in a similar way to pornography's drive to make sexual pleasure visible). In de Sade's *Philosophy in the Bedroom*, anticipating a sexual version of Bentham's *Panopticon*, Mme de Saint-Ange explains the presence of mirrors in her bedroom: '[b]y repeating our attitudes and postures in a thousand different ways, they infinitely multiply those same pleasures for the persons seated here upon the ottoman. Thus everything is visible, no part of the body can remain hidden: everything must be seen'.[114] Power is exercised through extreme visibility. In Thomas Harris' *Red Dragon* (1981) filmed as *Manhunter* (Michael Mann, 1986), psychopath Francis Dolarhyde films his victims and uses mirrors both as murder weapons and to record the terror of his victims. By placing small shards of broken mirror in the eyes of his victims, he creates a Blakean fantasy of attaining a God-like omnipotence, echoing Mark Lewis in *Peeping Tom* (Michael Powell, 1960) in making the male gaze both a recording tool and a weapon. Like Bateman (if we accept his version of events), Dolarhyde makes one of his victims, sleazy journalist Freddy Lounds, watch films of previous murders whilst being tortured: 'Do you see?...Do you see?'[115] By force, they both place characters within the narrative in the same viewing position that Max and Nicki choose in *Videodrome*.

Conclusion

For Susan Sontag, 'what pornography is really about, ultimately, isn't sex but death'.[116] Conventionally, sexual arousal and physical repulsion would be seen as mutually exclusive: if the contestants on Videodrome are volunteers, we have a masochistic text, if not, then we have a sadistic text. However, for artists like Cronenberg and Barker and their literary and philosophical forebears, de Sade and Masoch, these apparently competing elements are sometimes placed in complementary and even causal relationships. However, as Nicki says to Max at the close of *Videodrome*, 'You've gone about as far as you can with the way things are now'. In 1982, a narrative of 'Just torture and murder. No plot. No character. Very, very realistic', seemed to Max, as Cronenberg's alter ego, to be 'what's next'. By 1999, with the same sense of evolutionary fervour, Levi's sales pitch in *eXistenZ* for the game 'transCendenZ' warns 'It's coming soon'. Cronenberg is experimenting with the parergonal logic mentioned in the introduction, likely to inculcate a watchful and suspicious response in a viewer. In *Videodrome*, this is only partially successful as the political conspiracy plot requires a degree of identification with characters in order to work at all. By the time of *eXistenZ* (1999), an overtly existential narrative frees Cronenberg from the strictures of more conventional narratives (such as reliable narrators) and allows him to play games literally with the audience.

Judith Halberstam and Ira Livingston argue that 'a posthuman condition is upon us, and that nostalgia for a humanist philosophy of self and other, human and alien, normal and queer is merely the echo of a battle that has already taken place'.[117] It is still unclear if, as Brian O'Blivion foresees, the venue for this battle was the Videodrome of televisual, spectacular culture or, indeed, who won. In a sense, Bianca's explanation that her father 'was convinced that public life on television was more real than private life in the flesh' and that 'he wasn't afraid to let his body die' suggests that the real 'new flesh', rather than some kind of new techno-flesh mutation (as suggested by the cut final scenes), is existence on television.

Although the status of Warhol's remark about '15 minutes of fame' was very quickly eroded to the point of cliché, its relevance for a global media has not diminished. If the only transcendent state towards which most people aspire is appearance on television, Foucault's perceptions on institutional power become strangely prophetic in relation to a media environment that is increasingly turning inwards, creating the kind of unresolvable tensions between masochism and spectacle that Cronenberg explores in *Videodrome*. As murderously ambitious reporter Suzanne Stone (played by Nicole Kidman) says in *To Die For* (Gus Van Sant, 1995), 'You're not anybody in America unless you're on TV. On TV is where we all learn about who we really are. Because what's the point of doing anything worthwhile if nobody's watching'.

Notes

1. *Not a Love Story – A Film About Pornography* (Bonnie Sherr Klein, 1981).
2. J. G. Ballard, No. 19 in 'Answers to a Questionnaire', *War Fever* (London: Palladin, 1991), p. 81.
3. Stephen King, *Danse Macabre* (New York: Everest; London: Warner Books, 1981), p. 155, note 1.
4. Julian Petley, 'V.D. O'Nasty', in Wayne Drew (ed.) *David Cronenberg: Dossier 21* (London: British Film Institute, 1984), p. 38.
5. J. G. Ballard cited in Linda S. Kauffman, 'David Cronenberg's Surreal Abjection', in *Bad Girls and Sick Boys: Fantasies in Contemporary Art and Culture* (Berkeley; Los Angeles; London: University of California Press, 1998), p. 158.
6. J. G. Ballard, *High Rise* (London: Triad/Panther, 1977), p. 46 and Chris Rodley, 'Crash', *Sight and Sound* 6:6 (June 1996), p. 9.
7. Susie Bright 'Accidents Will Happen', The Salon Interview with David Cronenberg (http://www.salon.com/march 97/interview970321.html), p. 2.
8. Bruce Kirkland, 'Blue', Canadian Movie Guide, (http://www.canoe.ca/JamMoviesCanadianB/blue.html), p. 1. Cronenberg dismisses most of his acting work as 'terrible' but claims 'I did one thing, a little film called *Blue*, and I thought I wasn't bad in that'. *Shift* interview, (http://www.cronenberg.freeserve.co.uk/cr_rushd.html), p. 5.
9. Victor Sage, 'The Gothic, the Body, and the Failed Homeopathy Argument', in Xavier Mendik and Graeme Harper (eds.), *Unruly Pleasures: The Cult Film and its Critics* (Guildford: FAB Press, 2000), p. 143.
10. Mark Kermode, 'David Cronenberg', *Sight and Sound* 1:11 (March 1992), p. 12.
11. Bright, op. cit., p. 7.
12. Marty Roth, '*Videodrome* and the Revenge of Representation', *CineAction!* 43 (July 1997), p. 61.
13. Steven Shaviro, *The Cinematic Body* (Minneapolis; London: University of Minnesota Press, 1993), p. 54.
14. Ibid.
15. Ian Conrich, 'An Aesthetic Sense: Cronenberg and neo-horror film culture', in Michael Grant (ed.), *The Modern Fantastic: The Films of David Cronenberg* (Trowbridge: Flicks Books, 2000), p. 45.
16. Guy Debord, *Society of the Spectacle* (New York: Black and Red, 1970), paragraph 47 and paragraph 49.
17. 'William Burroughs: An Interview', *Paris Review* 35 (1965), cited in Eric Mottram, *William Burroughs* (London: Marion Boyars Publishers Ltd, 1977), p. 42.
18. Marty Roth, op. cit., p. 61.
19. J. G. Ballard, cited in James Goddard and David Pringle (eds.), *J.G. Ballard: The First Twenty Years* (Hayes: Brian's Head Books Ltd., 1976), p. 69.
20. J. G. Ballard, *The Kindness of Women* (London: Grafton, 1992), p. 299.
21. Ibid., p. 252.
22. Ibid., p. 299.
23. David Wojnarowicz, *Close to the Knives: A Memoir of Disintegration* (London: Vintage, 1991).

24. Elaine Scarry, *The Body in Pain: The Making and Unmaking of the World* (Oxford: Oxford University Press, 1985), p. 40.
25. Ibid., p. 52.
26. Leopold Sacher-Masoch, *Venus in Furs*, in Gilles Deleuze, *Masochism: Coldness and Cruelty* (Zone Books, 1989), p. 185, 223, 244, 268.
27. Masoch cited in Scarry, op. cit., p. 143, 144.
28. Masoch, op. cit., p. 155.
29. Theodore Reik cited in ibid., pp. 74-75.
30. Ibid., p. 149.
31. Ibid., p. 154.
32. Ibid., p. 180.
33. Linda Ruth Williams, 'The Inside-out of Masculinity: David Cronenberg's Visceral Pleasures', in Michele Aaron (ed.), *The Body's Perilous Pleasures: Dangerous Desires and Contemporary Culture* (Edinburgh: Edinburgh University Press, 1999), p. 37.
34. Masoch, op. cit., p. 269.
35. Ian W. Hill, '*Videodrome*: TV or not TV?', *Video Watchdog* 36 (1996), [A letter from a reader criticizing the MCA-TV version of *Videodrome*, with an editorial response], p. 78.
36. Steven Shaviro, op. cit., p. 57.
37. Hill, op. cit., p. 78.
38. James Woods cited by Tim Lucas, 'Videodrome', *Cinefantastique* 12:2/3 (April 1982), p. 6.
39. Masoch, *Venus in Furs*, in Gilles Deleuze, op. cit., p. 143.
40. William Burroughs, (with Claude Pelieu and Carl Weissner), *So Who Owns Death TV?*, (San Francisco: Beach Books, 1967).
41. David Cronenberg cited in Peter Morris, *David Cronenberg: A Delicate Balance* (Toronto: ECW Press, 1994), p. 94.
42. Marshall McLuhan, *Understanding Media: The Extensions of Man* (London: Sphere Books, 1967), p. 11.
43. William Burroughs cited in Mottram, op. cit., p.112.
44. David Cronenberg cited in Richard Porton, 'The Film Director as Philosopher: An Interview with David Cronenberg', *Cineaste* 24:4 (1999), p. 6.
45. Marshall McLuhan, *Understanding Media: The Extensions of Man* (London: Sphere Books, 1967), p. 25.
46. Christopher Sharrett, 'Myth and Ritual in the Post-Industrial Landscape: the Horror Films of David Cronenberg', *Persistence of Vision* 3-4 (summer 1986), p. 126.
47. Linda Badley, *Film, Horror, and the Body Fantastic* (New York: Greenwood Press, 1995), p. 30.
48. Sharrett, op. cit., p. 124.
49. Steven Shaviro, op. cit., p. 137.
50. Jean Baudrillard, *For a Critique of the Political Economy of the Sign* (St Louis, MO: Telos Press), pp. 164–185.
51. Barry Miles, *William Burroughs: El Hombre Invisible* (London: Virgin Books, 1992), p. 120.
52. Guy Debord, op. cit., paragraph 1.
53. Michel Foucault, *Discipline and Punish: The Birth of the Prison* [trans. Alan Sheridan], (Harmondsworth: Penguin Books, 1977), p. 201.
54. Kauffman, op. cit., p. 187.
55. Eric White, '"Once They Were Men, Now They're Landcrabs": Monstrous Becomings in Evolutionist Cinema', in Judith Halberstam and Ira Livingstone (eds.), *Posthuman Bodies* (Bloomington: Indiana University Press, 1995), p. 260.

56. Ibid., p. 262.
57. Ibid., p. 264.
58. Ibid., p. 264 and p. 265.
59. William Burroughs, *The Wild Boys* (New York: Grove Press, 1971), p. 82.
60. Clive Barker cited in Linda Badley, *Writing Horror and the Body: The Fiction of Stephen King, Clive Barker and Anne Rice* (New York: Greenwood Press, 1996), p. 73.
61. Ibid., p. 84.
62. Robin Wood, 'Introduction' in Robin Wood and Richard Lippe (eds.), *The American Nightmare* (Toronto: Festival of Festivals, 1979), p. 24.
63. Geoff Pevere, 'Cronenberg Tackles Dominant Videology', in Piers Handling, (ed.), *The Shape of Rage: The Films of David Cronenberg* (Toronto: Academy of Canadian Cinema, 1983; New York: New York Zoetrope Inc., 1983), p. 141.
64. Clive Barker cited in Badley, op. cit., p. 91.
65. Ramsey Campbell, 'Introduction' to Clive Barker's *Books of Blood*: Volumes 1-3 (London: Sphere Books, 1984), (*xii*).
66. Ibid., p. 7.
67. Ibid., p. 18.
68. Ibid., p. 32.
69. Ibid., p. 25.
70. Ibid., p. 24.
71. Badley, op. cit., p. 84.
72. J. G. Ballard cited in Iain Sinclair, *Crash* (London: BFI Modern Classics, 1999), p. 42.
73. Judith Halberstam and Ira Livingstone, 'Introduction', op. cit., p. 12.
74. Ibid.
75. See Michel Foucault, *The History of Sexuality, Volume I: An Introduction*, trans. Robert Hurley (Harmondsworth: Penguin Books, 1978), p. 12 and Linda Williams, *Hard Core: Power, Pleasure, and the "The Frenzy of the Visible"* (Berkeley: University of California Press, 1989), p. 3.
76. See 'Interview with David Cronenberg', by Serge Grünberg, *Cahiers du Cinéma* 453 (March-April, 1992), p. 24.
77. Clive Barker, 'The Age of Desire', in *Books of Blood*: Volume 4 (London: Sphere Books, 1985), p. 184.
78. Ibid.
79. J. G. Ballard, *The Atrocity Exhibition* (London: Triad/Panther, 1979), p. 77.
80. Barker, op. cit., p. 184.
81. Rodley, Chris (ed.), *Cronenberg on Cronenberg*, (London: Faber and Faber, 1992), p. 97.
82. David Cronenberg in 'The Image as Virus: The Filming of *Videodrome*', by Tim Lucas, in Piers Handling (ed.), op. cit., p. 155.
83. Rodley, op. cit., pp. 103–108.
84. Barker, op. cit., p. 190.
85. Ibid., p. 196.
86. Ibid., p. 185.
87. Ibid., p. 201.
88. David Cronenberg, cited in Tim Lucas, '*Ideadrome*: David Cronenberg from *Shivers* to *Dead Ringers*', *Video Watchdog* 36 (1996), p. 41.
89. Clive Barker, 'Jacqueline Ess: Her Will and Testament' in *Books of Blood*: Volume 2 (London: Sphere Books, 1984), p. 60.
90. Peter Michelson, *The Aesthetics of Pornography* (Herder and Herder, 1971), p. 5, cited in Linda Williams, op. cit., p. 10.

91. Barker, op. cit., p. 83.
92. Ibid.
93. Ibid., p. 84.
94. Ibid., p. 90.
95. See Linda S. Kauffman, op. cit., pp. 115–145.
96. Brett Easton Ellis, *American Psycho* (London: Picador, 1991), p. 112.
97. Rodley, op. cit., p. 94.
98. Ellis, op. cit., p. 69.
99. Ibid., pp. 179-180.
100. Ibid., p. 264.
101. Ibid., p. 205.
102. David Cronenberg cited in Kauffman, op. cit., p. 249.
103. Ibid., p. 188.
104. Paul Taylor, '*Videodrome*', *Monthly Film Bulletin* 50:598 (November 1983), p. 311.
105. Ellis, op. cit., p. 86.
106. Ibid., p. 206.
107. Ibid., p. 20.
108. Ibid., pp. 372-373.
109. Ibid., p. 304.
110. J. G. Ballard, *The Kindness of Women* (London: Grafton, 1992), p. 265.
111. Ellis, op. cit., p. 105.
112. Ibid., p. 265.
113. Ellis, op. cit., p. 208.
114. Marquis de Sade, *Philosophy in the Bedroom*, p. 203.
115. Thomas Harris, *Red Dragon* (London: Corgi, 1991), p. 172.
116. Susan Sontag, 'The Pornographic Imagination', in *A Susan Sontag Reader* (Harmondsworth: Penguin, 1982), p. 224.
117. Halberstam and Livingstone, op. cit., 'Preface', p. *vii*.

CHAPTER TWO

DEAD RINGERS: 'SCHIZOPHRENIA CANNOT BE UNDERSTOOD WITHOUT UNDERSTANDING DESPAIR'[1]

Of all of Cronenberg's films, *Dead Ringers* (1988) has the greatest number of articles devoted to it. Many of these take a psychological or feminist approach to gender roles, focusing on the characterization of the Mantle brothers and Claire Niveau, who disrupts their equilibrium. My approach will be slightly different. After several drafts using different writers and producers, Cronenberg wrote his own script and drew attention himself to additional items not in Norman Snider's original script but which he felt were central: 'the instruments; the dream sequences; the opening with the kids; the Mantle Retractor...they were touchstones'.[2] These are the four areas that I will focus on most of all, whilst also considering the film as a text in the tradition of 'the double'.

Twins, (a provisional working title for *Dead Ringers*), also opened in 1988, directed by a former colleague of Cronenberg's, Ivan Reitman, and reflects the concerns with duality in a more mainstream, comic arena. All subsequent references to *Twins* will denote the 1977 novel by Bari Wood and Jack Geasland. Thomas Doherty notes that Cronenberg 'said he immersed himself in the literature, psychology, and cinematic history of twins', including *The Dark Mirror* (Robert Siodmak, 1946), *The Parent Trap* (David Swift, 1961), *Dead Ringer* (Paul Henreid, 1964), and he even screened *A Zed and Two Noughts* (Peter Greenaway, 1986) for the crew.[3] However, Cronenberg does not specify what literature he referred to and it is this aspect of 'the double' upon which this chapter will focus.

The relationship of *Dead Ringers* to *Twins*
(character changes, homosexual subtext and parallel scenes)
Cronenberg came to the narrative through a newspaper article about real-life identical twin gynaecologists, Stuart and Cyril Marcus, found dead in a New York

apartment from drug misuse. Only subsequently did he read the 1977 Bari Wood and Jack Geasland novel based on the Marcus scenario. According to critic Owen Gleiberman, 'the basic premise' of Cronenberg's film 'is derived from the novel', whereby the twins, Michael and David Ross, become involved with an actress, Kathy Field, one falling in love with her, but lose her through their habit of substituting for one another sexually.[4] In the novel *Twins*, one of the twins is gay and one gets married, emphasizing differences between them, an approach that Cronenberg dismissed. He also rejected a subsequent re-write by Andy K. Lewis, who wanted to 'demystify' the brothers so they were not 'in any way be amazing or strange'.[5] For Cronenberg, their existence as identical twins made their situation special, not ordinary, both to the brothers themselves and characters around them. J. G. Ballard's definition of schizophrenia as representing 'the insane's idea of the normal', seems to be Cronenberg's starting point.[6] The innate seriousness of the Mantles is established from the prologue. They may not be rejected by adults quite so bluntly as they are by the unnamed girl in the opening but they are still nonetheless 'freaks', not so much for their identical appearance but their apparent humourlessness in response to their situation.

Cronenberg claims that his version of Norman Snider's 1981 script is 'a radical rewrite'. The two share screenwriting credit but Cronenberg claims his input was 'more surrealistic – the stuff with the kids at the beginning for example'.[7] His comments on the process prefigure claims he made about the role of Burroughs in the script of *Naked Lunch*, asserting that 'there are some things which I can't remember whether Norman wrote or I wrote', which, bearing in mind his precision about writing credits in most of his projects, seems frankly unlikely.[8] Peter Bloch-Hansen credits Cronenberg with the name change from *Twins* to *Dead Ringers*, but this is more a matter of choice than wholesale creation as this was the title of a 1974 *Esquire* article on the case that he had read previously that, according to Lucas, 'detailed the case history on which the novel was discretely based'.[9] Snider and Cronenberg 'felt that because the book had been written we had better option it' so that they could 'say the movie was based on the book', making the film's relation to its source more bound by legal convenience than creative inspiration and although the novel was first optioned in 1980, it was another eight years before the project could be realized, creating a lengthy gestation period.[10]

Cronenberg was unhappy with parts of Snider's early drafts 'due to his attempting to use some of the stuff from the book', so faithfulness to the source material does not *appear* to be integral to his vision of the film.[11] The casting of Irons meant that, for Cronenberg, the original conception of Claire's character as English had to be modified, to emphasize the element of change that she brings to the twins' symbiotic relationship. As a French-Canadian actress, Geneviève Bujold both had some shared cultural background with Cronenberg but, more importantly, her appearance in *Coma* (Michael Crichton, 1977) created useful connotations around her screen persona as intelligent, perceptive and combative when faced with the vested interests of the medical establishment. In *Tightrope* (Richard Tuggle, 1984), she had already played a figure who unsettles male sexuality, when she exposes suppressed sadomasochistic desires in detective Wes Block (played by Clint Eastwood).

Cronenberg does make some changes to the central female character of his source novel, *Twins*. Unlike the film, in the novel's description of the twins' relationship with a woman, there is no element of suspense. Kathy knows about the brothers' womanizing reputation before sleeping with them and is actually attracted by it.[12] The perversity in her character that Cronenberg expresses in her masochistic sexual tastes is more connected to polygamous lust in the novel as she muses, '[w]hy tell them apart? Why not have both?'[13] She is described as being the same age as the twins, forty-three, emphasizing the bond between them, rather than difference.[14] David later seduces Kathy to try and separate his brother from her emotional clutches but despite this, Kathy and Michael marry and have a child (echoed in Claire Niveau's motivation for coming to the Mantle Clinic). Cronenberg translates Kathy's career as an artist to Claire's as an actress and converts Michael spotting one of Kathy's paintings of their son in a gallery to Beverly's discovery of his surgical tools; in both cases a creative act leads back to respective female loves via a gallery.

In Cronenberg's film, homosexual subtext is suppressed rather than erased. Rodley notes in Cronenberg's realization of the Mantles 'there seems to be an equivalent of Ron Mlodzik's gay sensibility at work again, albeit at a subtextual level'.[15] Beverly's disavowal extends to being unable to recognize the nature of Claire's gay secretary (clearly signalled by a stereotypical camp voice) and the ferocity of the irrational outburst that the man has been 'fucking a mutant', suggests the surfacing of a suppressed identity. Claire questions him about why he has a woman's name, to which he reacts sharply wondering if she is questioning his masculinity and sexuality. Cronenberg removes those elements of the original narrative of the Marcus twins that are at odds with heterosexuality, i.e. incest and homosexuality, but they resurface. In the scene where Elliot dances with Cary, Beverly joins them so that 'women (are) providing an environment...in which they can touch each other'.[16] Eve Sedgwick identifies such 'triangulation' as a means of avoiding the threat of 'homosocial desire', which could be seen in Cronenberg's placement of Elliot with twin prostitutes.[17] The sexual subtext also resurfaces in both the dream scene retained and the one cut (see later), where the brothers are in bed together, irrespective of the presence of Claire.

In the novel, the elder twin, David, initiates some sexual touching, which Michael eventually reciprocates but this remains an isolated incestuous act until later in adult life when David 're-captures' Michael. David is openly bisexual, conducting a lengthy homosexual relationship with Romer, another doctor.[18] In therapy, Michael admits homosexual experiences and the therapist, Snyder, provokes a response from him that echoes Sedgwick's theories of disavowal:

How do you feel about the other man?
You make it sound like a love triangle.
Isn't it?[19]

The appearance of Cary as a girlfriend late in the film, far from ensuring 'the viewer's acceptance of the male protagonist's heterosexuality', is deliberately unconvincing, as shown by Elly hurling Cary aside to give mouth-to-mouth to the collapsed Beverly.[20] This episode derives from a scene in the novel, where, at a drunken party, Michael has sex with a local girl called Junie. David fanatically wants to 'go next', pushing a bystander away with such force that the man falls over.[21]

For Elaine Showalter, the Mantles' status as twins 'is a metaphor for an ultimate homoeroticism and autoeroticism', and Irons himself feels that the relationship of the Mantles is 'fundamentally homosexual, but Platonic.[22] It allows them the freedom to relate to other bodies...rather blind to emotional implications'.[23] Cronenberg's response to the novel's portrayal of *one* of the twins as gay was dismissive: 'that seemed psychologically false, it couldn't be true. I did not believe it. I could imagine two heterosexual twins or two homosexual twins but not that distinction'.[24] Cronenberg justifies the suppression of homosexuality and incest on the grounds that this was a distraction away from the similarity of the two men: 'the point of the story is how similar they are'.[25] Whilst balking at the commercial realities of producing a film featuring incest might be understandable, Cronenberg's 'heterosexualization' of a gay narrative, involves a shift to sexual acts between the sexes but with a strong element of voyeuristic and masochistic fantasy. Claire is intrigued when she finds that Beverly has a brother, enquiring 'Do you sleep together?' Later in the restaurant, she challenges Elliot: 'Can't you get it up unless your brother is watching?' and her demand to see the brothers together has sexual overtones as well as expressing a need to establish their separate identity.

Unacknowledged by Cronenberg in any interviews on the film, there are *three* occasions in the novel when Michael makes a phone call but cannot speak: the final one is to his girlfriend (as in the film) but the *first two are to his brother*. In the first call, David's gay lover, Romer, answers with David in the background.[26] Cronenberg translates this same-sex relationship into Beverly's jealous delusion surrounding Claire, casting homosexual relations as deviant, immature and hateful. Later Michael rings David again to explain that he is thinking of moving into a separate clinical area (cancer) but cannot speak.[27] Both calls are about a separation, the first sexual, the second professional.

In terms of narrative, the novel opens with a focus on the strange discovery of the twins' deaths and Kathy, who agrees to go and identify the bodies. It is deduced that Michael killed David with an injection of Seconal and Michael effectively committed suicide by flushing his anti-convulsant drugs (Dilantin) away, dying later near his brother, of withdrawal. The novel closes, not with a focus on the brothers in their final moments but with Kathy at the morgue. As she is one of the few who can tell them apart (like Claire in Cronenberg's film), she can mislead the authorities so that David appears the killer, thereby protecting her child. In an echo of *Scanners*, the novel ends as 'Michael became David', not in an act of fusion of brothers but a switch of identity after death with toe-tags re-written.[28] Identity is protean and mediated by television (the images of the bodies are seen on screen rather than directly). The narrative of the novel is based on a pursuit, with Michael trying to escape and David always reeling him back in, with David actually welcoming revelations about Michael's drug abuse as it gives him some leverage with Kathy. In the novel, they only go into gynaecological practice together because David has made Michael feel a failure in his cancer work, but Cronenberg takes their professional co-operation as a given from the outset of the film. The series of switching between the twins that appears from the outset of the film only appears in the novel when David pretends to be Michael for a medical emergency, so that substitution begins by chance, rather than calculation and in a professional rather than a private arena.

Cronenberg picks up many verbal cues. David's dialogue that 'Ander's girlfriend (Kathy) could mean trouble for us, Michael' and the omniscient narrator's description that 'David decided he didn't like Miss Field and the effect she was having on his brother', is translated by Cronenberg into Elliot's reference to Claire's effect on 'the Mantle saga'.[29] Mannerisms like Beverly's keening for his brother at the end of the film are anticipated in David calling plaintively to Michael at the lake and after sex.[30] Striking visual images that may appear original in the film have clear literary precursors. The Mantles trudging in step through their apartment at the end of the film is drawn directly from a hotel scene in the novel where bystanders watch in amazement as the Ross twins walk almost in step through the foyer. Minor characters and events in the novel appear in the film with only slight alteration. A rich sponsor, Mrs Calhoun, is treated by Michael rather than David and his rough and distracted manner provides a template for Beverly's examination of Mrs Bookman in the film.[31] At a dinner reception, Michael is embarrassing, not so much by being drunk and offensive in the sexually blunt terms of the film, but by problematizing notions of identity altogether, declaring 'He's Michael and I'm David'.[32] Overall, Cronenberg's unwillingness to acknowledge the extent of the debt that he owes to his literary source is, at the very least, disingenuous. So much of the novel resurfaces in the film, that it is just not possible to see the film as an entirely independent artistic entity.

Twins/Doubles
(the importance of similarity and difference in issues of identity)
Studies of the double motif often adopt a psychoanalytical approach, based on Freudian notions of narcissism and familial pressures to explain character motivation. Otto Rank in *The Double: A Psychoanalytical Study* (1914) suggests that 'fear and hate with respect to the double-self are closely connected with the

narcissistic love for it and with the resistance of this love'.[33] Whilst some comments can be useful, such as Rank's assertion that 'the double is often associated with the brother', Cronenberg tends to shy away from such schematic explanations for what he regards as a process that is far more intuitive and complex and prefers instead to draw on a literary sensibility rather than a psychological one.[34]

According to Malcolm Jones, what Dostoevsky added to the double motif in works like 'The Double' (1846) were 'the links between "the fantastic" in the romantic tradition and abnormal psychology, by rewriting the former in terms of the latter', which Cronenberg also does in *Dead Ringers*.[35] The shift of narrative voices in *The Double*, including dramatized conversations with imaginary adversaries, can also be found in Beverly's outburst at Claire's agent, the paranoid delusion that the insides of women like Mrs Bookman are 'all wrong' and finally addressing his own brother as 'Chang'. Jones asserts that 'the two principal voices of the hero, although they may change places, cannot dwell in harmony'.[36] Beverly's dilemma in *Dead Ringers*, aspiring to the suave confidence of Elliot, is paralleled in Jones' description of Dostoevsky's protagonist, Golyadkin, who is trying to 'reconcile the lowly, pathetic care-laden, guilt-ridden figure he has to be to survive in society with the successful, domineering, carefree conscienceless person he would like to be and projects as a separate, independent personality'.[37] Like Beverly, he is infatuated with a woman (his patron's daughter in Golyadkin's case) but 'in thus projecting himself he seems even more ridiculous in the eyes of others, and that he has neither the psychological nor the social means to sustain the role'.[38] As Elliot has been impersonating Beverly in Claire's bed, by the time the real Beverly consummates his relationship with her, he has the impossible task of out-performing what he perceives as Elliot's sexual prowess. Elliot's advice to 'Just do me' means that Beverly is acting out a subjective fantasy of his brother just as Elliot was, in relation to Beverly earlier.

For Jones, 'The Double' is about a 'hero who is driven to distraction by the refusal of others to validate his self-image'.[39] In *Dead Ringers*, this is a dilemma ultimately shared by both brothers, even though Elliot initially seems much more self-possessed than Beverly. In a scene largely neglected by critics, one of Elliot's coping mechanisms is the hiring of twin escort girls, Mimsy and Coral, one of whom he instructs to call him 'Bev' and the other 'Elly'. This is one means by which he can sustain the fantasy of a unified self and indulge in the subtext of incest and homosexuality whilst maintaining the appearance of excessive virile heterosexuality. As François Ramasse expresses the paradox of the scene, 'the two twins are one, one twin is two'.[40] Elliot is very bad with names. In obtaining a prescription for Claire, he gets the name of the chemist wrong, even though it is implied that he has used his services many times before and, similarly, one of the twin escort girls has to remind him of her name even though she only has just introduced herself. It seems that names (and by extension, individual people) are one of the sacrifices that must be made 'to keep life simple' as Elliot puts it, in order to achieve results.

As Elliot notes sardonically, 'the truth is, nobody can tell us apart'. This is part of the tragedy of the film as we can see, even if the brothers cannot, that one person can tell them apart: Claire. Cary is clearly marked as a less perceptive individual and unworthy long-term mate by her warning an increasingly addicted Elliot that 'It's getting hard telling you two apart'. Ironically, their game of substitution has become too successful. For Cronenberg, 'it's not so much a fascination with twins per se...as it is a question of doubles and identity'.[41] He frequently cites research on twins from the University of Minnesota, which suggests that what we assume to be a matter of free will appears to be biologically predetermined, contradicting Romantic notions of a unique self.[42] In Nabokov's *Despair*, the protagonist, Hermann, assures the reader that he is the absolute identical counterpart of Felix, his murder victim and even considers using 'The Double' as the title for his artistic account of his criminal masterpiece but later we discover they are *not* so at all, suggesting that only madmen really believe in the concept.

In *Dead Ringers*, there are two pairs of real identical twins (the boys at the beginning and the escort twins) and, in theory, Cronenberg could have used real twins as the adult Mantle brothers. However, doubles appear to be identical but actually are not (in terms of character in *Dead Ringers*, in terms of appearance in *Despair*) and Cronenberg is at pains to point out that the notion of identical twins is a cultural myth: 'I'm suggesting that it's impossible'.[43] His decision to opt for one actor playing both parts rather than using genuine twins means that he is, in effect, creating a *myth of twinship*, not present in the world beyond the film. His reason for doing so seems bound up with the wish to play an extended Nabokovian game with the viewer, challenging assumptions about identity and individuality and necessitating ground-breaking special effects, which draw attention to themselves both in mundane scenes like the twins walking abreast down a hospital corridor and climactic scenes like the restaurant episode.[44] As Hermann is made to realize in *Despair*, 'in the whole world there are not, and cannot be, two men alike, however well you disguise them', and in the novel *Twins*, Dr Benson states, '[i]t's like a template for a design. Everything that comes out of it should be the same but never is...not even in identical twins'.[45] This all undermines Cronenberg's attempts to explain the suppression of his homosexual subtext on the grounds of maintaining a similarity between the twins, when he appears to believe at the same time that such similarity is a myth.

Nabokov claims 'there are no real "doubles" in my novels', but his work abounds with characters, names and situations that clearly parallel one another, such as Humbert (whose full name is an example of doubling) and Quilty (*Lolita*, 1959), Hermann and Felix (*Despair*), Shade and Kinbote (*Pale Fire*, 1962) and Van and Ada (*Ada*, 1969).[46] As in *Dead Ringers*, the fulcrum about which the doubles revolve is death. Hermann kills Felix for an insurance fraud, Humbert kills his love rival Quilty and Shade is killed accidentally by Gradus. L. L. Lee observes that 'doubleness turned upon itself too far is more than parody...it can be a kind of insanity' and the pursuit of parallels and doubles in Nabokov's work has spawned a whole critical industry.[47] Wittgenstein refers to primitive forms of language acquisition as involving 'language-games' and uses the term 'family resemblances' (in relation to types of game) as a potential way of creating groups of similar activities, like competitive, ball or card games.[48] *Dead Ringers* dramatizes a working out of the 'game', through literal family resemblances.

Cronenberg's choice of the same actor to play both twins in *Dead Ringers* means that the viewer is forced to pay minute attention as to who is on screen at any one time. When we see Claire making love to one of the Mantle brothers, tied by medical ties and clamps, we do not know at that precise moment whether this is Beverly or Elliot. Similarly, in *Lolita*, Nabokov seems keen to *blur* rather than emphasize distinctions between Humbert and Quilty.[49] In the Pavor Manor death scene, the interweaving of pronouns suggests the interchangeability of homoerotic doubles in an echo of the wrestling scene in D. H. Lawrence's *Women in Love* (1920): '[w]e rolled over me. They rolled over him. We rolled over us', and their battle constitutes a 'silent, soft, formless tussle on the part of two literati'.[50] This latter 'tussle' could be seen as Nabokov engaging in a literary game with his predecessors and there is an element of this in Cronenberg's film too. The attempt to kill the alien Other is a convention of the double tale, as seen in *Despair*, 'The Double' and Edgar Allen Poe's 'William Wilson' (1839), which Cronenberg follows, as the operation 'to separate Siamese twins' will result in Elliot's death and, until the final shot, we do not know that Beverly will choose to die as well.

In *Despair*, Hermann appears to have an underlying insecurity about his wife's fidelity but as we only have his point of view, this is far from certain. For Stephen Parker, this indicates that 'the double provides Hermann with the projection of a preferred self-image, an abnegation of his true self in the face of his marital/sexual despair'.[51] Beverly's obsessive jealousy and paranoia about Claire convinces him that she is being unfaithful to him, despite the lack of any evidence. Hermann fails because 'his attempt at self-reproduction is based on the impossible assumption of his own reality totally perceived and thus capable of recreating itself' and it could be said that Beverly's relationship with Claire fails for the same reason.[52]

According to Alfred Appel Jr, before Nabokov began *Lolita* in 1949-50, 'he considered writing a novel about Siamese twins; Vera Nabokov dissuaded him: "The subject is too unpleasant!" – and he instead turned to nympholepsy'.[53] The rejected subject is displaced into a little-known short story. In 'Scenes from the Life of a Double Monster', Floyd describes himself and his twin brother, Lloyd, thus: '[e]ach was eminently normal, but together they formed a monster. Indeed, it is strange to think that the presence of a mere band of tissue, a flap of flesh not much longer than a lamb's liver, should be able to transform joy, pride, tenderness, adoration, gratitude to God into horror and despair'.[54] Cronenberg states that 'separation from your parents' is the most terrifying experience of all childhood fears and cites *Blue*

Lagoon (Frank Launder, 1949), where Susan Stranks and Peter Jones play adolescents marooned on a Pacific island, as his most memorable cinematic example of this.[55] *Dead Ringers* many years later carried the tag line 'Separation is a terrifying thing', with brothers standing in the place of parents, who are not shown in Cronenberg's film.

In discussing notions of duality, Karl Miller notes that 'the component parts may complete, resemble or repel one another'.[56] Before Claire disrupts the equilibrium of the brothers, each is effectively acting out the fantasy of the other, almost as if he wishes he could be the other, which in a social and sexual sense he can by swapping partners, and telling the other about it. However, as Steven Shaviro states, they are 'purchasing omnipotence by denying embodiment'.[57] Their ability to pass for one another will only work as long as neither develops any noticeable, individual traits. As soon as Beverly 'loses his heart' to Claire, the physical changes in him, exacerbated by drug use, lead him to displace that change onto the source of his sameness, women's reproductive organs, that are now 'all wrong'.

The novel *Twins* uses metaphors from Hollywood horror films and carnivalesque freak shows to convey the 'otherness' of the twins. When introduced to Harriet, a local girl, she exclaims:

> 'Oooh ! You're twins'.
> 'We're not twins', Michael said.
> 'We do it with mirrors', said David, and he stretched out his arms in front of him. 'Moooohaha', he moaned, staggering, stiff-legged, into the apartment imitating Frankenstein. 'Moooohaha...'
> Harriet backed away, smiling but a little uncertain'.[58]

In the film, when Claire sees the Mantle brothers together for the first time in the restaurant, she murmurs in amazement that 'it's uncanny'. Lucy Maddox asserts that for Nabokov 'a simple thing seen in isolation may be momentarily interesting, but when a complex thing is seen together with its mimotype, there is room for an entire world of wonders in the slight asymmetry between the two'.[59] Similarly in Angela Carter's *Wise Children* (1992), Dora Chance explains how she and her identical twin, Nora, high kicking at dance school before a long mirror, look 'like trick photography in flesh and blood...By ourselves, neither of us was nothing much but put us together, people blinked'.[60] The irony is, of course, that in the case of *Dead Ringers*, what Dora describes as 'not so much a twin, more of an optical illusion', is literally the case due to Cronenberg's use of computer-aided motion photography.[61] The scene dramatizes Wittgenstein's notion of how different objects can be perceived in different 'aspects', drawing on the examples of the duck-rabbit and later an acute triangle, which appears to have "fallen over". He describes how you can 'distinguish between the "continuous seeing" of an aspect and the "dawning" of an aspect', as if you 'suddenly see the solution of a puzzle picture.'[62]

In *Twins*, there is a parallel scene when a grandfather of a neighbour sees the Ross twins for the first time and recounts that in Jewish culture 'they say twins are cursed...not one person, yet less than two'.[63] This echoes the social anthropology of René Girard, who describes how twins can be seen as a violent omen, or the work of Mary Douglas, where they represent the violation of social taboos.[64] In the novel, this scene greatly disturbs Michael, who suffers a recurrent nightmare, in which the old man appears and warns him to get away from David. In the film, Cronenberg does not follow this Freudian paradigm of a traumatic event in childhood forming adult character, undermining the position of psycho-analytical critics like Barbara Creed, and he completely removes all references to the twins' parents, who, in the novel, are used to show development in the boys, such as when Michael talks with his father about whether he really wants to be a doctor.[65]

A useful comparison can be made with the narrative of Bruce Chatwin's novel *On the Black Hill* (1983).This describes the lives of Benjamin and Lewis Jones, Welsh hill farmers and identical twins with an ability to communicate with each other without speaking and which, Benjamin feels, will remain 'inseparable – even in death'.[66] The pseudo-marital relationship between the brothers recalls the Mantles with Lewis performing the more demanding manual tasks on the farm, while Benjamin, the more effeminate, younger twin, is far more emotional and prone to nightmares. Their professional expertise in an agricultural context mirrors the Mantles' gynaecological knowledge as Benjamin becomes expert at helping in birthing processes (of lambs) and is prepared to 'thrust his forearm into the womb to disentangle a pair of twins'.[67] Both *On the Black Hill* and *Dead Ringers* dramatize Wittgenstein's notion that pain is incommunicable or inalienable.[68] When Benjamin is stung by a wasp, Lewis is strangely able to 'draw the pain from his brother, and take it on himself'.[69] This could be said to be Elliot's motivation in sharing Beverly's drug habit and gradually adopting a more passive role in their final scene together as he lies back and allows himself to be operated on for the benefit of his younger brother.

In Chatwin's novel, the brothers visit a flower show, their first major excursion beyond the family home. A rather predatory female childminder, Mrs Griffiths, stands them next to each other and is not happy until she spots a tiny mole behind Benjamin's ear, yelling, 'I've found a difference',which prompts the pair to run away in fright.[70] In *Dead Ringers*, female curiosity to differentiate apparently identical individuals leads to fear, anguish and ultimately closer bonds between the twins. Cronenberg dramatizes Wittgenstein's suggestion that 'it would also be imaginable for two people to feel pain in the same – not just the corresponding – place. That might be the case with Siamese twins'.[71] Wittgenstein challenges his reader to 'imagine a case in which people ascribed pain *only* to inanimate things; pitied *only* dolls!'[72] This is the scenario that Cronenberg presents, including the opening with the Mantle boys, playing with anatomical dolls rather than other children of their own age, Beverly's insensitivity with Mrs Bookman and Elliot's doll-like escorts.

The Jones twins have their own secret language and feel resentment towards any presence that they perceive coming between them. After the arrival of their baby sister, Rebecca, they are discovered 'writhing convulsively on the kitchen floor...playing at making babies'.[73] This is what the Mantle boys, in a more controlled way, are doing at the start of Cronenberg's film and also arguably in the final operation, where Beverly creates a 'womb' for Elliot (and by extension, for himself). Like Cronenberg's twin heroes, the Jones brothers spend the narrative within a very limited geographical compass and are terrified of separation. Lewis gets work at a nearby farm, immediately causing a mixture of emotions in Benjamin: 'he hated Lewis for leaving and suspected him of stealing his soul'.[74] Like Beverly, when he is left alone, Benjamin becomes 'sadder and sadder and he soon grew thin and weak'.[75] In Chatwin's novel, unlike Cronenberg's film, tragedy is avoided by allowing one brother to come back and the pair work together, although unlike the Mantles' smooth-running practice at the beginning of the film, 'it took the twins another ten years to work out a division of labour'.[76] The Mantles seem paralysed if they are apart for any length of time. Elliot initially seems much more self-sufficient but following Beverly's return to Claire in the final section of the film, it is Elliot who declines and is found in a state of emotional collapse, apparently unable to function.

The father of the Jones twins, Amos, tries to exempt them both from First World War conscription on the grounds that 'his sons were not two persons, but one', and their mother, Mary, 'sensed that, one day, they would both slide back into the old, familiar patterns of dependence'.[77] This is exactly what happens when she dies and they regress back to an insular, child-like existence, dressing even more alike and sleeping in the same bed. The 'juvenilization' of the Mantle twins begins before their retreat to the flat, marching in step, dressed in identical clothes (the blazer over boxer shorts looking a little like an early teen school uniform). Cary's advice to Elliot to 'stay away' and 'cut yourself loose' from Beverly (which, literally, he does) sounds more like advice from a parent to steer clear of disruptive teen influences. Beverly's whining for ice cream and pop casts him as the baby brother, even though only minutes separate him from Elliot. The birthday cake is then broken roughly by hand, as Elliot's body will be.

Prior to *Dead Ringers*, Cronenberg had examined the potentially destructive relationship of brothers in *Scanners* (1980), the film that, according to Serge Grünberg, convinced Burroughs that Cronenberg was the man to realize *Naked Lunch* on screen.[78] In *Scanners*, the battle between brothers becomes a simplistic Good versus Evil dichotomy, which Cronenberg was at pains to avoid in *Dead Ringers*. In Leon Whiteson's novelization of *Scanners*, Vale's scan of Consec's computer in his attempt to destroy Dr Ruth's 'Ripe Programme' is described in terms of *Dead Ringer*'s conjoined nervous system: 'Cam, Kim and the computer were Siamese triplets welded together by a potent electronic bond'.[79] In effect, at the end of *Dead Ringers*, Beverly is a scanner, who has lost the only being that shares his special communicative power, his brother Elliot.

The Prologue
(displaced features from *Twins* and two further parallel texts)

In the opening scene of *Dead Ringers*, the Mantle twins consider why humans reproduce in the way they do and not like fish, ultimately concluding 'Because humans don't live underwater'. The remainder of the film is, to some extent, an exploration of what would happen if they did, via the *mise-en-scène* of oceanic blues that dominates all the scenes of the twins in their apartment, which they increasingly feel unable to leave. As precocious children, the brothers play with an anatomical doll and one of the twins muses that if humans reproduced like fish, then there would be 'a kind of sex...where you wouldn't have to touch each other'. The definition of scuba, that is carefully spelled out for us ('self-contained underwater breathing apparatus'), in effect, describes the use of the Mantle Retractor and Beverly's medical instruments that allow the Mantles to operate, medically and existentially, in an underwater environment, an other world of their own making, that casts female sexual difference as mutancy. At the 1983 Toronto Festival of Festivals, Cronenberg named *The Creature from the Black Lagoon* (Jack Arnold, 1954) as one of his favourite films. The Mantle boys constitute creatures that have not made the journey successfully from one medium to another. They ask a girl to have sex with them in the bath as if not totally happy on land, caught between the elements, just as they are hovering between the transitional states of child and adult. Later, Claire throws water in Beverly's face, perhaps suggesting that at a deeper level she recognizes his true element and in the film's final section Elliot is found lying, fully clothed, in a shower. Beverly dives for oxygen in the operating theatre, claiming that he needs to 'slow things down' as if yearning for a floating, aquatic state.

Twins opens with a citation from Hermann Melville's *Moby Dick* (1851) in which the narrator, Ishmael, states that whilst on board, during a particularly hazardous whale hunt, he was tied to Queequeg, a whaler whom he idolizes. The bond that connects them is described: 'usage and honour demanded that instead of cutting the cord, it should drag me down in his wake...Queequeg was my own inseparable twin brother'.[80] The text omitted here describes the cord as a 'Siamese ligature' and the umbilical-like 'cord' binds the pair together and would pull them both down to a *watery* grave.[81] In *Twins*, David is a champion swimmer and Michael describes him as 'like a goddamn fish', later saving his life in a swimming pool.[82] As adults, the twins repeat a boyhood fishing trip and the magical description of a lake suggests a close affinity with water.[83] Later, Michael buys a brass manta ray as a gift for cancer patient, Louise Perera, with whom he falls in love. The description of a distorted flat fish ('its metal tail twisted above its flat triangular body') and as 'a caricature with cross eyes that made the fish look bewildered' is converted by Cronenberg into the Mantle Retractor.[84] Like the Retractor, the ray seems slightly grotesque and out of kilter with what surrounds it and acts as a visual metaphor for the twins' aquatic origins and their natural element: 'the little brass ray didn't fit for some reason. It was shining and clean; a token from some other time'.[85]

Michael fully intends to take the ornament to Kathy and places it in his pocket but returns with it to his brother, where it is found on a bedside table.

William Burroughs uses a cinematic metaphor to describe the social factors that affect sexual development: '[w]hat is sexually exciting to someone is essentially...an old film, a film usually laid down in childhood on a reception screen'.[86] In *Dead Ringers*, we see what that film might be: an obsession with female genitalia, in itself not uncommon in growing boys but here development is arrested, the film remains paused as it were, because the obsession is purely medical, rather than social, linked closely to notions of doubling. The Mantle twins appear to learn not from their parents but from experimentation in mock operations and 'practicals' in propositioning girls. To adopt the terms used by the young girl in *Dead Ringers*, it could be questioned as to whether either of the protagonists 'really know what "fuck" is', and by following careers in gynaecology, they spend their lives trying to find out.

Another useful parallel text is Rose Tremain's novel *Restoration* (1989), set at the same time as the anatomical art expressed in the opening credits of *Dead Ringers*. The restoration of the title, apart from the political import, refers to the hero, Robert Merivel, and his attempt to deny the fascination that medicine, and more precisely the body, has for him, which he is forced to recognize through the course of the narrative (a little like Cronenberg's own film career and his developing views on embodiment). The opening is strikingly similar to Cronenberg's film with two very brief juxtaposed scenes, which are numbered, like shots in a storyboard:

'1. In 1636, when I was nine years old, I carried out my first anatomical dissection. My instruments were: a kitchen knife, two mustard spoons made of bone, four millinery pins and a measuring rod. The cadaver was a starling...I worked until, with the body of the starling opened and displayed before me, I had, I suddenly recognised, caught a glimpse of my own future'.

'2. At Caius College, Cambridge, in 1647, I met my poor friend, Pearce...We were both by then students of anatomy and...our rejection of Galenic theory, coupled with our desire to discover the precise function of each part of the body in relation to the whole, formed a bond between us'.[87]

In *Dead Ringers*, the opening narrative sequence includes a precocious play version of a dissection using improvised medical instruments with a model, followed by a jump to a dissection scene at a top medical school (set in 1967, very close chronologically to Cronenberg's own medical studies, which he ended in 1965). Tremain is not dealing with brothers but, like the Mantles, Pearce and Merivel form and maintain an almost fraternal bond until death, sealed through their study of anatomy, both reject orthodox methodology, are at the cutting edge (literally) of their field and are driven by an obsessive curiosity to open up the body, to make the insides *visible*. Like Cronenberg, Tremain dramatizes a process of disavowal, jealousy, envy and unrequited love between two men.

A key image in this process is an anonymous man who presents himself before the pair. Beneath a removable steel plate, the result of a surgery on damaged ribs, he claims to have a visible heart, which for a small fee, they may actually touch:

 'Carefully, he unbound the linen and revealed to us a large hole in his breast, about the size of a Pippin apple, in the depths of which, as I leaned forward to look more closely at it, I saw a pink and moist fleshy substance, moving all the time with a regular pulse.

 "See?" exclaimed Pearce..."See it retract and thrust out again? We are witnessing a living, breathing heart!"'[88]

It is not simply the viewing of bodily interiors, which fascinates and repels Merivel but the wish to touch them:

 'My hand entered the cavity. I opened my fingers and with the same care I had applied, as a boy, to the stealing of eggs from birds' nests, took hold of the heart'.[89]

The experience (particularly the fact that the man feels no pain) impresses upon Merivel a sense of mortality and an almost existential awareness of how human culture attributes to the heart features which the organ itself does not possess. Wittgenstein refers to the gesture of pointing at the heart as a mark of sincerity: '[d]oes one, perhaps, not *mean* this gesture? Of course one means it. Or is one conscious of using a *mere* figure? Indeed not – it is not a figure that we choose, not a simile, yet it is a figurative expression'.[90] In interview, Cronenberg, reprising Beverly's 'beauty contests for the insides' speech almost verbatim, explains how in an alternative aesthetic of the body, 'people would unzip themselves and show you the best spleen (and) the best heart'.[91] Both Tremain's protagonists and the Mantles spend their lives trying to see and thereby explain the workings of an area of the human body (the heart and the womb respectively), which is hidden from plain view, ascribed a metaphysical status unsupported by scientific knowledge, and without having to touch or be touched by it.

A further parallel text can be found in the work of Margaret Atwood, a fellow Canadian who graduated from Toronto University only a couple of years before Cronenberg. *The Handmaid's Tale* (1987) postulates a future fascist state, where all women are subject to rigid social and sexual rituals that class them in one of five categories. The most important (as in the Mantle clinic) is the potentially pregnant woman, the handmaid, due to widespread sterility, a scenario Cronenberg had already touched upon in *Crimes of the Future* (1970). The handmaids are forced to wear a uniform, which may have been the inspiration for Denise Cronenberg's costume designs for the operating scenes in *Dead Ringers*. Atwood describes the garment as 'like a surgeon's gown of the time before', apart from its most dominant feature: it is all red.[92]

A newly pregnant Handmaid Ofwarren is described by the first-person narrator (only identified in retrospect as Handmaid Offred) as 'a magic presence to us, an object of envy and desire, we covet her'.[93] The reason for the Mantle's wonder at Claire is her unusual uterus rather than pregnancy but its effect on them is similar to that described by Atwood. The connotations of the terms used by the Mantles to describe Claire's internal organs ('fabulously rare') are fairly pejorative. This particular phrase might normally refer to a steak or an unusual object (usually collectable), casting the woman as consumable object, judged on its sensual or economic attraction. If used in relation to a specimen, it has more ghoulish connotations, even evoking popular myths about Jack the Ripper, who may have had medical training and possibly collected trophies from his victims, including uteruses.

Atwood's novel traces the future consequences of the kind of interventionist medical patriarchy that the Mantle clinic represents in the 1980s. Atwood's handmaids face compulsory monthly visits to the gynaecologist to check their fertility status, and for Anne Balsamo, 'the regime of surveillance described in humiliating detail in the novel is less fiction than biography', so that the novel can be read as 'ethnography rather than as science fiction'.[94] The woman lies with her legs apart, naked but bisected at the neck by a suspended sheet so that the doctor 'deals with a torso only' and the sterile intrusiveness that Atwood describes might equally be used of Beverly's first examination of Claire: 'a cold finger, rubber-clad and jellied, slides into me, I am poked and prodded'.[95]

Offred recalls being made to watch a film of how the birth process used to be in the late twentieth century, which was 'made in an olden-days hospital: a pregnant woman, wired up to a machine, electrodes coming out of every which way so that she looked like a broken robot...some man with a searchlight looking up between her legs...a trayful of sterilised knives, everyone with masks on'.[96] The brusque manner in which the Mantles speak to the women who come to them, and the sense of an assembly line from waiting area to examination room, is reflected in Offred's description of her status: 'we are two-legged wombs, that's all'.[97]

Beverly's Instruments ('take a set of surgical instruments – innocent in an operating theatre, but in Myra Hindley's handbag?')[98]
Barbara Creed's lengthy historical analysis of the credit sequence of *Dead Ringers* identifies 'an array of instruments' from the sixteenth century 'then used in anatomical dissections: knives, scissors, clamps, saws, ropes'.[99] However, without this specific cultural knowledge, the status of the objects, as art, tool or instrument

of torture, is more ambiguous. Far from William Beard's confident assertion that 'everybody immediately recognises them as weapons', there are a range of responses to the instruments, both within the film itself and in critical reaction to it.[100] Some commentaries focus on the deliberately anachronistic design, for example, Karen Jaehne describes the tools as 'fascinatingly medieval', and Daniel Shaw describes the tools as 'positively prehistoric'.[101] Other commentators suggest a possible animal derivation: Stuart Klawans calls them 'parts of insects' bodies', whilst Stephanie Bunbury talks of 'handles like dinosaur bones', and Shaw describes them as 'resembling the claw of a winged dinosaur'.[102]

However, Creed's analysis omits a key feature. The camera zooms in *and past* the drawings and sculptures (anticipating the forward-moving, kinetically driven credits of *Crash*) as if swerving away from looking directly at them. Only the final image of both opening and closing credits uses a static shot, suggesting an attempted evasion and disavowal of the true nature of the brothers' relationship. The final drawing by Ambrose Paré shows Siamese twins, a boy and a girl joined at the back, both possessing male and female genitals, in an image that echoes Cronenberg's image of the New Flesh, ultimately cut from the final scene of *Videodrome*.[103] The credits 'are presented as if the viewer were touring an exhibition or a museum: the sketch moves into the frame, the camera glances at them and then slides away'.[104] Evoking the use of steadicam in gallery sequences in the opening of Nic Roeg's *Bad Timing* (1980) and the romantic pursuit in Brian de Palma's *Dressed to Kill* (1980), Cronenberg is implicitly linking the instruments we see to *works of art*. Beverly meets Claire by chance in a gallery, the Mantle apartment is filled with stylish Italian furniture and Beverly visits Wollek's studio twice, firstly to commission the production of his instruments and later to take back what he regards as his artwork.

The status of the instruments raises the question of what constitutes a work of art. When Beverly first brings the designs for the instruments to the gallery, he clarifies that 'No, they're not Art. I'm a doctor. I need them for my work'. However, it takes an artist to make them and the instruments appear on display in Wollek's gallery, where they are shown as the work of an artist, and therefore do constitute Art. They are also marked by a red dot on the case as having been sold, i.e. they are now being consumed as a commercial commodity. In this sense, the tools are an accurate metaphor for Cronenberg's own work as a director (with himself as Wollek, the creative artist), taking a prototype through from design to production and ultimately sale to the public. Like Wollek's work, this involves industrial processes (particularly the split-screen technology here) but ultimately produces something that can be regarded as Art.

Cronenberg has used artworks as metaphors for plot, character development and theme prior to *Dead Ringers*. Ben Pierce's sculptures in *Scanners* (constructed by Montreal artist Tom Coulter) are described by Cronenberg as 'the physical equivalent of my movies'.[105] In Arno Crostic's gallery, there is a montage of Pierce's work, including papier maché doctors dressed as if for an operating theatre with distorted and demonic expressions and what appears to be a baby trying to break away from their clutches. It is only with the information in Revok's final speeches that we can see these figures as representative of the medical patriarchy responsible for the administering of ephemerol to unsuspecting mothers in the 1950s. Pierce confides to the hero, Cameron Vale, whilst sitting inside a giant head in his studio, described in the novelization as a self-portrait.[106] Pierce tried to kill his whole family at the age of 10 (the age of the Mantle boys in the first scene) and has been released from prison to pursue 'rehabilitation through art', subsequently claiming himself that it is 'art that keeps me sane', a process repeated (albeit unsuccessfully) in Beverly's designs. Outside on the darkened street, looking at the lighted casement containing his instruments, Beverly has to break into the womb-like space of the gallery to steal his creation. It seems that he is placed in situations where he can either see but cannot touch (as here) or touch but cannot see (as in the initial examination of Claire).

Creed's assertion that the illustrations are 'of both a mythical and realistic kind' is a little misleading as the scientific distinction between these two states is far clearer now than it would have been in the sixteenth century.[107] Without Creed's historical knowledge, the objects may well appear as potential, or actual, instruments of torture: Linda Badley talks of them as looking like 'medieval torture devices' and Thomas Doherty describes the drawings as 'portraits of medieval-looking stainless steel torture tools'.[108] Elaine Scarry, in tracing the cultural history of torture, observes that 'the first degree of torture was the sight of the instruments', and cites testimony from victims who were 'made to stare at the weapon with which they were about to be hurt'.[109] This is facilitated here by the film's credit sequence.

In *Restoration*, as Merivel drifts from his vocation in medicine, the King sends him a special gift: a set of silver-plated surgical tools set out on a velvet cushion. Merivel 'took them up, one by one, the hook, the probe, the cannula, the perforator, the hammer, the osteoclast, the dipyrene, the spathomele and, last of all, the scalpel. I turned each one round in my hands and looked at it'.[110] There is no letter with the instruments: '*they themselves were the message*'.[111] At key dramatic moments in *Restoration* and *Dead Ringers*, language, whether written (as here) or spoken (Beverly in the phone booth at the end), is redundant. Similarly, after Beverly steals the tools from Wollek's gallery and returns to Claire, she finds one of the instruments and in the shot where she holds it up, Cronenberg keeps her in darkness and slightly out of focus so that the claw-like device emerges in clear light and in sharp focus from the bottom of the screen.[112] As in *Restoration*, there is no comment on the instruments. The unfamiliarity of the archaic terms used by Tremain is paralleled in *Dead Ringers* by the bewildered reaction to the tools from all characters who come into contact with them, other than the Mantles. When

Beverly suddenly whips back a sheet to reveal them in an operating theatre, the experienced nurse assisting with the operation does not recognize them and 'can only place them in an arbitrary numerical order, like the letters in an alphabet', in Cronenberg's version of a language-game.[113]

The Mantle Retractor
The instrument that the young Mantle boys use on the anatomical doll in the Prologue is referred to as a 'Reticulator'. According to a reference work contemporary with the film, the 1988 Oxford English Dictionary, the word 'reticulator' does not exist. What do exist, however, are a range of related terms: reticulated: 'divided into a network or into small squares with intersecting lines'; reticule: 'a woman's bag of woven or other material, carried to serve the purpose of a pocket'; reticulum: 'a ruminant's second stomach, a net-like structure'; and reticle: 'a network of fine threads or lines in the focal plane of an optical instrument to help accurate observation'.[114] Cronenberg's blended term thus has connotations of an instrument, which can be used to judge depth and a means by which men could attempt to appropriate a womb-like pouch, reminiscent of Samantha Eggar's external growths in *The Brood* (1979).

Maggie Humm traces Cronenberg's interest in the Retractor to work abandoned from *Total Recall* ('the penis-like earthworms – "Sandsubs" – and mutations – "Ganzibulls"' and also claims that 'an exhibition of ancient torture instruments stimulated his interest (Florence 1991)'.[115] However, the original idea pre-dates this by many years. Whilst living in Tourettes-sur-Loup in southern France in the late 1960s, Cronenberg produced a sculpture, which he called *Surgical Instrument for Operating on Mutants* made from aluminium.[116] He claims, rather implausibly, to have completely forgotten about this episode and only remembered it upon unearthing an old notebook detailing his previous ideas as a 17-year-old in France.[117] The Retractor holds a talismanic power in the film, to the extent where, along with the instruments, it has been viewed as 'a kind of metaphor for the way the twins probe and manipulate the world'.[118] The name 'Retractor' suggests taking something back or recanting an ideological position and the brothers do certainly 'retract' and 'draw back' to their origins with Beverly later cradling the Retractor as a doll or comfort toy. The medical function of the Retractor seems to be to hold the female body in position during surgery, i.e. to allow visibility of internal female organs of the lower abdomen, a function shared with hardcore pornography.

Late in the film, Beverly is examining Mrs Bookman (whose name suggests bodily inscription and that she is viewed almost as a textbook example from a male point of view) and she winces after he has used the Retractor on her. He dismisses this ('we have the technology, it couldn't possibly hurt') and she apologizes for appearing to question his authority. Florence Jacobwitz and Richard Lippe take exception to the exchange in which Beverly quizzes the woman about what she had intercourse with, and recounts the story of a previous patient who had sex with a

Labrador retriever. However what they dub as 'Cronenberg's frat-house sensibility', misses the point.[119] Malcolm Jones, in describing Dostoevsky's 'The Double', states that 'the reader is drawn irresistibly along by the process of the hero's slide into insanity and fascinated by the accompanying slippage between perception and reality, signifier and signified, sign and referent'.[120]

Beverly talks about he and Elly sharing everything, to which Claire points out sharply that 'I'm not a *thing*'. By the close, Beverly seems increasingly unable to distinguish between inanimate objects and living people, especially women, as seen in his examination of Mrs Bookman. In the opening sequence, a girl rebuffs the boys' sexual curiosity and so they experiment at home on a doll. In the second part of the opening sequence, where the twins are using the Retractor, their supervisor tells them that it may work on cadavers but not on living patients. The Mantles cannot tell the difference between the laboratory and the world beyond it, the living and the dead.

Dreams
(neglected scenes, the fantastic, parallel plot lines/themes)
Dead Ringers originally had two *substantial* dream sequences, the second one with Beverly visualizing 'an aged version of his other brother growing out of his abdomen', which, according to Lucas, was 'very similar to a scene that previously appeared in Cronenberg's unfilmed screenplay for *Total Recall*'.[121] Although Cronenberg asserts 'I felt they were crucial to the movie', he eventually cut the second one, a decision that Rodley suggests 'seems to have been based largely on audience squeamishness'.[122] Make-up artist Gordon Smith describes the prosthetics of the second dream sequence as 'a parasite twin about one quarter of Irons' actual size growing out of his lower abdomen, a bladder puppet that pulsated'.[123] Apparently 'the puppet character had about 10 lines in the scene' and with its planned aggressive ripping from Beverly's abdomen, it would have presented something like John Hurt's first encounter with the eponymous creature in *Alien* (Ridley Scott, 1979).[124] In the sequel, *Aliens* (James Cameron, 1986), what primarily persuades Ripley to go to the colonized planet is the recurrent dream of a xenomorph moving and stretching her stomach flesh upwards as it is about to burst outwards, and Beverly also acts (begins to take drugs) to stop him repeating his dream. In Nabokov's *Despair* (1932), reflecting the sense of inversion and forced separation in this second dream sequence, Hermann dislikes those 'monsters of mirrors', which distort that which they reflect and a man's insides are 'pulled out like dough and then torn in two'.[125]

A key feature that seems to have largely been missed by critics is that, as stated explicitly in the dialogue, whereas Chang and Eng were joined '*at the chest*', in Beverly's dream we see the Mantle twins joined *at the stomach*. Both Rodley and, more significantly, the man who designed it, Smith, describe the second dream creature as originating from Beverly's *abdomen*, not his chest. The final operation is a displacement then onto that part of the body that the rest of the film associates with female fertility, i.e. the womb, articulating the anxiety associated with a myth of male bonding. Beverly calls Elliot 'Chang' during the operation, which he ironically conducts wearing gloves, suggesting the ritual significance of the process is more important than any rational, medical purpose.

In an echo of Wordsworth and Coleridge's 1798 *Lyrical Ballads*, Cronenberg claims that the aim of *The Fly* was 'to make the fantastic seem absolutely real', whereas in *Dead Ringers* it was 'to make reality seem fantastic'.[126] Tim Lucas claimed *Dead Ringers* will open 'a completely new wing in the fantastic film genre' and that Cronenberg's 'traditionally realistic interpretation of the fantastic is inverted, forging a kind of magic realism'.[127] The dream sequences play a significant part in this process. According to the theories of Todorov, the fantastic requires a state of hesitation, between ascribing a supernatural or rational explanation for an event.[128] However, in the final chapter of his study, Todorov begins to sketch out a more modern version of the fantastic, exemplified by Kafka's 'Metamorphosis' (1916), which begins with a supernatural event as a given and is written within a cultural framework that does not have access to religious belief and therefore lacks a 'hesitation' phase. Todorov suggests that 'psychoanalysis has replaced...the literature of the fantastic' and in *Dead Ringers* Claire certainly tries to understand the Mantle brothers in terms of psychoanalysis, suggesting that Beverly is 'subtly schizophrenic'.[129] However, this seems unsatisfactory, not just to Beverly, who screams 'what is this bullshit psychoanalysis?' but also to Cronenberg, who does not find that psychoanalysis sweeps away the fantastic, rather it evolves into a further hybrid, which we might term 'the literary fantastic'.

In *Dead Ringers*, the whole notion of hesitation linked to a belief in a supernatural state depends on the inter-related factors of whether viewers find the spectacle of identical twins beyond their everyday experience and/or whether the notion of Jeremy Irons playing two parts simultaneously on screen breaches their 'suspension of disbelief'. Within the fiction, the brothers represent a technological version of the supernatural, achieving the impossible in making apparently infertile women conceive (although this is inferred rather than actually seen with Claire, Mrs Bookman and an anonymous client all representing failures on the Mantles' part). Moreover, they magically appear in two places at once through their professional and sexual games of substitution, although we are shown how such tricks work from the outset. At the beginning of 'Metamorphosis', there is a very fleeting notion of hesitation as Gregor Samsa wakes and tries to rationalize what has happened to him. However, as Todorov notes, this is almost immediately 'drowned out in the general movement of the narrative'.[130] In *Dead Ringers*, after the prologue, the audience is almost instantly engaged in trying to distinguish between the twins, rather than admire at a distance the effects of motion-control photography. Like Todorov's modern fantastic, the narrative of the film follows its own nightmarish logic and could be said to 'naturalize' a supernatural event, if this latter category can include the phenomenon of identical twins and special effects technology.

Todorov concludes that 'the difference between the fantastic tale in its classic version and Kafka's narratives (is) *what in the first world was an exception here becomes the rule*'.[131] Part of the complexity of *Dead Ringers* lies in that it follows Todorov's modified fantastic in some ways but also includes the characteristic moments of hesitation that Todorov describes in the main body of his study. The three conditions that Todorov specifies for the fantastic to exist do occur in *Dead Ringers*, although not in a static and unproblematic mode. Firstly, the characters, though odd, are a recognizable part of human society. Secondly, the sense of hesitation is experienced by a character within the fiction (Claire, prior to the restaurant scene, and more importantly through Beverly's dreams). Thirdly, the viewer may reject allegorical or 'poetic' interpretations initially but as the twins' behaviour becomes more difficult to explain, it becomes increasingly difficult to resist ascribing metaphorical significance to actions, such as the final evisceration.

Important in this process is a dream sequence, which is often missed. We are prepared for the main dream sequence by an earlier brief scene where we see Beverly wake, apparently from a nightmare. This means that the second time the same actions appear, shot in the same strong blue light, we expect the sequence to be 'real'. This is especially so as we first see Beverly and Claire in bed and only then cut to Elly. It is not immediately clear that this is a fantastical nightmare. Although it would contradict the character motivation of Beverly, the idea that the brothers would share Claire is not so outlandish as to be easily dismissed. It is only in the three-shot, where we see the fleshy bond that links the brothers, that we know that this is definitively a dream and that the hesitation that Todorov describes begins to dissipate.

Conclusion ('The Autoptic Vision')[132]
Towards the end of de Sade's *Juliette* (1797), Noirceuil addresses one of his victims whilst sodomizing her, suggesting, 'that it would be enough to cut the dividing membrane, to completely nullify the action against which you protest'.[133] He is referring here to cutting away whatever flesh divides vagina from anus, thereby making his act legal. This is the solipsistic logic of the Mantles. When Beverly complains that the women look 'normal' from the outside but on the inside they are 'all wrong', he too is articulating the notion of a fragile border between legal/criminal, male/female and places the male in the position of suggesting corrective surgery for a perceived imperfection in the female body.

Dead Ringers ends with a dissection of a kind, not an operation to separate literally (only by killing in effect) but a medical procedure to remove internal organs to see how they function. In *Lolita*, Humbert admits that 'my only grudge against nature was that I could not turn my Lolita inside out and apply voracious lips to her young matrix, her unknown heart, her nacreous liver, the sea-grapes of her lungs, her comely twin kidneys,' and as Elliot says, 'I've often thought there should be beauty contests for the insides of bodies.'[134] The closing scene could be said to constitute such a contest.

The final operation, like the first one we see, appears to be 'inter-ovular surgery'. Elliot asks Beverly why he is crying, to which he replies, 'Separation can be a terrifying thing'. We see the main cutting tool approach Elliot's stomach but not the actual incision. Beverly wakes in an identical posture to Elly but in another gynaecological examining chair. He murmurs that 'I had a terrible dream', in an attempt to cast the operation into the realm of the fantastic, a fantasy he perpetuates by avoiding direct eye contact with Elly's corpse lying prostrate in the chair in the background of the shot. Beverly's increasingly forlorn calling of Elly's name underlines the delusion of its apparent function. He knows his brother lies dead behind him so this is less a calling to him than an elegy for him. Cronenberg's camera placement almost acts as an accomplice in this delusion by not cutting in on the axis to give the viewer a clearer view of Elly but keeps him in the background as Beverly shuffles off camera-right.

Beverly removes clothes from a line, apparently imposing order on the situation but the direction of the slow tracking shot is unconventional, from right to left, suggesting that this semblance of domestic order is masking a deeper unease. The social ritual of dressing for work is followed meticulously as Beverly shaves in front of a mirror and apparently ready to begin a new life, he emerges from the flat, appearing smarter and *much more like his suave brother than he has been at any other point in the film.* Just as Elliot has shifted towards the role of his brother, trying to get himself in synch with Beverly's drug habit, retreating into their flat and finally submitting himself to the position of passive female to be operated upon, so Beverly has moved towards a male dynamic (according to the dialectic of the film), more associated with a public, active position (he is moving out into an exterior environment we have scarcely seen, particularly in connection with him, outside the amniotic blue of the clinic and the flat). However, despite the appearance of normality, and the bag that Beverly carries, which would suggest that he plans a new life with Claire, he cannot answer the voice at the other end of the phone. Put simply, he cannot answer the question she asks: 'Who is this?' All through the narrative, his character has been defined by its opposition to Elly. Through repeated social and sexual substitution, and disavowal of his feelings for Claire, he has forfeited his sense of himself as an individual entity. Perhaps Beverly cannot answer Claire as he no longer sees himself as Beverly but as Eng, the younger of the Siamese twins and the phone booth acts as an umbilical link with Claire, which he severs.

In *Birth of the Clinic* (1973), Foucault traces how for doctors at the beginning of the nineteenth century, the new 'sovereign power of the empirical gaze' in the developing practice of anatomy involves a process of visual revelation, making the invisible, visible,' so that 'a new alliance was forged between words and things, enabling one *to see* and *to say*'.[135] Unfortunately, the Mantle twins can only fulfil the first half of Foucault's equation. In de Sade's *Juliette* (1797), towards the end of the narrative, Juliette asserts that 'Philosophy must say everything', the meaning of which depends on whether 'say' or 'everything' is stressed.[136] *Dead Ringers* focuses on the importance of the former. Experience is only validated by speech. As Elliot tells Beverly, 'You haven't fucked Claire Niveau until you tell me about it', casting their reality as a shared delusion created by verbal descriptions of sex acts in 'yummy detail'. The brief glimpse that we see of Elliot's speech to a packed lecture hall seems strategically placed in the film, between Beverly's nightmare and his scene with the twin prostitutes. His text talks of the 'demand for a philosophy that mixes compassionate curiosity with social responsibility' but it is a blend that the brothers never really achieve, apparently unable to communicate with people outside the clinic.

If the Mantle brothers are seen as a husband and wife team then their relationship has some similarities to that of Shakespeare's Macbeth and Lady Macbeth. The award scene, where Elliot tries to project the public face of the clinic, appearing calm and in control, has strong overtones of the banquet scene (act III, scene iv). Unlike Banquo, Beverly has not been murdered, but does steal into the gathering, apparently unnoticed by Elliot, and only makes his presence felt when Elliot makes a toast to him and wishes that he were there. Like Lady Macbeth, Elliot smoothes over the potential threat to their public image, making excuses for irrational behaviour and disclosures which are damaging (Beverly's crude descriptions about their division of labour) and, like Shakespeare's couple, it is the Mantles' *inability to talk* about matters that used to be freely discussed that drives a wedge between them. Karl Miller notes that in much literature of the double 'there is an urge to confess to the other', but by Beverly honouring Claire's entreaty to 'don't tell *anyone*' about her, he creates a tragic division from his brother.[137]

Discussing literary manifestations of the double, Miller describes how 'this is a literature which does the impossible', such as characters being in two places at once.[138] Cronenberg is also interested in notions of impossibility but not restricted simply to proxemics. The Mantle twins are reminiscent of Brundlefly's flawed attempt at purifying his essence by trying to fuse with a pregnant Veronica in *The Fly*, which can only lead to an eternal regression, exemplifying the dilemma articulated by John Barth in *Petition*: '[t]o be one: Paradise! But to be both and neither is unspeakable'.[139] In discussing what she terms 'the paranoid Gothic', as exemplified by texts like *Dr. Jekyll and Mr. Hyde*, Showalter feels that 'such texts involved doubled male figures...and the central image of the unspeakable secret'.[140] In terms of *Dead Ringers*, this 'unspeakable secret' might be the brothers sleeping together; that they are actually different; that because no one can see their individuality, they may as well be the same; or that what binds them together is literally unspeakable (that they have a common nervous system, which allows them to communicate without necessarily verbalizing their thoughts, hence Beverly's silence to Claire at the end). Scarry discusses the difficulty, if not near impossibility, in expressing physical pain, which annihilates everything else as 'physical pain does not simply resist language but actively destroys it'.[141] Wittgenstein asserts that 'what we cannot speak about we must consign to silence', and it is this inability to express verbally the pain of existence, which lends the end of *Dead Ringers* its often-noted elegiac quality.[142]

The sight granted to the Mantle twins in the evisceration scene can only be gained at the cost of death. They both want to be conscious so they can *see*. To perform an autopsy on a living body represents an attempt to record the unrecordable, the precise moment of death. In seeking a vision of such bodily interiors, they are seeking a vision and a consciousness of death that is impossible. Effectively, they are aspiring to emulate Edgar Allen Poe's Monsieur Valdemar, who is frozen in a mesmeric state right at the point of death and on being awoken, is able, before crumbling into putrefaction, to utter the nonsensical phrase 'I am dead'.[143]

The detritus of the Mantles' flat with Beverly shuffling through discarded household and medical waste, echoes the chaos of furniture behind the boys in the opening scenes.[144] However, unlike the montage of ordinary living space at the end of *Halloween* (John Carpenter, 1978), the horror is not of the social and domestic but of the existential and human. Beverly has lifted Elly down from the chair and lies across his lap, the light from the Venetian blinds falling on his open eye. Some Renaissance anatomical art shows the subject as complicit in the process and in an emotional relationship with the figure performing the procedure. Jonathan Sawday describes how 'the lover who seeks anatomization is demanding from the beloved anatomist access to a form of sexual self-surrender, which, whilst it hints at transgressive fulfilment, also endlessly defers the moment of dissolution.'[145] At the end of another Carpenter film, *The Thing* (1982), Carpenter's hero, Mac, surrounded by a burning Antarctic research station and the cold closing in, without any sense of hope, says to Childs, the only other surviving character, 'Why don't we just...wait here for a little while...See what happens'. The denouement of *Dead Ringers* also suggests that this is what characterizes human existence: deferral and a waiting for death.

Notes
1. R. D. Laing, *The Divided Self* (Harmondsworth: Penguin Books, 1965), p. 38n.
2. Chris Rodley, *Cronenberg on Cronenberg* (London: Faber and Faber, 1992), p. 139.
3. Thomas Doherty, 'David Cronenberg's *Dead Ringers*', *Cinefantastique* 19:3 (March 1989), p. 39.
4. Owen Gleiberman, 'Cronenberg's Double Meanings', *American Film* 14:1 (October 1988), p. 42.
5. Cronenberg cited in Rodley, op. cit., p. 138.
6. J. G. Ballard, *A User's Guide to the Millennium* (London: Harper Collins Publishers, 1996), p. 278.

7. Cronenberg cited in Peter Bloch-Hansen, 'Double Trouble', *Fangoria* 78 (October 1988), p. 55.
8. Ibid.
9. Tim Lucas, 'Videodrome', *Cinefantastique* 12:5/6 (July-August 1982), p. 7.
10. Rodley, op. cit., p. 136.
11. Ibid.
12. Bari Wood, and Jack Geasland, *Dead Ringers* (London: Sphere Books, 1988), [re-release of the original novel *Twins*, on which the film was based. First published in the U.S. in 1978 by Signet Books], p. 60.
13. Ibid., p. 64.
14. Ibid., p. 8, 11.
15. Rodley, op. cit., p. 146.
16. Linda Badley, *Film, Horror, and the Body Fantastic* (New York: Greenwood Press, 1995), p. 134.
17. See Eve Sedgwick, *Between Men: English Literature and Male Homosocial Desire* (New York; Guildford: Columbia University Press, 1985), pp. 21–27.
18. Wood and Geasland, op. cit., pp. 30-31.
19. Ibid., p. 154.
20. Florence Jacobwitz and Richard Lippe, '*Dead Ringers*: The Joke's On Us', *CineAction!* (spring 1989), p. 66.
21. Wood and Geasland, op. cit., p. 37.
22. Elaine Showalter, *Sexual Anarchy: Gender and Culture at the Fin de Siécle* (London: Virago, 1992), p. 140.
23. Cronenberg cited in Karen Jaehne, 'A Visit to the Doctor', *Film Comment* 24 (September-October, 1988), p. 27.
24. Cronenberg cited in Michel Ciment, 'Entretien avec David Cronenberg', *Positif* 337 (1989), p. 33.
25. Rodley, op. cit., p. 163.
26. Wood and Geasland, op. cit., p. 84.
27. Ibid., p. 117.
28. Ibid., p. 346.
29. Ibid., p. 58 and p. 59.
30. Ibid., p. 35 and pp. 301-302.
31. Ibid., p. 262.
32. Ibid., p. 296.
33. Otto Rank, *The Double: A Psychoanalytical Study*, translated, edited and with an introduction by Harry Tucker Jr (New York: Meridian Books, 1971), p. 73.
34. Ibid., p. 75.
35. Malcolm Jones, *Dostoevsky After Bakhtin: Readings in Dostoevsky's Fantastic Realism* (Cambridge; New York: Cambridge University Press, 1990), p. 37.
36. Ibid., p. 39.
37. Ibid., p. 50.
38. Ibid., p. 42.
39. Ibid., p. 55.
40. François Ramasse, 'La chair dans l'âme', *Cahiers du Cinéma* 416 (January-February 1989), p. 29.
41. Cronenberg cited in Bloch-Hansen, op. cit., p. 54.
42. Ibid
43. Cronenberg cited in Rodley, op. cit., p. 144.

44. William Beard strangely asserts that there are 'no special effects' in *Dead Ringers*. See *The Artist as Monster: The Films of David Cronenberg* (Toronto: The University of Toronto Press, 2001), p. 234.

45. Vladimir Nabokov, *Despair* (Harmondsworth: Penguin, 1971), p. 170 and see Wood and Geasland, op. cit., p. 14.

46. Vladimir Nabokov cited in Alfred Appel Jr, *The Annotated Lolita* (New York: McGraw-Hill, 1970), p. 118.

47. L. L. Lee, *Vladimir Nabokov* (Boston: Twayne's United States Authors Series, 226, 1976), p. 147.

48. Ludwig Wittgenstein, *Philosophical Investigations*, trans. G.E.M. Anscombe (Oxford: Blackwell, 1963), thesis 67, p. 32.

49. See Alfred Appel Jr, op. cit., p. *lxiv*.

50. Vladimir Nabokov, *Lolita* (London: Corgi Books, 1961), p. 315.

51. Stephen Jan Parker, *Understanding Vladimir Nabokov* (Columbia: University of South Carolina Press, 1987), p. 44.

52. Ibid., p. 46.

53. Alfred Appel Jr, *Nabokov's Dark Cinema* (New York: Oxford University Press, 1974), p. 85.

54. Vladimir Nabokov, *Nabokov's Dozen* (London: Doubleday, 1958), p. 122.

55. Cronenberg cited in David Breskin, *Inner Views: Filmmakers in Conversation* (London: Faber & Faber, 1992), p. 207.

56. Karl Miller, *Doubles: Studies in Literary History* (Oxford: Oxford University Press, 1987), p. 21.

57. Steven Shaviro, 'Bodies of Fear: David Cronenberg', in *The Cinematic Body* (Minneapolis; London: University of Minnesota Press, 1993), p. 151.

58. Wood and Geasland, op. cit., p. 62.

59. Lucy Maddox, *Nabokov's Novels in English* (Athens, Georgia: University of Georgia Press, 1983), p. 110.

60. Angela Carter, *Wise Children* (London: Virago, 1992), p. 60.

61. Ibid., p. 30.

62. Ludwig Wittgenstein, op. cit., p. 194 and p. 196.

63. Wood and Geasland, op. cit., p. 23.

64. See Mary Douglas, *Purity and Danger* (London: Routledge and Kegan Paul, 1966). Douglas describes how 'in some West African tribes, the rule that twins should be killed at birth eliminates a social anomaly', (p. 39) or that the birth of twins would lead to sexual abstinence for a whole community (p. 152), or that such a birth signifies an ability 'to break through the normal human limitations', (p. 168), i.e. of conventional single births.

65. Wood and Geasland, op. cit., p. 40.

66. Bruce Chatwin, *On The Black Hill* (London: Picador, 1983), p. 192.

67. Ibid., p. 11.

68. Wittgenstein, op. cit., theses 246–252, pp. 89-90 and theses 253–255, p. 91.

69. Chatwin, op. cit., p. 42.

70. Ibid., p. 43.

71. Wittgenstein, op. cit., thesis 253, p. 91.

72. Ibid., thesis 282, p. 97.

73. Chatwin, op. cit., p. 45.

74. Ibid., p. 99.

75. Ibid., p. 98.

76. Ibid., p. 88.

77. Ibid., p.105 and p. 88.

78. Serge Grünberg, 'Sur les terres de Cronenberg', *Cahiers du Cinéma* 446 (July-August, 1991), p. 38.
79. Leon Whiteson, *Scanners: a novelisation based on the original screenplay by David Cronenberg* (New York: Tower Books, 1991), p. 135.
80. Herman Melville, *Moby Dick* (New York: Airmont Publishing Company, 1964; originally published in 1851), p. 264.
81. Ibid.
82. Wood and Geasland, op. cit., p. 33 and p. 223.
83. Ibid., pp. 142-143.
84. Ibid., p. 212 and p. 11.
85. Ibid., p. 12.
86. William Burroughs cited in Eric Mottram, *William Burroughs: The Algebra of Need* (London: Marion Boyars, 1977), p. 200.
87. Rose Tremain, *Restoration* (London: Sceptre, 5th Edition, 1991), p. 15.
88. Ibid., pp. 15-16.
89. Ibid., p. 18.
90. Ludwig Wittgenstein, op. cit., p. 178. See also p. 154.
91. David Cronenberg cited in Anne Billson, 'Cronenberg on Cronenberg: a career in stereo', *Monthly Film Bulletin* 56:660 (January 1989), p. 5.
92. Margaret Atwood, *The Handmaid's Tale* (London: Virago, 1987), p. 19.
93. Ibid., p. 35.
94. Anne Balsamo, *Technologies of the Gendered Body: Reading Cyborg Women* (Durham; London: Duke University Press, 1996), p. 86.
95. Atwood, op. cit., p. 70.
96. Ibid., p. 124.
97. Ibid., p. 146.
98. J. G. Ballard, *The Kindness of Women* (London: Grafton, 1992), p. 241.
99. Barbara Creed, 'Phallic Panic: Male Hysteria and *Dead Ringers*', *Screen.* 32:2 (summer 1990), p. 127.
100. William Beard, op. cit., p. 255.
101. Karen Jaehne, 'Double Trouble', *Film Comment* 24:5 (Sept.-Oct. 1988), p. 21 and Daniel Shaw, 'Horror and the Problem of Personal Identity: *Dead Ringers*', *Film and Philosophy* 3 (1996), p. 18.
102. See Stuart Klawans, cited in Showalter, op. cit., p. 140; Stephanie Bunbury, 'David Cronenberg Doubles Up', *Cinema Papers* 71(Jan. 1989), p. 24 and Shaw, op. cit., p. 18.
103. See Creed, op. cit., p. 128.
104. Leonard G. Heldreth, 'Festering in Thebes: Elements of Tragedy and Myth in Cronenberg's Films' in Robert Haas, (ed.) Special issue: David Cronenberg, *Post Script* 15:2 (winter-spring 1996), p. 54.
105. Paul M. Sammon, 'David Cronenberg', *Cinefantastique* 10:4 (spring, 1981), p. 32.
106. Whiteson, op. cit., p. 58.
107. Creed, op. cit., p. 127.
108. Badley, op. cit., p. 132 and Doherty, op. cit., p. 38.
109. Elaine Scarry, *The Body in Pain: The Making and Unmaking of the World* (New York; Oxford: Oxford University Press, 1985), p. 40 and p. 27.
110. Rose Tremain, op. cit., p. 127.
111. Ibid.
112. See Rodley, op. cit., p. 142.
113. Mary Russo, *The Female Grotesque: Risk, Excess and Modernity* (New York; London: Routledge, 1994), p. 115.

114. Joyce M. Hawkins (ed.), *Oxford Paperback Dictionary* (Oxford: Oxford University Press, 1988), p. 691.
115. Maggie Humm, 'Cronenberg's Films and Feminist Theories of Mothering', in *Feminism and Film* (Edinburgh: Edinburgh University Press, 1997), p. 86.
116. See Rodley, op. cit., p. 34.
117. Cronenberg cited in 'Entretien avec David Cronenberg', by Iannis Katsahnias, Charles Tesson, and Vincent Ostria, *Cahiers du Cinéma* 416 (January-February 1989), p. 64.
118. Terrence Rafferty, 'Secret Sharers', *New Yorker* 64 (3 October, 1988), p. 92.
119. Florence Jacobwitz and Richard Lippe, op. cit., p. 68.
120. Malcolm Jones, op. cit., p. 54.
121. Rodley, op. cit. p. 149 and Tim Lucas, 'Cronenberg and the Flesh', *Video Watchdog* 36 (1996), p. 45.
122. See Rodley, op. cit., p. 150.
123. Gordon Smith cited in Gary Kimber, 'Dead Ringers', *Cinefantastique* 19: 1-2 (January, 1989), p. 87.
124. Gordon Smith cited in Bloch-Hansen, op. cit., p. 53.
125. Vladimir Nabokov, *Despair* (Harmondsworth: Penguin, 1971), p. 27.
126. Cronenberg cited in Linda Badley, op. cit.,p. 131.
127. Tim Lucas, 'David Cronenberg's *Dead Ringers*: Part One', *Fangoria* 79 (December 1988), pp. 26-27 and 'Ideadrome: David Cronenberg from *Shivers* to *Dead Ringers*', *Video Watchdog* 36 (1996), p. 38.
128. See Tzvetan Todorov, *The Fantastic: A Structural Approach to a Literary Genre*, trans. Richard Howard (Ithaca, New York: Cornell University Press, 1975).
129. Ibid., p. 160.
130. Ibid., p. 169.
131. Ibid., p. 174.
132. Jonathan Sawday, *The Body Emblazoned: Dissection and the human body in Renaissance culture* (London and New York: Routledge, 1995), p. 1.
133. Marquis de Sade, *Juliette*, trans. Austryn Wainhouse (New York: Grove Press, 1968; originally published in 1797), p. 560.
134. Vladimir Nabokov, *Lolita* (London: Corgi Books, 1961), pp. 173-174.
135. Michel Foucault, *The Birth of the Clinic: An Archaeology of Medical Perception*, trans. Alan Sheridan (New York; London: Routledge, 1973), Preface, p. *xii*.
136. Marquis de Sade, op. cit., p. 586.
137. Miller, op. cit., p. 26.
138. Miller, op. cit., p. 25.
139. John Barth cited in Shelley Kay, 'Double or Nothing', *Cinema Papers* 74 (July 1989), p. 35.
140. Showalter, op. cit., p. 222n.
141. Scarry, op. cit., p. 4.
142. Wittgenstein, op. cit., thesis 7, p. 31.
143. Edgar Allen Poe, 'The Facts in the Case of M. Valdemar' in *Selected Tales* (Oxford: Oxford University Press, 1967), p. 354.
144. See Rodley, op. cit., p. 104.
145. Sawday, op. cit., p. 84.

CHAPTER THREE

NAKED LUNCH:
'NOTHING IS TRUE: EVERYTHING IS PERMITTED'[1]

In an article on Cronenberg's male protagonists, Michael O'Pray raises, but leaves unanswered, a crucial concern for understanding Cronenberg's work: '[a]s a young aspiring writer in the 60s, David Cronenberg fell under the spell of two charismatic literary figures: Nabokov and Burroughs'. He goes on to note that 'a case could be made for interpreting Cronenberg's entire film output since then...in terms of these two fatally charming writers'.[2] O'Pray however does not seem to want to be the one to make that case. Cronenberg, growing up as an adolescent in the late 1950s and early 1960s, around the time that *Naked Lunch* (1959) and *Lolita* (1961) first appeared in Canada, has stated that 'as for specific influences I often point to Vladimir Nabokov and William Burroughs' and Peter Morris records that 'almost everything Burroughs wrote, Cronenberg seems to have read assiduously'.[3] Morris claims that 'Burroughs seems to have been the most lasting influence', but fails to say *how*.[4] Nabokov and Burroughs initially inspired Cronenberg to be a writer, but it was a sense that he could not escape their influence, which led to a rejection of that particular ambition.[5] However, although he changed mediums from the page to the screen, the influence of his literary mentors did not necessarily disappear altogether.

Cronenberg's *Naked Lunch* (1991) is not a conventional adaptation of a literary text but a hybrid of Burroughs-related material. There are motifs and stylistic elements from Burroughs' *Naked Lunch* but also elements from actual biographies, such as Ted Morgan's *Literary Outlaw: The Life and Times of William S. Burroughs* (1988), semi-autobiographical references from *Queer* (1986) and *Exterminator!* (1973), and letters written by Burroughs to his lover Allen Ginsberg. Rather than attempting to render a cinematic equivalent of a cut-up narrative, Cronenberg focuses instead on the circumstances that surround the composition of *Naked Lunch* and the notion of Burroughs as a creative artist.

'All desire is homosexual'[6]
In Rodley's plot summary of Cronenberg's 1994 film *M Butterfly*, 'he (Rene) is unaware that the object of his desire is really a man'.[7] In Cronenberg's *Naked Lunch*, Hank asks Martin, 'Is rewriting really censorship Bill, because I'm completely fucked if it is'. The title of Cronenberg's 1990 *Nike* advert, 'Transformation', not only reflects arguably the dominant theme of his oeuvre but also anticipates what he does with Burroughs' *Naked Lunch*. Cronenberg makes changes to crucial aspects of the novel, which appear to constitute self-censorship precisely and literally to prevent male characters from being, as Hank puts it, 'completely fucked'. William Beard's conclusion that 'all sexuality, all desire, is transgressive and, hence, potentially monstrous', ignores the possibility that some desires are potentially more transgressive than others.[8]

Amy Taubin asserts that Cronenberg's *Naked Lunch* is 'less an adaptation of William Burroughs' novel than David Cronenberg's fantasy about how it came to be written'.[9] It becomes a subjective view of how Burroughs suffered literary paralysis after killing his wife, the depths of despair to which this drove him and his escape from writer's block by re-enacting the event with his wife's alter ego. What Taubin finds most surprising is not so much that Cronenberg uses 'a bare-bones but not unconventional, *noir* narrative' but that the focus of this structure is 'the body of a woman'.[10] David Thompson suggests that Joan 'fulfils the Romantic role of literary muse' so that in re-shaping Burroughs' narrative around her death, Cronenberg is sending his protagonist in the film, Lee, 'more on a guilt trip than a drug-induced one'.[11]

A real event, the death of Joan, that does not appear directly anywhere in *Naked Lunch* or in Burroughs' letters, is chosen by Cronenberg to stand at the centre of his film. In an introduction to *Queer*, Burroughs states that 'the book (*Queer*) is motivated and formed by an event, which is never mentioned, in fact is carefully avoided: the accidental shooting of my wife, Joan'.[12] In a strangely prophetic way, Ballard's *The Atrocity Exhibition* (1970) fuses elements of material that will re-surface in the novel *Crash* with tensions underlying Burroughs' writing of *Naked Lunch*: 'Travis had embarked on the invention of imaginary psychopathologies, using her body and reflexes as a module for a series of unsavoury routines, as if hoping in this way to recapitulate his wife's death'.[13] The notion of the author is linked explicitly to sexuality in *Naked Lunch* as Burroughs himself admits: 'I am forced to the appalling conclusion that I would never have become a writer but for Joan's death'.[14]

Burroughs' description of the event in *Naked Lunch* is brief and embedded within an episode referred to obliquely by Timothy Murphy: 'significantly, this pimp can only communicate with other men through female intermediaries'.[15] Murphy only suggests Burroughs' discomfort in accepting responsibility for Joan's death but it could also be said that both Burroughs and Cronenberg use women as a means of looking at men and communicate with other men through female intermediaries. As Eve Sedgwick suggests in *Between Men* (1985), relations between men and women are effectively conduits for the expression and policing of male homosocial desire. Just as Burroughs 'identifies his writing as an involuntary psychological defence mechanism', so Cronenberg's work might be seen in a similar way acting as a device of homosexual disavowal.[16] Cronenberg states that 'I knew that I wanted a woman to be an important character' and for the film to have 'narrative cohesiveness', claiming that this was not 'because it was a movie that was going to cost x million dollars'.[17] However he does not say exactly *why* these features were important to him.

He creates a love affair between Lee and Joan Frost, a character based on writer Jane Bowles, 'despite the fact that the real Jane Bowles was a lesbian'.[18] The love scene between Bill and Joan is signalled by an erect phallus emerging from the typewriter, although it is unclear at this stage whether this is a response to their growing intimacy or a reflection of it. At no time does Burroughs' novel place a woman as the object of male sexual desire and the 'heterosexualization' of Cronenberg's narrative is underlined by the use of what he terms the 'sex blob', that leaps onto Joan and Bill as they embrace. Fashioned as a hybrid of crayfish and ammonite but with shining, thrusting, humanoid buttocks, this creature seems literally and metaphorically like a fish out of water, quivering on the floor, trying to come between the couple. The break of the shot-reverse-shot convention in this sequence creates a sense of cinematic transgression to reflect displaced desire. The 'blob', which seems to suggest only the lower half of the human form, is intercut with the upper half of the human torsos, reflecting a conflict between conscious and cerebral heterosexuality and a lower, deeper, abiding homosexual aesthetic.

In *Twins* (see previous chapter), Kathy Field comes upon the Ross twins on the floor writhing together 'like one animal...half of the shape on the floor was her husband, but if someone had put a gun to her head and told her to pick which, she couldn't have done it'.[19] Cronenberg appears interested in Freud's notions of 'polymorphous perversity' and 'omnisexuality', in which sex transcends gender, social and cultural expectations. In particular, the 'sex blob' is a personification of this with its many orifices and as David Breskin notes, 'it's humping the floor'.[20] Cronenberg admits that he is 'fascinated by scenes in *Prick Up Your Ears* where twenty guys would be fucking each other in a public toilet, with the lights out, not knowing who anybody was, or what anyone looked like. Part of me says, I'd love to try that. And if you're doing that, it doesn't matter if it's men or women or a combination of them'.[21] Such statements (which would have been manifested in the final cut scene from *Videodrome*), strongly echo Burroughs' ideas on evolutionary changes that might even 'involve the sexes fusing into an organism'.[22] Again, in *Queer*, there is a precursor of this notion, where Lee starts to talk in baby language to the object of his lust, Eugene Allerton, as a clumsy seduction technique: 'wouldn't it be booful if we should juth run together into one gweat big blob'.[23]

One of the very few direct quotations that Cronenberg takes from Burroughs is the 'talking asshole' routine.[24] Its inclusion could be explained by the fact that this is one of Burroughs' most infamous sequences and that Cronenberg is expressing a similar sense of bravado and flouting of conventional tastes that is part of the notoriety of the original. The sequence has been read as 'a conflict between the oral and the anal', and for Burroughs, the supremacy of the anus is clear as it subsumes the function of the mouth completely.[25] However, in Cronenberg's version, homosexuality only scores a pyrrhic victory. To a degree, it could be said that the passage represents 'a grim parable about giving too much power to transgressive desire' but although Cronenberg's Lee quotes the passage in full, the context in which Burroughs' text is placed, recasts its meaning.[26] As Beard observes, 'passages written or narrated directly in the book are in the film put in the mouth of Lee, who recites them to other characters'.[27] It appears that there is only a relativist distinction between various transgressive impulses, which could be creative, homosexual or murderous, and that it is possible and, perhaps, even necessary, to slide from one category to another.

The homosexual subtext of Cronenberg's *Naked Lunch* reasserts itself through the operation of writing and its related technology. The 'blob' is forced by Fadela over the balcony. We cut to the scene at ground level, where Tom is looking, not at the creature but a smashed typewriter. We see the results of the creature's fall, but we are not certain whether the creature was merely a drug-induced subjective hallucination of Bill and Joan's or whether Cronenberg intends to equate deviance in writing (pornography) with deviance in displacing and denying deep-seated desires. In this atmosphere of uncertainty, when Fadela angrily asserts that 'this is an evil and insane thing you are doing', it is unclear whether she is referring to Bill in terms of the drug-taking and sex with Joan or directed at the creature and its attempt to break up the heterosexual party. As a figure with some associations of same-sex relationships herself, Fadela might be addressing Bill and challenging him not to deny his true homosexual nature.

In the film, after Bill apparently commits himself to a homosexual lifestyle, the Mugwump head on which he types, has a penile extension, from which drips some kind of seminal fluid. The pep talk that the creature gives Bill as he writes might refer to a number of different things. When it says, 'this is very potent', it might be referring to the quality of Bill's writing, the pleasure it gains from his touch, the seminal fluid, the drugs that are producing this hallucination or the lifestyle he is now leading. The Mugwump hopes that Bill is devoting himself to being a writer as 'the two are very closely related', without specifying exactly what is being allied to writing. If the condition of being an agent is the object of comparison, then, in effect, the Mugwump is relating writing to being true to oneself, which here is the embracing of a homosexual lifestyle, as well as a new partner, Kiki. In Cronenberg's narrative, although Joan appears to inhabit the role of Romantic muse, it is Lee's gay lover who acts as a catalyst in Lee's literary development, offering Bill support to 'help you become a writer'.

Burroughs' infamous 'talking asshole' sequence is literalized in Cronenberg's conception of the bug, which speaks through its anal-like orifice. The transgressive imagery is compounded by Cronenberg, who converts a substance designed to kill, the bug powder, into a drug of choice. Cronenberg appears keen for us to make this connection as the shot lingers on the powder being applied to the lips of the bug. The implicit connection between Joan and the bug suggested by her earlier line that she 'feels like a bug', is enhanced by the bug's instruction here to 'Rub powder on my lips', which is then used by her later. This adds to the bug's assertion that Joan is an Interzone agent but also that Joan herself may be part of Lee's subjective hallucination. The connection between the female protagonist and a repulsive insect also reflects misogynistic tendencies in Burroughs, which Cronenberg does not appear to be questioning. Cronenberg has the bug derisively refer to Joan three times as 'the little woman', question her whole status as a human and, most clearly, instruct Lee to destroy her. In Interzone, the bug typewriter tells Bill that 'women are not human' but a 'different species with different wills and different purposes', which appears to represent a retrospective imposition by Cronenberg of misogynistic motivation for the fictional death of Joan Lee.

Her interest in other men and her slide into drug misuse could be seen as a search for stimulation and attention after being neglected by her husband, who in turn seems increasingly drawn to hallucinations with a strong homo-erotic content. The bug, who denounces Joan, via an anal mouthpiece, as a non-human Interzone agent, is only the first in a number of transgressive creatures. Kiki's description of the Mugwump as one who 'specialises in sexual ambivalence' might equally apply to their original creator Burroughs but also to Cronenberg as the individual who has verbalized and visualized much of what was previously implicit in his source material.

In this context, the first time that we see Lee openly injecting himself, indicating his addiction more clearly, could be his attempt to get closer to Joan by imitating her behaviour, in effect to get their habits in sync like the Mantle brothers in *Dead Ringers* (1988). As in the earlier film, this is unsuccessful due to underlying sexual tensions. The nature of Lee's hallucinations, the outcome of both versions of the William Tell game, and his apparent indifference to his wife's sexual boredom, suggest that Lee is in a state of homosexual disavowal. Later when the bug typewriter first appears, we inhabit Lee's point of view as he scans the room for a weapon with which to crush the creature, which is a potent metaphor for his attempt to deny the possibility that he is attracted to the ideas suggested by the bug.

Cronenberg's version is imbued with this sensibility. In giving Lee the mysterious liquid made from centipedes as part of a supposed cure for Joan's addiction to bug powder, the mysterious Dr Benway refers to its contents as 'in a larval state' and 'just waiting for the proper moment to hatch out', providing an image of Lee's latent sexuality. Another simile makes the point more blatantly. Benway describes the concoction as 'like an agent who has come to believe his own cover story' and later the typewriter bug tries to reassure Lee by stating that 'Homosexuality is the best all round cover an agent could have'. As the creature speaks, it starts to moan, aroused by its own suggestion and reflecting Bill's own suppressed arousal at the bug's masochistic pleasure, as it challenges him to 'hurt me'. The relish with which the bug refers to the words and how 'glad' he is that these words are going into the report portray writing as a penetrative act, in which words themselves become sexual objects and how in combination, as a report, they can produce a literal body of work. The juxtaposition of espionage, homosexual disavowal and writing is prefigured in *Queer*, where the frustration of Lee's barely suppressed attraction to the young man Allerton, is made more intense, not just by Allerton's apparent lack of awareness of the effect he is having but also his prattling on about checking reports during the war as a counter-intelligence officer.[28]

As Murphy suggests, Cronenberg really does 'reify the word', particularly through his talking bugs, who seem to spend more time talking about sex than actually engaging in any.[29] Words generate more words as the typewriter bug comments on words almost as soon as he has produced them: 'That is a great sentence. These are words to live by'. The typewriter bug goes on to articulate potential anxieties felt by Lee as he is forced to question his own sexuality: 'We appreciate that you might find the thought of engaging in homosexual acts morally, and possibly even physically, repulsive and we are encouraged that you are able to overcome these personal barriers to better serve the cause to which we are all so devoted'. Bill's reaction is instructive. He does not argue or fight, he *walks away*. He avoids and denies confronting his deepest impulses.

When Lee returns home to find his wife having sex with Hank whilst Martin recites poetry, Cronenberg portrays literature as possessing the properties of an aphrodisiac. Joan's explanation that the sex represents 'nothing serious; we're just bored', anticipates the tired and strangely passionless sexuality of Cronenberg's *Crash* (1996), particularly in the latter film's opening three scenes. Cronenberg's matter-of-fact dialogue dramatizes broader statements from Burroughs' 'algebra of need' covering the loss of libido on drugs ('the orgasm has no function in the junky'), to convey a sense of sex as an instinctive compulsion invoked unconsciously to counteract boredom rather than a conscious expression of affection.[30] When Joan says that Hank has gone, the following exchange occurs:

Lee: Not before you came I hope?
Joan: Hank's on junk. He doesn't come.
Lee: Not before you came I hope.
Joan: I'm on bug powder. I don't need to come.

Before first meeting a Mugwump, Lee is asked 'Are you a faggot?' to which he replies, 'Not by nature, no. However circumstances have forced me to consider the possibility that...' Cronenberg takes the teasing that Burroughs endured as a youngster and adds an overt statement of his own about the ambiguity of sexual identity. The 'circumstances' that are mentioned could well refer to Lee's killing of Joan and whether this was an accident or a willed act. As Tom Frost states ominously later, 'there are no accidents'. Creed seems to accept Lee's disavowal entirely at face value, but if Tom and Joan Frost 'come here for the boys', this could be Bill's motivation too.[31] Later, Cloquet remarks, 'I've seen you around but I had no idea you were queer'. We may be surprised by the overt recognition explicit in such a phrase because we have been denied specific confirmation by Bill that he has homosexual impulses.

Bill's state of denial is mirrored in the narrative, which displaces overt images of Bill's homosexuality onto the figures around him, most notably the pawnshop ornament. The implication is that the ornament literally may be a possession of Bill as he tries to gain enough money for passage to Interzone but metaphorically it reflects an attempt to distance himself from an intrinsic part of his being. Ironically, far from escaping this side of his nature, Interzone has the opposite effect, liberating it more clearly. Bill continues to deny this however. When Tom says that Bill could seduce Cloquet if he wanted, Bill can only incoherently stutter, 'I'm not...I don't...' unable to articulate a process within him that he does not want to acknowledge. This disavowal also operates in Cronenberg's process of adaptation. He is evoking, without acknowledgement, a scene from *Queer*, where Lee buys a camera from a pawnshop as a way of imposing a sense of obligation upon Allerton, thereby pressurizing him to become his paid companion. A commercial transaction disguises a calculating sexual manoeuvre.

Cronenberg also takes lines directly from *Queer* as Bill admits, 'the Lees have always been perverts. I shall never forget the unspeakable horror that froze the lymph in my glands and the baneful words seared my reeling brain: I was a homosexual'.[32] The self-loathing felt by Burroughs at this point is reflected by Cronenberg in another borrowing from *Queer*: Bill's recounting of the strangely surreal demise of Queen Bobo by having his internal organs sucked out.[33] Burroughs' notion of '*schlupping*: the complete assimilation of another person', is used as a verb, 'to schlup' or physically and mentally consume.[34] However, Cronenberg converts this into a repulsive adjective to describe the sound of what happens to Bobo. Like the ghoulish Beverly Hills elite in *Society* (1989), Cronenberg is also interested in 'the idea of parasitic symbiosis', but in more overt sexual terms than the class and political allegory of Brian Yuzna's film.[35] For Burroughs, 'this was an extension of the bond that he sought with Ginsberg to 'become soul-mates and somehow merge into one entity'.[36] Ginsberg found these ideas progressively more repulsive: 'Bill became more and more demanding that there be some kind of mental schlupp. It had gone beyond the point of being playful and humorous. It seemed that Bill was demanding it for real'.[37] Cronenberg presents the process repulsively both in the image of the figurine and its live counterpart because it represents the denial of artistic individuality, the Romantic notion underpinning his reading of Burroughs.

The film opens with an intertitle from Burroughs' *Naked Lunch*: '[h]ustlers of the world, there is one mark you cannot beat: The Mark Inside'. If Cronenberg's reading of Burroughs is of someone who was still trying to reconcile contrary sexualities at the time of writing *Naked Lunch*, then the film can be read as 'the drama of a character who denies and misrecognises his own deepest impulses' and 'whose resulting inner turmoil gives rise to hallucinations and the acting-out of repressed desires under "cover" of a self-invented alibi'.[38] This is oddly reminiscent of Max Renn's position in *Videodrome* and might suggest that there is an element of denial occurring there too, also linked to sexuality but of a heterosexual, sadomasochistic variety.

Specifically, the relationship between Cronenberg's Lee and Cloquet is important. The kind of effeminate homosexuality which the latter represents was repulsive to Burroughs himself, but Lee apparently sacrifices the attractive empathetic character of Kiki in an act that could be read as sadistic wish fulfilment.[39] Beard sees the homosexuality in the film as either cool and detached, as in Lee's scenes with Kiki and Cloquet or horrific and repulsive, such as the statue of Cloquet and Kiki and its later hallucinatory echo in the parrot cage scene. He claims overt eroticism is reserved for heterosexual exchanges between Joan and Lee. However, in one of her drug-taking scenes, she asks Lee to 'rub some of that powder on my lips', echoing the talking anus bug-typewriter that represents more overtly homosexual desire. Beard feels that Cronenberg's *Naked Lunch* is not homophobic as such but 'it does impute a kind of predatoriness to Lee's homosexual impulses'.[40] It is disingenuous of Cronenberg to say that 'it's not saying that gay sex involves a kind of centipede-like sexuality'.[41] If the imagery is designed to be, and is, repulsive, such a scene can only perpetuate images of homosexuality as predatory, unnatural and repulsive.

One of the clear changes from Burroughs to Cronenberg's conception of *Naked Lunch* occurs in the realization of the Mugwump creatures themselves. Cronenberg consciously moves their genitalia from their usual position to being placed on the heads of his creatures. For Beard, 'by transporting these sexual organs to the head, and by creating a Mugwump-head-typewriter which dispenses a liquid that is connected to powerful writing, the film emphasises the relation between artistic inspiration and sexual desire'.[42] The creatures become literal images of D. H. Lawrence's notions of 'sex in the head' but whereas for Lawrence this was seen as evidence of a spiritual descent, for Cronenberg this is a more explicit extension of the sexual evolution that he had posited earlier in *Shivers* (1976) and particularly *Rabid* (1977), with Rose's armpit growth. It picks up Burroughs' idea of 'undifferentiated tissue' that can mutate apparently at will, thereby linking experimental artistic expression with physical change and asserting that to create artistically *does* actually change the fabric of the real world.[43]

The talking bug typewriter is crucial in Cronenberg's reading of Burroughs. However, when Beard asserts talks of a connection, which 'extends from insect-disgust to homosexual-desire and thence to artistic creation', the three-stage process, which he outlines, proves problematic for Cronenberg.[44] Whether the process works forwards or backwards, there still needs to be a stage involving the acknowledgement of homosexual desire and it is this that Cronenberg seems to wish to skip over. If we accept Beard's reading of the Martinelli-bug-typewriter as 'more or less representing Lee's heterosexual attraction to Joan' and the Mugwump-head-typewriter as 'representing his homosexual desire for Kiki', then Cronenberg's film would seem to suggest that true creativity can only take place once one's deepest desires have been acknowledged.[45] It is the Martinelli that produces the writer's block that is only released by its rejection in favour of the Mugwump machine and Lee is only able to write fluently whilst living with Kiki and feeding on Mugwump jism. Whether Beard's reading is convincing or not, Cronenberg is drawing on another Burroughsian episode here. In *Queer*, Joe Guidry, a gay acquaintance of Lee, moans that a passing lover, Maurice, has stolen his typewriter. Maurice is also gay but, according to Joe, 'he won't accept it. I think stealing my typewriter is a way he takes to demonstrate to me and to himself that he is just in it for all he can get'.[46] Knowledge of this passage casts Cronenberg's portrayal of Tom Frost as less paranoid about the theft of his property and more frustrated that Lee will not accept his true sexuality.

Beard interprets Lee as 'sacrificing Kiki to predatory homosexual desire' in the horrific image of Cloquet as a giant centipede buggering the hanging man: the definitive Burroughsian image of transgressive desire.[47] In later critical work on the film, Beard notes, but does not explore, how this scene has been prefigured by the figure in the pawnshop window, albeit held in shot very briefly and possibly only consciously noted on repeated viewings.[48] In Burroughs' *Naked Lunch*, the author asserts that:

> 'The Word will leap on you with leopard man iron claws, it will cut off fingers and toes like an opportunist land crab, it will hang you and catch your jissom like a scrutable dog, it will coil round your thighs like a bushmaster and inject a shot glass of rancid ectoplasm...'[49]

Cronenberg takes this abstract notion, four pages from the end of Burroughs' *Naked Lunch*, and converts it into a concrete image, albeit only glimpsed momentarily. The figurine in the pawnshop combines 'leopard man iron claws', in a grotesque image of hanging, that 'will coil round your thighs...and inject a shot glass of rancid ectoplasm'. Furthermore, the 'sex blob' apparently out of its natural element visualizes this 'opportunist land crab', and is beaten away 'like a scrutable dog' by Fadela, only to be developed later in the market where she is described in Cronenberg's film as cutting up 'some kind of sea creature'. One of Burroughs' working titles for the novel was *Word Hoard* and in fleshing out Burroughs, sometimes literally, Cronenberg creates an equivalent 'image hoard'. Word is, indeed, made Flesh.

Richard Dellamora sees the shot of the figure (which he debatably terms 'prolonged') as a 'foreshadowing' of what he calls 'a scene of sexual assault' (by implication, the parrot cage scene) and also an allusion to Andres Serrano's photographic work *Piss Christ* (1987), all acting as focal images for the far right in US debates about gay representation.[50] The pawnshop setting implies that Cronenberg's Lee is seeking a transaction. Transgressive desire is being set aside as if it can be ignored temporarily. A complete transaction of ownership has not taken place and the desire is placed in a kind of limbo that can be re-activated at any time. As seen elsewhere in this chapter, Cronenberg is appropriating material from a range of Burroughsian sources. *Queer* contains a market scene in Guayaquil, Ecuador, where Lee is surrounded by a sense of deviancy in the design of 'salt shakers and water pitchers', which display 'nameless obscenities: two men on all fours engaged in sodomy formed the handle for the top of a kitchen pot'.[51]

The glimpse of the figure in the pawnshop suggests that the fantasy that it depicts is part of Lee's make-up. Cronenberg himself has spoken of his ability to identify sexually with this. He talks of Burroughs' fantasies of 'sodomizing young boys as they're hanging. I can actually relate to that to quite an extent. I really understand what's going on'.[52] Perhaps Cronenberg is showing a greater depth of honesty here about sexual ambiguity than most individuals would be brave enough to admit but it is still difficult to reconcile such overt statements with assertions about his predominant heterosexual sensibility. He states, 'I'm not gay and so my sensibility, when it comes to the sexuality of this film is going to be something else. I'm not afraid of the homosexuality, but it's not innate in me and I probably want women in the film'.[53] The effect of such statements exemplifies Judith Butler's description of 'the parodic or imitative effect of gay identities worked neither to copy nor to emulate heterosexuality, but rather, to expose heterosexuality as an incessant and *panicked* imitation of its own naturalised idealisation'.[54] Cronenberg justifies the scaling down of homosexuality in his version of *Naked Lunch* by the biographical claim that 'Burroughs had not at that point come to terms with being homosexual' and that 'this is a fusion of several things together: me and Burroughs for one thing', apparently underlining his heterosexual credentials again.[55]

The character of Kiki is not found in Burroughs' *Naked Lunch* but a minor character with the same name appears as an object of consensual homosexual lust in *The Ticket That Exploded* (1968).[56] However, in Cronenberg's film, Kiki's nature is made more predatory and constitutes 'every straight man's worst nightmare about gay sex', particularly in the parrot cage sequence.[57] Cronenberg's explanation of this scene is that Lee has not accepted his own homosexuality and that 'when he talks to his typewriter, he's talking to himself'. The machine thus acts as his unconscious, forcing him to come to terms with himself.[58] Cronenberg verbally explains the scene (perhaps an admission in itself of flawed expression in cinematic terms), by claiming that what Lee hears is Kiki and Cloquet together. According to Cronenberg, some time has elapsed during which Lee has taken a drug that makes it seem just a few moments later and that on seeing the men engaged in sex together, 'he has to construct a horrific, unbearable, repulsive image...because his response is revulsion, guilt, fear'. To say that Lee 'hallucinates this thing that he can run away from' is all very well but as Cronenberg admits himself, although 'it should be obvious' what is happening, it may not be 'the first time through'.[59] Burroughs frequently uses centipedes, towards which he admits to having a personal aversion as a metaphor for predatory homosexuality.[60] Burroughs notes that 'he (Cronenberg) got the centipede motif from me'.[61] For example, in *The Western Lands* (1987), apart from an AIDS-like plague of centipedes, the hero, Kim, is shown a picture of 'a man strapped to a couch, a huge centipede, six feet in length, is curling over the bound figure', to which he reacts with 'horror and disgust', which, in turn, reiterates an image from *Queer* of 'a man tied to a couch and a centipede ten feet long rearing up over him'.[62]

David Thompson states in his review of Cronenberg's *Naked Lunch* that 'the outrageous homoerotic elements in Burroughs have been awkwardly muted' and that Weller's performance 'barely registers any impact of the "gayness within"'.[63] However a penchant for acting styles that are understated and muted is one of Cronenberg's key directorial features and Thompson takes this position even further to the unsupportable generalization that 'homosexuality has never been to the fore in Cronenberg's cinema'.[64] He is a little harsh in judging that 'the only homosexual act directly visualised is the shock effect of the oily Cloquet...becoming one with the fey Kiki amid a welter of Chris Walas gunk'.[65] Such criticism seems unfair considering how uncomfortable both censors and mainstream audiences would probably have felt about more explicit images and his dismissive tone also seems to contradict subsequent comments that 'this is probably the most extreme image Cronenberg has yet given us of the physicality of sexual union'.[66] To have included a greater number of sexual images would have detracted from the horror of this scene, which, Thompson fails to note, was also foreshadowed in the figure in the window display earlier.

During Burroughs' composition of *Naked Lunch*, he wrote to Ginsberg about how he had 'glimpsed a new dimension of sex: Sex mixed with routines and laughter, the unmalicious, unrestrained, pure laughter that accompanies a good routine, laughter that gives a moment's freedom from the cautious, nagging, ageing, frightened flesh'.[67] If Cronenberg's conception of the 'sex blob' attempted to visualize such a view, this might well explain the scene's amused reception by critics like Thompson and Jaehne. It also reflects how, in the film, rather than in pronouncements in interviews, Cronenberg distances himself from direct linkage with Burroughs' homosexuality and 'treats homosexual relations obliquely when sympathetic and with comic disgust when direct'.[68]

Whilst Burroughs was producing the material in Tangiers that would later become *Naked Lunch*, he was obsessively in love with Allen Ginsberg, indeed to the point where much of the novel could be seen as Burroughs' attempt to win Ginsberg back. None of this appears in Cronenberg's film and Ginsberg and Kerouac appear more as 'Tweedledum and Tweedledee'.[69] Cronenberg's explanation that 'this is only secondarily a film about the Beats' fails to fully explain this omission.[70] He does give Lee a lover, Kiki, but this is alluded to more than stated openly and clearly he feels uncomfortable about the issue: 'it was something that I just didn't feel I could delve into'.[71] His defence that 'I myself am not homosexual and do not feel prepared to create a character as extreme in his homosexuality as in *Naked Lunch*', seems somehow hollow for a director so closely associated with images of the extreme.[72] His claims to have 'struggled with it aesthetically and morally, because it seemed a kind of transgression' is ambiguous as to what the 'it' in this sentence actually refers to.[73] The 'transgression' here could be the idea of 'selling out' on gay representation but it also links the notion of transgression to homosexuality itself, possibly reflecting a more deep-seated, repressed conservative and censorious view of same-sex relations. Cronenberg has stated that his film's portrayal of the Burroughs/Ginsberg relationship 'is an enquiry into the particular kind of intelligence they had which does not depend upon homosexuality', which appears to be delivered with either extreme naivety or perversity to gay audiences.[74]

For Taubin, 'Cronenberg's *Naked Lunch* never resolves the incompatibility between the heterosexual drive of its narrative and the remnants of Burroughs' homoerotic fantasy'.[75] Dellamora notes the casting of Peter Weller (best known for his macho cyborg role in *RoboCop*), Lee's horrified reaction in the parrot cage scene and the focus on special effects (which Dellamora links rather stereotypically with young heterosexual males), as all serving to distance Cronenberg from presenting an empathetic view of same-sex relationships.[76] Cronenberg's explanation of Lee's adoption of homosexuality is also a little unclear. His insect controller does order him to play this role but as Cronenberg points out, 'he (Lee) has created this; he's making it his excuse. He's demanding of himself that he must do it. But it's for "other reasons", not because he's homosexual'.[77] These reasons are never fully explained, other than alluding to an assumption of homosexuality as a cover, constituting some 'noble, social act'.[78] Cronenberg claims that 'the sex in *Naked Lunch* is beyond gay. It's sci-fi sex; it has metaphorical meaning every way'.[79] However this presents problems when Cronenberg claims to be pursuing a metaphorical aesthetic journey and yet his images often emphasize their literal, metonymic features. Ultimately as far as Burroughs is concerned, Cronenberg seems to view 'homosexuality as a somewhat unwelcome accident of circumstance and plot' and that 'he simply did not, as an artist, find that aspect of "Lee" to be significant to the story he wanted to tell in the film'.[80]

This chapter does not constitute a judgement on Cronenberg's own sexuality (he even jokes about 'coming out of the closet as a bisexual'), but concerns his treatment of the issue of male desire.[81] In recalling how he was propositioned after a screening of *Stereo* (1969), partly due to casting Ron Mlodzik in the lead role, Cronenberg accepts '[h]ow directly that connects with my own sexuality or not, it certainly connects very directly to my aesthetic sense of his space and his medieval gay sensibility, which I like a lot'.[82] Interestingly, at the same time that Cronenberg was writing the script for *Naked Lunch*, he was playing the protagonist in Clive Barker's *Nightbreed* (1991), Dr Decker, a psychopathic homosexual psychiatrist. This was more than just a cameo, as he emphasizes himself: 'I was three months in London. You don't do that just for fun'.[83] During filming, Barker relates how Cronenberg kept 'freaking out the film's crew by remarking how comfortable the Buttonhead mask became after a while' and kept it on during 'lengthy breaks' between scenes, which reflects, over and above a macabre sense of humour, an enduring fascination with occupying, and role-playing, different sexual identities.[84]

'Operation Re-write'
(the writer of a creation and the creation of a writer)

For Mark Kermode, Cronenberg's 'recurrent central thesis' is 'the acceptance and celebration of mutation'.[85] It could be said that beyond physical mutation, Cronenberg is also interested in *literary* mutation, in particular how written texts affect visual images. The overt subject of the film is *the author and his work*: 'I also knew that I wanted it to be about writing: the act of writing and creating something that is dangerous to you'.[86] In this, Cronenberg faces a familiar problem: 'the act of writing is not very interesting cinematically...It's an interior act'. His solution is to 'turn it inside out and make it physical and exterior'.[87] This is entirely consistent with earlier films like *The Brood* (1979) with internal anger displaced to create external womb sacs or Beverly's suggestion of beauty contests for the insides of bodies in *Dead Ringers*.

Cronenberg himself states '[i]t's appropriate that the movie of *Naked Lunch*, which is very much about writing and new realities that are made through the creative process, should present me again with this problem of metaphor...This is something I struggle with all the time. The use of metaphor in literature is crucial, and there is no direct screen equivalent'.[88] Cronenberg's solution is that 'often I end up using special effects for just this purpose. There's a very specific example in *Naked Lunch* where we have a creature, which evolves out of a typewriter that is all-sexual, a polymorphously perverse thing'. This 'is really an allegorical being that you would probably call lust if you were writing in the fourteenth century. It would be the embodiment of the lust of these two people. So I'm doing something very literary here, but in a very cinematic way'.[89]

The novel *Naked Lunch* presents some clear difficulties and challenges in transferring it to a cinematic medium. Burroughs' novel is a hallucinatory narrative, written in the first person. One of Cronenberg's main challenges is to visualize this subjectivity. Burroughs deters direct empathy with characters by making them repulsive, engaged in repetitive acts and adopting a non-linear narrative, whereas Cronenberg creates dramatic engagement with the audience by blending fragmented Burroughsian material into a linear narrative. Rodley feels that 'the emergent film was clearly more Cronenberg than Burroughs', and yet he goes on to state that 'the film had become as much an adaptation of Ted Morgan's biography of Burroughs, *Literary Outlaw* (the most visible book on set), as it was *Naked Lunch*'.[90]

The opening shot in his first scene inhabits the point of view of a subjective persona standing in front of a door, calling the word 'Exterminator!' The first spoken word and the subjective camera position align us with Burroughs the author of *Exterminator!*, in which he recounts in semi-autobiographical style his own experiences as a pest controller. The subjectivity is maintained for a little longer as the door is subsequently opened by an unseen occupant and we see shots of powder being sprayed down the back of units: an action that could conceivably be acted out by the 'viewer-persona'. It is only when Peter Weller appears in shot that the shift towards a conventional third-person narrative occurs. However, subjectivity is drip-fed through the film to undermine any consistent narrative viewpoint. When Lee goes to collect more bug powder, the non-diegetic laughter in the background creates an unsettling atmosphere and we share Lee's sense that he is being humiliated by the lack of clear motivation for the sound effect.

In the police station when Lee is first arrested, there is a mixture of conventional objective omniscient point of view and implied subjective view, which problematizes whether we are inhabiting Lee's consciousness or not. When the detectives produce a bug, Cronenberg uses devices employed by conventional thrillers to create dramatic suspense. We hear a scuttling noise before we see the bug itself, thereby using sound that is literally unmotivated by the visuals that accompany it, creating momentary curiosity in the viewer. Later in the same scene, the camera drops below the level of the table to show Lee carefully removing his shoe ready to kill the bug. This device and the brief hesitation as Lee raises the improvised weapon creates momentary dramatic suspense as to whether he will strike. It is a virtual parody of Hitchcock's definition of suspense and creates some empathy towards Lee as a fictional character distinct from the viewer, particularly because the object of antagonism, the bug, is so repulsive.[91]

However, it is not enough to throw up one's critical hands and declare as William Beard does that 'it is most often quite impossible to say or even guess what is "really" going on in the film'.[92] Like our awareness of Max in *Videodrome*, which Beard also admits to finding confusing, we are only gradually made aware that we are experiencing the narrative through the view of a character, who is less than wholly reliable.[93] Burroughs' novel refuses to deliver a conventional cause-and-effect narrative but Cronenberg's version is not a wholesale adoption or reversal of this. Even when there is the semblance of a causal relationship between motivation and its consequences, this is often undermined almost immediately. At home after escaping from the first bug, Lee breathes heavily on some cockroaches by a mirror and the fact that they fall implies that Lee has been abusing bug powder himself, undermining the credibility of everything we have seen so far in the film. This is made explicit in the dialogue as he acknowledges that he has started to hallucinate and admits, 'I'm not even sure how I got out of there'. He asserts that he and Joan must leave as they have 'been made', which only makes sense if they had created some kind of crime or that Lee felt guilty for something. In a sense, he has 'been made' by the audience, who now cannot wholly suspend their disbelief and trust his viewpoint.

Serge Grünberg highlights the bus station scene as particularly important in this process, with the dressing of the set emphasizing that we are actually in New York. Bill is puzzled and wonders if he is hallucinating, to which Hank replies, 'My dear Bill, this must be the first time for a long time that you're *not* hallucinating!' Grünberg asserts that this is 'the first time that the eye of the camera "unveils" an illusion, a fantasy or an hallucination'. However, within a matter of lines he contradicts himself by claiming that unlike in *Videodrome*, where we were not allowed to stand outside the subjective view of Max Renn, *Naked Lunch* 'is peppered with these calls to order'.[94]

The latter position has far more evidence to substantiate it. There are a number of clues in Cronenberg's version of *Naked Lunch* that Interzone is really only a mental, rather than a physical, state. On visiting Joan Frost, although the exteriors suggest a Tangiers-style location, the slow, over-the-shoulder steadicam shot up to the door reprises the style and content of the opening sequence and once inside Bill also comments that 'There's a restaurant just like this in New York'. Towards the end of the film, Bill is muttering about an 'exchange of hostages' at the same time as putting the Mugwump head in a bowling bag. With its antenna dripping seminal fluid, this is both grotesque and comic, further undercutting Bill's status as a serious and reliable narrator. Cronenberg also prefaces some hallucinatory interludes with a character taking some kind of stimulant, as when Joan takes hash, motivating the subsequent 'sex blob' creature. Burroughs does not do this quite so overtly, devoting sections of his *Naked Lunch* to the mechanics of addiction and then cutting to visionary passages, leaving it to the reader to piece together a causal link.

For Eric Mottram, 'throughout *Exterminator!* the elegiac is sharply juxtaposed to the satirical and demolishing' and the same hybrid tonal quality is present in Cronenberg's film.[95] In the pawnshop, Lee's growing paranoia is underlined by his exaggerated behaviour in adopting the persona of a shifty secret agent, promising Martin that he will send him a report. He then almost immediately corrects himself to say he will send a copy, not the actual report itself, indicating how he is being swallowed up by the internal logic of his role as agent. His small aside also reflects the process of constant editing, in which Burroughs and Cronenberg both engaged to produce their relative versions of *Naked Lunch*. Cinematographer Peter Suschitzky describes how Cronenberg 'endlessly rewrites' and there is a similar restlessness about the images that remain in the finished film.[96] It is as if Cronenberg makes an assertion and then undercuts it almost immediately. Martin's observation that 'I hear Interzone is nice this time of year' smacks of the clichéd code words of spy novels but the jaunty way in which it is delivered shows a key difference between the two figures: for Martin, this is a light-hearted game; for Bill, deadly serious.

Despite the fragmentation of the linear narrative by Burroughs' use of cut-up and fold-in methods, it is not possible for a writer to escape a reliance on the written word. Burroughs is really only replacing one set of grammatical concepts by another. This is implicitly recognized by his admission that in the tetralogy 'there was too much rather undifferentiated cut-up material' and Cronenberg's linearization of Burroughs' *Naked Lunch* reflects Burroughs' own shift through the 1980s away from cut-up as a writing tool and a return to more conventional narrative style.[97] One of Cronenberg's few allusions to cut-ups comes in the opening credits with the titles running in three different planes and the score dominated by *the* quintessential fragmented musical style: jazz. However, the very first scene undercuts this fragmentation by the clear adoption of classically conventional editing. The close-up on a numbered door and the subtitle of 'New York City, 1953' places the scene in terms of a recognizable screen space and time.

Cronenberg's equivalent for Burroughs' attempt to erase language is to bring into question the basic building block of his medium, the image. The subjective universe that Cronenberg's Bill inhabits is signalled by two particular incidents of mistaken identity, one minor and barely noticeable, the other more prominent and connected with a climactic scene. The first one occurs in the pawnshop as Bill, on being asked if he has got the tickets, produces, by mistake, the centipede given to him by Benway. In a sense, this is his 'passage', the means by which he crosses into Interzone, the metaphysical realm of higher consciousness accessed by drug-induced perceptions.

The second incident occurs on the beach, when Hank and Martin discover Bill sleeping rough and carrying a pillowcase, into which we have seen him stuffing the broken typewriter in the preceding scene. On being shown the contents of the bag, we do not see the Martinelli as we might expect, but a collection of pills and bottles. It is the clearest indication yet that not only are we not inhabiting the viewpoint of an omniscient narrator, but that we are purposely given a viewpoint that shifts, without any narrative markers, between objective and subjective positions. This is more than a Hitchcockian 'Macguffin', it is a narrative feature that is mutually exclusive, i.e. the pillowcase cannot contain both machine and pills, *we* must decide which is the more likely. The *mise-en-scène* here contributes to the sense of subjectivity with an initial establishing shot positioning Bill as nearly buried under a mound of sand, which is almost the same brownish-yellow colour as the bug powder that had triggered his initial hallucinations, explicitly visualizing the sense of a shrunken hero, whose addiction has grown to the extent of almost engulfing him. By emphasizing the fragility of the cinematic narrative, Cronenberg creates a process of *visual disavowal*, in which statements are made and then unmade, images are created only to be dismantled and screen 'reality' is apparently established only to be undermined.

Cronenberg's *Naked Lunch* reflects the repetitive nature of Burroughs' original novel but achieves this via different elements and for different effects. In Interzone, we see Bill repeating actions that he had taken whilst in New York, for example, injecting himself in the heel and breathing on an insect in order to kill it. Cronenberg repeats an earlier long tracking shot that takes us to the insect, inhabiting Bill's subjective and drug-affected point of view, giving us time to adjust to this before showing the grotesque object of the hallucination. It is by repeated actions, camera motifs and character doubles in the two Joans, that Cronenberg attempts to echo Burroughs' use of 'routines'. He also develops the term itself, using it in a broader theatrical sense by having Tom compliment Bill for a 'routine', a sequence of seductive behaviour, which impressed Cloquet.

For Jaehne, Cronenberg's *Naked Lunch* 'uses Burroughs' life and art as a reason to explore the writer as addict' and reflect a vision in which 'life, like writing, is boring or repulsive'.[98] Cronenberg asserts, 'there is this act that occurs between the life of the person creating and the work of art that transforms and separates the two of them. That's what this movie is about'.[99] Cronenberg has claimed that '[w]hen I'm writing I do go into a trance-like state which I can be in and out of in an instant...It's a kind of out-of-body thing'.[100] As so much of Cronenberg's work surrounds attempts to escape the body, this might suggest that flights of imaginative literary creativity provide one of the few means to this end, albeit temporarily. Commercial considerations may also have led Cronenberg to focus on the figure of the writer, thereby providing the film with the conventional narrative 'through-line' of a biography. In this way, elements that audiences cannot easily understand immediately, such as the birdcage scene at Cloquet's house, can be designated as subjective hallucinations of a drugged narrator.

Tom's confession that he has been killing his wife 'slowly over months' appears in a climactic scene, cited at length by Beard but not analysed.[101] At the only point in the film, we hear Tom's dialogue on the soundtrack ('If you look carefully at my lips, you'll realize I'm actually saying something else'), but his mouth does not move in sync with the words. Creed claims that 'the episode makes it clear that we should not necessarily believe Bill when he says he does not desire other men'.[102] This is fair but could also be an oblique way of signalling that this is part of Bill's subjective paranoia, brought on by his drug habit, seeing conspiracy theories where they do not exist or it could be that momentarily Tom acts as a Cronenberg-archetypal character, the scanner. Tom's apparent ability to communicate telepathically could be seen to draw Bill into a complicit pact against women, ultimately resulting in the needless second murder of the second Joan.

Taking the notion of the human body as a 'soft machine', Burroughs advocates that the only way to break the bond between word as parasite and human as host is 'don't answer the machine – shut it off'.[103] More precisely, 'one must give the machine scrambled, cut-up recordings of its own memory/control words and let it fall into a self-destructive feedback loop'.[104] Tom's apparent ventriloquism could be seen as Cronenberg's visualization of Burroughs' attempt to 'rub out the word'. As such, it is only partially successful, however, as 'the word' is not removed, merely displaced chronologically, so that it is still audible but not when we might expect. According to Burroughs' accounts in *The Job*, he played a small role in Antony Balch's underground film *Bill and Tony* (1972), using facial projection and cross-dubbing to confuse and problematize the identity of the cast. Such experimental cinematic techniques find their parallel in Cronenberg's work too, albeit as 'process' rather than 'product'. During the filming of the doubling scenes in *Dead Ringers*, a sound recordist describes how an acting double would lip-sync a playback of Irons' recorded dialogue: 'it was actually quite spooky to see the acting double standing there, moving his lips, with Jeremy's voice coming out'.[105]

Cronenberg is strangely contradictory in explaining the inclusion in his film of *two* shooting incidents. To state that Burroughs had to 'relive that trauma repeatedly' so that the film is 'meant to be about his suffering' seems fair enough. However, his assertion that the film is 'not about him getting rid of the woman in his life so that he could be creative' is followed immediately with 'it was only after he came to terms with her loss that he began to write seriously again'.[106] As Serge Grünberg points out, 'it would be just as wrong to see the two Joans as identical as the twins in *Dead Ringers*'.[107] If the act of creation (here writing a novel) is seen as standing for the birthing process more overtly represented in earlier films like *The Brood* and *Dead Ringers*, then Cronenberg is depicting a male usurping the position of a woman, who is removed from the narrative, not just once but twice. The significance of the second death is related to, but *not the same as*, the first. The first killing is of an unfaithful, drug-addicted wife, the second is of a *writer*, so that 'if the murder of the first Joan triggers off in Bill a compulsion to write (and its denial), the murder of the second Joan definitely locks it up in the *trap* of art'.[108] In the film, shooting a second Joan dramatizes a wish-fulfilling scenario that was always denied to Burroughs in real life. Cronenberg's Bill, on entering Annexia, breaks, or annexes, all connections with the past.

Cronenberg's Lee at the typewriter, his version of Vaughan with his scrapbook in *Crash* (1996) and his realization of Spider, scribbling in a private notebook, all reflect an enduring fascination with the figure of the writer. Burroughs also shows frequent recourse to using writers as narrators (often with only thinly veiled autobiographical links), such as Kim Carsons, Tom Dark and William Seward Hall in *The Place of Dead Roads* (1983) and Joe the Dead and Hall again in *The Western Lands*. Taubin's assertion that 'the film's central image is of Lee alone in his wretched hotel room sitting in front of this insect writing machine',[109] echoes the close of *Cities of the Red Night* (1982) with Audrey Carsons 'at a typewriter in his attic room, his back to the audience'.[110] *The Western Lands* appears to convey a more resigned view of writing which cannot transform the world in ways which had been hoped. Hall, 'the old writer', switches back and forth between the narratives of Kim and Joe, apparently trying to break out of a writer's block but ultimately arrives at 'the end of words, the end of what can be done with words'.[111] Since many of Burroughs' works, not just the self-conscious cut-up novels, concern themselves centrally with writers and writing, it is perhaps not so surprising that Cronenberg's version of *Naked Lunch* should reflect a notion of writers, who discover themselves as such through the course of the narrative and through the act of writing itself.

Conclusion

In referring to his film *Naked Lunch*, Cronenberg asserts that '[i]t probably has more of me in it than of William Burroughs, because he had very little to do with the process' and goes on that 'I think of it as the product of a dream I would have about Burroughs and his book, a dream to which I bring all my particular obsessions and idiosyncrasies'.[112] If this is so, then Cronenberg's 'obsessions' and 'idiosyncrasies' seem, in terms of their expression, inextricably bound up with other Burroughsian texts, particularly *Queer*, as we find repeatedly that episodes and images from this text reappear in the film of *Naked Lunch*. In several interviews, when Burroughs himself has been asked about Cronenberg's adaptation of *Naked Lunch*, he replies with a paraphrase of Raymond Chandler, who when asked, 'How do you feel about what Hollywood has done to your novels?' is alleged to have replied, 'My novels? Why, Hollywood hasn't done anything to them. They're still right there, on the shelf'.[113]

In making *Naked Lunch*, Cronenberg rejected any notion of a direct translation and instead attempted to get himself in aesthetic sync with Burroughs. Cronenberg described this process in a simile from another of his own works: '[i]t's like Burroughs and myself fusing in the telepod of *The Fly*'.[114] Such comparisons imply equal artistic merit at the same time as suggesting faithfulness to the source material and the notion of the integrity of the original creative artist. However, like the Mantle twins' attempts to harmonize their drug habit in *Dead Ringers*, Cronenberg's attempts to fuse with Burroughs do not work for reasons related to the suppressed subtext of the earlier film. Burroughs' wholesale embracing of a homosexual aesthetic is denied by Cronenberg but this denial only results in displacement.

Cronenberg initially operates like the absent scientist of earlier films like *Shivers*, who has created an experiment that appears to be spiralling out of control.

However, here Cronenberg subsequently intrudes into his own experiment to direct it towards the outcome he wants or, more importantly, to deflect the narrative away from the logical direction of its own development: homosexual desire. Grünberg is correct when he describes the adaptation as 'a grafting or a vision, as if the director had plugged directly into the brain of the writer in order to produce a monster with two heads'.[115] The Janus-like product is a result of a complex process of artistic disavowal. Just as Cronenberg has drawn upon Burroughs' own process of writing the novel *Naked Lunch*, the film version he has produced reflects artistic tensions underlying his own creative processes. When Cronenberg speaks of his protagonist, he is also talking about his own aesthetic sensibility: 'I'm probably giving you the same sort of avoidance-denial cinematically that I'm saying Lee is doing psycho-emotionally...I'm saying Lee is denying and avoiding certain realities about himself.'[116] As Dellamora states, 'Cronenberg describes *Naked Lunch* as a "coming out" movie, but, as usually occurs when adapted by heterosexuals, the phrase is recontextualised: Cronenberg comes out – *as a writer*'.[117]

Notes

1. William Burroughs, *The Ticket That Exploded* (New York: Grove Press, 1968), p. 54.
2. Michael O'Pray, 'Fatal Knowledge', *Sight & Sound* 1:11 (March 1992), p. 10.
3. Chris Rodley (ed.), *Cronenberg on Cronenberg* (London: Faber & Faber, 1992), p. 152 and Peter Morris, *A Perfect Balance* (Toronto: ECW Press, 1993), p. 30.
4. Morris, op. cit., p. 29.
5. William Beard, 'Insect Poetics: Cronenberg's *Naked Lunch*', *Canadian Revue of Comparative Literature/Revue Canadienne de Littérature Comparée* 23:3 (September 1996), p. 827.
6. Steven Shaviro, *The Cinematic Body* (Minneapolis; London: University of Minnesota Press, 1993), p. 73.
7. Rodley, op. cit., p. 172.
8. Beard, op. cit., p. 842.
9. Amy Taubin, 'The Wrong Body', *Sight and Sound* 1:11 (March 1992), p. 8.
10. Ibid.
11. David Thompson, '*Naked Lunch*', *Sight and Sound* 2:1 (May 1992), p. 56.
12. Burroughs, *Queer* (New York; London: Pan, 1986), Introduction, p. 14.
13. J. G. Ballard, *The Atrocity Exhibition* (London: Triad/Panther, 1979), p. 88.
14. William Burroughs, *Queer* (Pan, 1986), Introduction, p. 18.
15. Timothy S. Murphy, *Wising Up the Marks: The Amodern William Burroughs* (Berkeley; London: University of California Press, 1997), p. 12.
16. Beard, op. cit., p. 826.
17. Rodley, op. cit., p. 165.
18. Al Wesel, 'Bugging Out: David Cronenberg Exterminates Homosexuality', *QW* 9 (August 1992), p. 36.
19. Bari Wood, and Jack Geasland, *Dead Ringers* (London: Sphere Books, 1988), [re-release of the original novel *Twins*, on which the film was based. First published in the U.S. in 1978 by Signet Books], p. 301.
20. David Breskin, *Inner Views: Filmmakers in Conversation* (London: Faber & Faber, 1992), p. 251.
21. Cronenberg cited in ibid., p. 252.

22. William Burroughs, *The Adding Machine: Collected Essays* (London: Calder, 1983), p. 126.
23. Burroughs, *Queer* (New York; London: Pan, 1986), p. 96.
24. William Burroughs, *Naked Lunch* (London: Paladin, 1991), pp. 131–133.
25. Ted Morgan, *Literary Outlaw: The Life and Times of William S. Burroughs* (London: Pimlico, 1988), p. 357.
26. Beard, op. cit., p. 838.
27. Ibid., p. 824.
28. William Burroughs, *Queer* (New York; London: Pan, 1986), p. 39.
29. Murphy, op. cit., p. 71.
30. William Burroughs, *Naked Lunch* (London: Paladin, 1991), *Naked Lunch*, p. 41.
31. Barbara Creed, 'The naked crunch: Cronenberg's homoerotic bodies', in Michael Grant (ed.), *The Modern Fantastic: The Films of David Cronenberg* (Trowbridge: Flicks Books, 2000), p. 96.
32. Burroughs, op. cit., p. 50.
33. Ibid., p. 51.
34. Burroughs cited in Barry Miles, *William Burroughs: El Hombre Invisible* (London: Virgin Books, 1992), p. 59.
35. Ibid.
36. Ibid.
37. Ibid.
38. Ibid., p. 834.
39. See William Burroughs, *Queer* (New York; London: Pan, 1986): 'I was a homosexual. I thought of the painted, simpering female impersonators I had seen in a Baltimore night club. Could it be possible that I was one of those subhuman things?' (p. 50).
40. Beard, op. cit. p. 847.
41. Cronenberg cited in Breskin, op. cit., p. 250.
42. Murphy, op. cit., p. 839.
43. William Burroughs, *Naked Lunch* (London: Paladin, 1991), p.110.
44. Beard, op. cit., p. 834.
45. Ibid., p. 839.
46. Burroughs, op. cit., p. 30.
47. Beard, op. cit., p. 839.
48. William Beard, *The Artist as Monster: The Films of David Cronenberg* (Toronto: The University of Toronto Press, 2001), p. 322.
49. William Burroughs, *Naked Lunch*, op. cit, pp. 180-181.
50. Richard Dellamora, 'Queer Apocalypse: Framing William Burroughs', in *Postmodern Apocalypse: Theory and Cultural Practice at the End* (Philadelphia: University of Pennsylvania Press, 1995), p. 152.
51. William Burroughs, *Queer* (New York; London: Pan, 1986), p. 92.
52. Rodley, op. cit., p. 99.
53. Rodley, op. cit., p. 162.
54. Judith Butler, 'Imitation and Gender Insubordination', in Diana Fuss (ed.), *Inside/out: Lesbian Theories, Gay Theories* (New York; London: Routledge, 1991), pp. 22-23.
55. Rodley, op. cit., p. 163.
56. William Burroughs, *The Ticket That Exploded* (New York: Grove Press, 1968), pp. 106–109.
57. Al Wesel, op. cit., p. 36 .
58. Cronenberg cited in Breskin, op. cit., p. 249.
59. Ibid., p. 250.

60. William Burroughs, *The Western Lands* (New York; London: Pan, 1988), p. 86.
61. Regina Weinreich, 'Mind Set: No-one Gets a Free Lunch', (previously unpublished, 1991); cited in Allen Hibbard (ed.), *Conversations with William S. Burroughs* (Jackson: University Press of Mississippi, 1999), p. 206.
62. William Burroughs, op. cit., p. 75 and *Queer* (New York; London: Pan, 1986), p. 92.
63. Thompson, op. cit., p. 56.
64. Ibid.
65. Ibid.
66. Ibid. There are other, more worthy candidates for this lofty honour, most notably the original final scene in *Videodrome*.
67. Burroughs cited in Miles, op. cit., p. 68.
68. Dellamora, op. cit., p. 154.
69. Karen Jaehne, "David Cronenberg on William Burroughs: *Dead Ringers* Do *Naked Lunch*", *Film Quarterly* 45:3 (spring 1992), p. 4.
70. Ibid.
71. Ibid., p. 5.
72. Ibid.
73. Ibid.
74. Ibid.
75. Taubin, op. cit., p. 10.
76. Dellamora, op. cit., p. 157 and p. 154.
77. Rodley, op. cit., p. 164.
78. Ibid.
79. Cronenberg cited in Taubin, op. cit., p. 8.
80. Burroughs cited in Ira Silverberg (ed.), *Everything is Permitted: The Making of Naked Lunch* (New York: Grove Weidenfeld, 1992), p. 15.
81. Breskin, op. cit., p. 262.
82. Rodley, op. cit., p. 23.
83. Cronenberg cited in Gavin Smith, 'Cronenberg: Mind Over Matter', *Film Comment* 33:2 (March/April 1997), p. 23.
84. Cronenberg cited in Maggie Humm, 'Cronenberg's Films and Feminist Theories of Mothering', in *Feminism and Film* (Edinburgh University Press, 1997), p. 70.
85. Mark Kermode, 'David Cronenberg', *Sight and Sound* 1:11 (March 1992), p. 11.
86. Rodley, op. cit., pp. 164-5.
87. Ibid., p. 165; Breskin, op. cit., p. 262.
88. Cronenberg cited in Kermode, op. cit., p. 12.
89. Ibid.
90. Rodley, op. cit., p. 171.
91. Alfred Hitchcock, interview with François Truffaut in *Hitchcock* (New York: Simon & Schuster, 1983), p. 73.
92. Beard, op. cit., p. 280.
93. See ibid. Beard admits that 'trying to determine what is the "real" or "objective status of most of the main figures"…is a hopeless task'. (p. 155).
94. Serge Grünberg, 'Humains trop humain', *Cahiers du Cinéma* 453 (March-April 1992), p. 13.
95. Eric Mottram, *William Burroughs: The Algebra of Need* (London: Marion Boyars Publishers Ltd, 1977), p. 207.
96. Serge Grünberg, 'Sur les terres de Cronenberg', *Cahiers du Cinéma* 446 (July-August, 1991), p. 41.
97. Burroughs cited in Mottram, op. cit., p. 95.

98. Jaehne, op. cit., p. 2.
99. Ibid., p. 5.
100. Kermode, op. cit., p. 13.
101. See William Beard, op. cit., pp. 316-17.
102. Creed, op. cit., p. 96.
103. William Burroughs, *Nova Express* (New York: Grove Press, 1964), p. 153.
104. Murphy, op. cit., p. 135.
105. Gary Kimber, 'Dead Ringers', *Cinefantastique* 19: 1-2 (January, 1989), p. 87.
106. Jaehne, op. cit., p. 4.
107. Serge Grünberg, 'Humains trop humain', *Cahiers du Cinéma* 453 (March-April 1992), p. 13.
108. Ibid., p. 14.
109. Ibid., p. 10.
110. Ibid., p. 10. See William Burroughs, *Cities of the Red Night* (New York; London: Pan, 1982), p. 284.
111. William Burroughs, *The Western Lands* (New York; London: Pan, 1988), p. 258.
112. Cronenberg cited in Jaehne, op. cit., p. 2.
113. Burroughs cited in Murphy, op. cit., p. 73.
114. Ibid., p. 162.
115. Serge Grünberg, 'Sur les terres de Cronenberg', *Cahiers du Cinéma* 446 (July-August, 1991), p. 34.
116. Cronenberg cited in David Breskin, op. cit., p. 264.
117. Dellamora, op. cit., p. 159.

CHAPTER FOUR

CRASH:
'NOT A FILM ABOUT PORNOGRAPHY –
A LOVE STORY'[1]

'The world had seen so many Ages. The Age of Enlightenment; of Reformation; of Reason. Now, at last, the Age of Desire. And after this, an end to Ages; an end, perhaps, to everything'.[2]

Iain Sinclair asserts that Cronenberg's *Crash* (1996) is 'part of the heritaging of Ballard; making his subversion safe'.[3] However, rather than neutralizing his influences, I would suggest that Cronenberg fulfils and develops them, so that, according to Harold Bloom's categories of influence, the film of *Crash* could be classified as a *tessera*, a work that '"completes" his precursor'.[4] Ballard's statement that 'Cronenberg began the film where my novel ended' and 'that which remains latent in the novel becomes overt in the film', would suggest that this is how he views the film too.[5] Much of the critical energy in Sinclair's book on the film *Crash* is devoted to background and autobiographical material and useful though that is, there has still been very little sustained analysis of exactly how J. G. Ballard's novel of *Crash* (1973), *The Atrocity Exhibition* (1969) or his short stories, relate *directly* to Cronenberg's project.

Linda Kauffman wonders '[w]ere David Cronenberg and J. G. Ballard separated at birth? Like the twins in *Dead Ringers*, both began their careers as medical students; both are fascinated with anatomy, biology, sexuality, and postmodern post-mortems'.[6] Paralleling Cronenberg's academic path, Ballard switched from medicine at Cambridge to English at London University (although he only studied for a year) and while Ballard rejected the novelization of *Alien* (Ridley Scott, 1979), Cronenberg turned down the offer to direct *Alien Resurrection* (Jean-Philippe Jeunet, 1997).[7] To minimise confusion, I shall use the term 'Ballard' to refer to the author J. G. Ballard and 'James' when referring to the fictional character James Ballard in the novel or film versions of *Crash*. Ballard himself usually refers to the film carefully as 'Cronenberg's *Crash*' but is slightly more generous in his praise for the adaptation[8] than Burroughs' refusal to be drawn into a judgement of Cronenberg's *Naked Lunch*.

'A surprisingly tight and straightforward adaptation'[9]
(alterations and additions to Ballard's *Crash*)

Stuart Laing asserts that 'all the main characters retain their structural positions in the plot and patterns of character involvement', and William Beard believes that 'the film is actually quite faithful to the slim narrative content of Ballard's book', but this is far too simplistic.[10] According to Sinclair, Cronenberg's strategy in realizing Ballard's novel is very straightforward: 'rely on memory, retype the novel, strip out the Elizabeth Taylor element, the London particulars, and nudge the sexual polarity back towards James and Catherine Ballard'.[11] These shifts of emphasis are true as far as they go but there is more to say here.

As with all the chapters in this book, it is very important to look closely at both literary source and film. As John Ellis notes, 'the adaptation trades upon the memory of the novel, a memory that can derive from actual reading, or as is more likely with a classic of literature, a generally circulated cultural memory'.[12] Michael Delville's study *J. G. Ballard* (1998), which does not mention Cronenberg at all, even in passing, seems to contain just such a case of Cronenberg's more recent film 'overstamping' memories of Ballard's original source novel. Although discussing the book rather than the film, Delville recounts James and Catherine's act of describing to each other 'their recent and future infidelities while having sexual intercourse' as a 'daily ritual'.[13] However, in the book Ballard only mentions the *general* tendency to share infidelities to add sexual spice to their relationship.[14] The third scene of the film, where James and Catherine compare sexual notes, draws on a scene towards the close of Ballard's novel, when Catherine starts to tell James about Vaughan following her. He finds himself 'slipping into the same erotic reverie in which I sometimes used to question Catherine about the flight instructor she lunched with, drawing one detail after another about some small amorous encounter'.[15]

Sinclair notes omissions from Ballard's novel but strangely asserts 'nothing is added', apparently neglecting (amongst other features) the James Dean crash scene, the tattooing and the ending.[16] One reason for this glossing over of difference is due to Cronenberg's method of adaptation. There is relatively little direct speech in Ballard's novel and Cronenberg's solution is to lift passages of James' stream of consciousness straight into dialogue, e.g. '[a]fter being bombarded endlessly by road-safety propaganda it was almost a relief to find myself in an actual accident'.[17] Beard claims that 'Cronenberg has resisted any temptation to port Ballard's virtuoso descriptions and elaborate perceptions over into the script', but, in fact,

Cronenberg's faithfulness to Ballard's novel even extends to using exactly the same metaphors and similes through the entire screenplay.[18] For example, at the hospital, Vaughan's scars are described 'as though residues from some terrifying act of violence'.[19] This virtual word-for-word borrowing is most obvious in passages of poetic description, such as Ballard's 'chromium bower' image in the car wash scene and at times, it is tempting to agree with the spirit of Sinclair's reservations about Cronenberg's originality.[20]

Bart Testa feels the 'narrative throughline is extremely feeble' and the 'handling of Ballard's conception...is way too elliptical'.[21] By its very nature, any film lasting only 96 minutes is likely to be elliptical compared to the prose source from which it is derived. Gene Walz asserts that he is 'not enough the engaged storyteller' and Sinclair claims that Cronenberg's version 'scrupulously avoids drama',[22] but the film is concerned with a different kind of existential, internal drama, not the obvious external variety of car chases and spectacle. Brian McIlroy's attempts to dismiss 'the film's emotional coldness' are rather undermined by the admission 'I suppose I should read the book'.[23]

Fred Botting and Scott Wilson's argument that 'the deficiency that determines his (Vaughan's) obsession', i.e. hints that he may have been castrated in a former crash, are flawed. To criticize Koteas' performance as 'so excessive' whereby 'he evokes incredulity, and fails to provide the point of identification that could enliven his project for a cinema audience', assumes the kind of classical Hollywood product of suture that Cronenberg is precisely at pains to avoid.[24] They implicitly acknowledge this by noting how 'the wounds, bruises and scars repeatedly thrust by the camera into watching faces serve to abject, rather than incorporate or elevate, the look' and they recognize that 'the car crashes do not take place as part of a compelling narrative'.[25] Stylistically and technically, they assert that *Crash* refuses to evoke the sensational and spectacular effects that one would expect: 'no big bangs, no sensuous slow-motion smashes, no romantic chases or erotic duels', although the last point is debatable bearing in mind the exchange between the three protagonists and the final scene.[26]

In Ballard's novel, Helen changes careers from immigration at the airport to a medical officer at The Road Research Laboratory, making the trajectory of her character motivation slightly clearer than Cronenberg's film, which omits this link. In Ballard's novel, both Catherine in the showroom scene and later Helen whilst being driven by James, recognize that he has bought exactly the same car.[27] Cronenberg reduces repetition, using the second example only, allowing him to save the showroom scene for Gabrielle later. Ballard's passages of drug-induced transcendence where the expressway is translated into a symbolic landscape are also cut from Cronenberg's film. Perhaps having covered the extreme subjectivity of *Naked Lunch*, Cronenberg did not want to muddy the metaphorical waters and possibly create sympathy or empathy for his protagonists whom he keeps detached from one another throughout.

Cronenberg also makes changes between his published screenplay and the finished film, which fall into specific areas. Superfluous plot details disappear, such as details of Helen's husband's job and Catherine's flying lessons and peripheral characters, like Renata and Karen, are pared down, so as to focus on a smaller group of key figures. Elements from Ballard's *Crash* are condensed. Cronenberg replaces Catherine making up James' face with a scene of soulless masturbation whilst Catherine describes the state of his car after the accident. This uses dialogue from slightly later in the script, in an equivalent of 'talking dirty', prefiguring the later scene in their flat. Dialogue which is too literal, such as James' outburst at Vaughan the first time he chases Catherine in the Lincoln and Vaughan's explanation that she finds such acts exciting, is also cut from the finished film.

Scenes featuring Catherine and her secretary, Karen, trying on underwear, whilst being watched by James, also disappear. For Sinclair, these were only ever part of 'a chain of erotic encounters' and would have distracted attention away from James' growing consciousness as Vaughan's disciple.[28] However, Cronenberg displaces the male voyeuristic viewer of lesbian desire (James) in a clothes shop to the omniscient audience view (although still associated with a male fantasy) of the back seat of a crashed car and from Catherine and Karen to Helen and Gabrielle as they embrace in the breaker's yard. In the novel, James' sex acts with Helen are contextualized as part of 'a period of unthinking promiscuity through which most people pass after a bereavement', as part of an attempt to bring her dead husband back to life.[29] In Cronenberg's film, James just becomes one in a long line of fairly nondescript sexual partners, whom Helen recalls by occupation only. Like the series of stalking incidents at the close of Ballard's novel between Vaughan and Catherine, Cronenberg selects one typical example from a series.

'Sadism demands a story'[30]
(Cronenberg's *Crash* as a Sadean text)
According to Ballard himself, we should 'think of the film as straightforwardly Sadean', but it is ambiguous how we might see Sadean influences in *Crash* as 'straightforward'.[31] In Volume I of *A History of Sexuality*, Michel Foucault discusses 'the modern compulsion to speak incessantly about sex', seeking to translate 'every desire, into discourse'.[32] This urge to talk about sex serves three main purposes within Cronenberg's *Crash*: to arouse a listener deliberately (in both an immediate situation and possibly to imitate an action described), to reflect a prurient interest in the sex lives of others, and to show the inability of language to appropriate fully the experience of sexual desire. In the first three scenes, Cronenberg's *Crash* would appear to offer a sensual overload, as we first see sex acts *and* hear them described afterwards. In Ballard's novel of *Crash*, Catherine's 'erotic interest in her secretary seemed an interest as much in the idea of making love to her as in the physical pleasures of the sex act itself', to the extent that sexual climax becomes impossible without linguistic foreplay.[33] In Cronenberg's *Crash*, talking about sex becomes a matter of foreplay (the third scene where James and Catherine 'compare notes')

and stimulation during sex (James and Catherine in their apartment), echoing de Sade's maxim that 'the sensations communicated by the ear are the most enjoyable and have the keenest impact'.[34]

It is almost as if sexual acts cannot take place unless they are described beforehand and afterwards. Stephen Pfohl notes how de Sade's libertines are busy 'describing everything, counting everything, leaving nothing unclassified, unspoken or uncontrolled'.[35] In Cronenberg's Naked Lunch, what critics like William Beard see as complicity between sexual desire and misogynistic violence in the Mugwump's prurient prompting to Lee not to 'leave out any of the tasty details' in the shooting of Joan, might also be seen as the use of language as a catalyst for desire by creating piecemeal images to fantasize about. In Dead Ringers, it is the retelling of the encounters that really excites Elly, and Bev's unwillingness to do this marks a significant breach in their relationship. It is the recounting afterwards of 'all the juicy details' that appears to be more stimulating than the act itself and also appears to validate its reality to the point where if an event is not shared, i.e. verbalized, it has not fully existed: 'You haven't had her until you've told me about it'.

Prurience and arousal are easily interwoven. For de Sade, '[y]our narrations must be decorated with the most numerous and searching details'.[36] In Dead Ringers, Elliot says if Beverly refuses to take his place with Claire, he will do terrible things to her. Beverly is suddenly curious and asks 'What terrible things?' We assume Elliot must have explained the details, judging from the cut to the following scene of Claire tied up with a man whom she thinks is Elliot (but really Beverly). In Lolita, Humbert does not passively accept Lolita's description of the sexual acts she and Quilty have performed ('weird, fancy, filthy things'), pressing her to verbalize this more precisely: 'What things exactly?'[37] Karen Jaehne recounts a scene cut from Dead Ringers, in which Claire demands a 'chemistry set', which might equally refer to the medical devices they use as sex aids or her drug habit.[38] Elliot warns her, 'You're going to come apart in a million pieces' to which she replies, 'Does that excite you?'

In Ballard's Crash, linguistic foreplay develops to the extent that 'these descriptions seemed to be a language in search of objects, or even, perhaps, the beginnings of a new sexuality divorced from any possible physical expression'.[39] For Pierre Klossowski, 'ecstasy cannot be conveyed by language; what language describes is the way to it, the dispositions that prepare for it', so that 'for the reader there remains only the reiteration described and the wholly exterior aspect of the ecstasy, the orgasm described, which is counterfeit ecstasy'.[40] This also prefigures the scene in Crash, where we come to the sexual exchange between Ballard and Helen in media res where Helen's recounting of her sexual history (an addition by Cronenberg to his source novel) has both acted as a stimulus to the act but in a sense is needed to complete the act, to complete this particular story. The immediate continuation of a post-coital conversation and the matter-of-fact dressing places the sexual exchange as a brief punctuation of little significance, in which neither character seems particularly interested. Rather than being an example of *coitus interruptus*, this uses a sexual act function as an example of *fabula interruptus*, as a narrative is broken by an event of apparently lesser importance. What has just taken place in the car is immediately placed as the most recent segment of an ongoing narrative. There seems to be a constant desire for characters to place themselves and events in a narrative, as if without this, identities drift aimlessly seeking attachment to some person, place or action.

Angela Carter muses on the similarity of Marilyn Monroe and de Sade's Justine: '[s]ee how alike they look! Marilyn Monroe, the living image of Justine; both have huge, appealing, eloquent eyes...their dazzling fair skins are of such a delicate texture that they look as if they will bruise at a touch, carrying the exciting stigmata of sexual violence for a long time'.[41] Cronenberg conflates Monroe and de Sade's Justine in his realization of Catherine Ballard. His comparison of James and Catherine claiming Vaughan's Lincoln with the fantasy of claiming Monroe's body[42] also echoes Clive Barker's 'Son of Celluloid', where the hero, Ricky, has a vision of Marilyn Monroe and feels immediate desire for her: '[w]hat the hell if she was just a fiction: fictions are fuckable if you don't want marriage'.[43] This may partly explain the switch of Hollywood icons from the raven-haired Elizabeth Taylor to the blond Mansfield and changing Catherine from a brunette in the published screenplay to a blond. Ballard's *Crash* opens with Vaughan's death, his car having only narrowly avoided the limousine of Elizabeth Taylor. She watches the carnage and 'as I knelt over Vaughan's body, she place a gloved hand to her throat'.[44] Cronenberg cuts Taylor as a figure linked to a particular chronological era and displaces her fetishized clothing onto Helen and Gabrielle. The gesture of touching one's own neck, which Ballard links with Taylor in the novel, is translated into the rough caress favoured by Vaughan in the sex scenes with the prostitute and later with Catherine in the car wash.

In discussing the car wash scene, Creed feels that 'unlike the anal sex scenes (which almost always commence with the woman offering her breast to the man), and the episode of "wound" sex, this one is not only "disconnected", it is sadistic'.[45] However, Catherine *does* offer her breast as before, her lengthy staring at Vaughan in the car does indicate attraction, and what Creed sees as a weakness, dismissing the scene as 'sadistic', is arguably a crucial point for Ballard and Cronenberg. For them, Creed's criticism, that 'the possibility of union between human and machine is displaced, in the main, on to the woman's body', represents a creative development in the range of human sexuality in which concepts of gender seem less important than a potential fusion with technology.[46] Similarly, Creed describes the parrot cage scene in Cronenberg's *Naked Lunch* (1991) as 'horrific and sadistic', but this is attributing to the characters the emotions of this particular viewer.[47] Sadism can be pleasurable and it is ambiguous whether Kiki is either horrified or that he is being 'raped' as Creed asserts.

Klossowski notes how 'the pervert pursues the performance of one sole gesture; it is done in a moment. The pervert's existence becomes the constant waiting for the moment in which this gesture can be performed'.[48] As Amelie wishes to be destroyed by Borchamps in *120 Days of Sodom*, 'to be the cause of a crime in her death', so Vaughan yearns for extinction by crashing with screen icon Elizabeth Taylor.[49] The Ballards' search for the perfect moment of sexual affirmation ('Maybe the next one…') that becomes entwined with Vaughan's dream death-crash ('Maybe the next time…').

Crash divides critics in the impact of its eroticism. Susie Bright feels it 'shows us what pornography might look like if it were made with imagination, intelligence and daring', and Sinclair claims that Cronenberg 'makes pornography safe and elegant'.[50] Conversely, Testa sees *Crash* as 'a cynical, flat, inert set of tableaux that are not even sexually interesting'.[51] However, what he identifies as structural weaknesses are precisely those generic cinematic tropes associated with pornography *and* Sadean narratives: 'the film's structure is serial: one sex scene after another with clunky dialogue scenes seeming to interrupt the sex scenes to provide the film with a "philosophy."'[52] As Steven Marcus expresses it, '[t]he ideal pornographic novel…would go on forever'.[53] The experience of reading Sadean texts reflects much critical reaction to *Crash*: 'although they contain a wealth of pornographic and sadistic detail, they are not sexually arousing…and many readers see the texts as too rambling and boring to warrant careful study'.[54]

As Carter notes, de Sade 'rarely, if ever, makes sexual activity seem attractive as such,' and Testa's complaints about philosophical interruptions are a little odd as it is the long ruminations about the significance of the traffic, which Cronenberg has cut from Ballard's novel (possibly suggesting that Testa has not read it).[55] As Jane Gallop notes, 'de Sade alternately presents pornographic scenes and philosophical harangues. The result of this mixture is that each undercuts the other'.[56] Cronenberg cut most of Ballard's sententious passages, apart from Vaughan's explanation of his project to James whilst driving. In a sense, unlike de Sade and disciples like Klossowski whose novels 'juxtapose graphic sexual description and scholastic, theological debate', Cronenberg extracts overt philosophical statements from his narratives and puts them instead in interviews.[57] In this way, reading illustrated articles about *Crash* often evokes Sadean narrative structure with erotic pictures juxtaposed with philosophical text.

Is *Crash* pornographic?
Kauffman describes de Palma's *Body Double* (1984) as 'a textbook example of how *not* to make a porno film', and 'by satirising porn's clichés, de Palma thwarts the viewer's pleasure'.[58] Kauffman's proposed guidelines for making such an 'anti-film' involve revealing the mechanics of film production, using multi-layered references to films-within-the film and feminizing the hero.[59] *Videodrome* clearly has references to the TV industry in Max's low-life cable channel, repeatedly uses the

TV screen as a means to convey hallucinations and focuses on a hero who develops a vaginal slit in his stomach. However Crash also features a protagonist who directs TV commercials, who watches tapes of slow-motion crashes with his newly found friends and has a hero in James, who is softly spoken, dominated (sexually) by an older man and seems unable (and unwilling) to stop Vaughan in his death mission. Although it could be seen as debatable to ascribe the adjective 'feminine' to some of these latter features, there is still enough material here to suggest that, according to Kauffman's definition, both Videodrome and Crash could be seen as 'anti-porn' films and certainly this is how Cronenberg views the latter film, describing it as 'anti-pornographic'.[60] Vladimir Nabokov, like Cronenberg, denies the viewer the prurient pleasures of sexual gazing that his texts appear to offer, describing Lolita as 'the copulation of clichés'.[61]

In analysing Hollywood musicals, Richard Dyer has suggested three types of narrative forms that might apply equally to pornography: texts that separate the narrative from the number; those that work to integrate the two through devices designed to mask the transition like verbal cues; and those that dissolve the gap between number and narrative.[62] Crash aspires towards the third category, but the generic expectations appear to condition audiences (and critics) to see pornographic sequences only as interludes between more weighty narrative sections. Part of the criteria, by which a genre picture is judged to be a commercial and critical success, is its ability to integrate its key generic elements with the cultural expectations of narrative. Hence, Linda Williams suggests parallels between the sex scenes in a porn film and the song and dance numbers in a musical in which both kinds of 'routine' are used to solve underlying narrative problems, 'through the relation of number to narrative and number to number'.[63] She takes this further to suggest that, metaphorically, masturbation is represented by solo songs, straight sex is like a classic heterosexual duet, and orgies are ensemble numbers.[64] In this sense, Cronenberg's Crash is like a series of duets (with minor variations), each ending on a note of incompleteness apart from the scene between Catherine and James in their apartment.

The conventional soundtrack of sex acts in pornographic films is also missing in Cronenberg's Crash. There are no orgasmic moans, partly because only on two occasions, in the apartment scene between James and Catherine and the car wash scene with Catherine, Vaughan (and James as driver), do we see the sex act to any sense of completion. In mainstream pornography, most cries are usually female and function as 'aural fetishes of the female pleasures we cannot see'.[65] Unlike conventional porn, there are no actively involved third parties (only James as voyeuristic driver with Vaughan, first with a prostitute and then with Catherine and the 'talking dirty' scene between James and Catherine with Vaughan as the verbally present third party); all sex acts are essentially between couples in enclosed spaces.

In Ballard's *Crash*, while the narrator describes Vaughan's sexual arousal at watching crash tests in person, in Cronenberg's film this is displaced to a scene of group masturbation in which the viewing of test crashes is experienced as repeatable pleasure (present in the novel through more primitive Ampex machines) as the group mesmerically watch videos at Seagrave's flat.[66] The choice of removing the sight of Vaughan masturbating could be calculated to avoid the social stigma still attached to such activity in mainstream heterosexual culture. By contrast, Cronenberg adds a scene of James being masturbated by Catherine in the hospital and a shot at the end of the film where James is stroking Catherine at the car pound. This seems even-handed (so to speak) but, in each case, the additions and omissions remove references that might damage the status of male characters and appear to enhance the viewing pleasure of a heterosexual male audience, such as the inclusion of the fantasy of an intimate 'bed-bath' in a public place. At the pound, Catherine is shown in thrall to her lover and if Cronenberg had wanted to accord female pleasure the same level of filmic status as male, then he could have retained references in Ballard's novel to Catherine masturbating, which do not appear in the film at all.[67] Victor Sage strangely misreads the final scene in the film, describing how Catherine 'masturbates against the blunt knife-edge of the car's window frame'.[68] Perhaps this is a scene which this viewer feels *should* be there.

'The death of affect'[69]
(the scarcity of jouissance in Cronenberg's *Crash*)
Much criticism of both Ballard and Cronenberg assumes a conventional model of mimetic naturalism that both men are at pains to subvert. Delville points out that Ballard is engaged in 'a deliberate attempt to depict a society which is essentially post-emotional, one in which human beings emerge as strangely distanced and detached observers of their own affectless condition', and Sinclair describes Cronenberg's film as 'an elegy to boredom, loss, futility...'[70] In an analogous text, *The Kindness of Women* (1992), Ballard recounts a trip to a Soho nightclub, where he watches strippers go through their routines. He confesses that 'the strippers seemed to parade their sexual possibilities with all the fervour of anatomy demonstrators in a dissecting-room taking their students through the urino-genital system'.[71] In retrospect, 'it was this stylisation of sex that most appealed...not the act itself'.[72]

Ironically, what is seen as a critical deficiency is at the heart of Cronenberg's aesthetic here: absence is not a flaw, it is what *Crash* is about. The hospital ward in which James finds himself is 'permanently reserved for the possible victims of an air-crash', a Foucault-influenced image of human existence as a hospital ward, an accident waiting to happen.[73] Carl's fate in *Naked Lunch* is described as 'an example of prison-hospital humiliation, a mere specimen whose semen is used for experiment', and James' hospital experience, particularly (and literally) at the hands of Catherine with her apparently uninvolved masturbatory bed-bath and her verbally flat delivery, casts him almost in the role of sperm donor.[74]

Cronenberg's protagonists, despite their numerous sex acts, seem to gain only limited satisfaction from them. Following de Sade's libertines who perform sexual acts 'in absolute apathy', both Ballard and Cronenberg include a sudden jump into a sex act between Helen and James *in media res* as she asks 'Have you come?'[75] His non-commital answer would seem to indicate that he has not. In a change from Ballard's novel, Cronenberg's first dialogue between James and Catherine emphasizes that neither achieved orgasm and the impression of the first three scenes is an almost desperate seeking after novelty as a catalyst to what is really lacking: desire.

The Atrocity Exhibition
(narrative structures, parallel scenes and plot-line echoes)
It has largely gone unnoticed that Ballard's collection *The Atrocity Exhibition* (1969) is closer to the structure of Cronenberg's film than the novel of *Crash*. The earlier work is constructed in sections, equivalent to related short stories rather than chapters in a novel and each section is composed of a series of separated paragraphs, each with a sub-heading in bold.[76] This kind of structuring creates a tableau-based narrative, constructed of juxtaposed episodes that have some links in terms of suggestion and allusion, rather than a more conventional sequential narrative.

Coherence is created in this literary montage by games with names, such as the protagonist in the different sections being variously named Travers, Travis, Tallis, Traven (amongst others). Victor Sage asserts that the disruption of a linear narrative means that 'people die before and after they are dead. Death is conceptual', which Cronenberg picks up in Seagrave's playing dead in the Dean crash reconstruction and then really dying in a pre-emptive reconstruction of the Mansfield crash.[77] T. (as Gregory Stephenson calls him) is pursued by two figures, a bomber pilot and a disfigured woman.[78] In the novel of *Crash*, Ballard slims this down by removing the pilot and making scarification an interest of all the main characters. Cronenberg continues this distillation by condensing the characters of Catherine Austin and Karen Novotny (both glacial heroines, unmoved by the sex acts they perform) into the figure of Catherine Ballard. Cronenberg also appropriates sententious passages of explanatory dialogue almost verbatim, e.g. 'the car crash is seen as a fertilising rather than a destructive experience...mediating the sexuality of those who have died with an erotic intensity impossible in any other form'.[79]

Cronenberg also lifts passages of descriptive prose straight from *The Atrocity Exhibition* into his stage directions in *Crash*. The scene where James gently touches Catherine's body after the rough sexual interlude in the car wash, derives directly from an isolated incident in *The Atrocity Exhibition*, where Nathan tentatively examines an anonymous, but similarly bruised, sexual partner of Travers: '[y]et something about the precise cross-hatching suggested that their true role lay elsewhere'.[80] Nathan struggles to explain this to Catherine watching disinterestedly by the window: '[h]e was trying to make contact with her, but in a new way'.[81] The scene with the airport prostitute in Cronenberg's *Crash* is anticipated as Travers describes how he had watched Vaughan pick up two teenage girls and then 'grappling with them in a series of stylised holds. During this exercise in the back seat his morose eyes had stared at Travers through the driving mirror with a deliberate irony'.[82] Cronenberg retains the voyeuristic elements of the scene but cuts the reciprocal gaze, reduces the number of prostitutes from two to one and greatly downplays the clear signals in Ballard of non-consensual sexual violence (the girls are 'almost raped' in Ballard's version).[83]

In Ballard's novel, Vaughan's enigmatic rejoinder 'the case could be made' does *not* follow his speech about 'benevolent psychopathology' as in Cronenberg's film. It follows James' question, 'I take it that you see Kennedy's assassination as a special kind of car-crash?'[84] For Ballard, the iconography that surrounds Kennedy exercises a particular fascination, reflected in other work such as 'The Assassination of Kennedy Considered as a Downhill Motor Race' in *The Atrocity Exhibition* and his use of a Lincoln as the prime showpiece in his 1969 'Crashed Cars' exhibition in Camden. Cronenberg retains the Lincoln but refocuses on philosophy rather than specific cultural icons, so that it is the existential question of existence, which Vaughan pursues in the film, rather than a particular impact with a specific screen icon, Elizabeth Taylor. By dropping Taylor, Sinclair suggests Cronenberg's film 'is left with a lacuna at its centre'.[85] However, the change from Taylor to Mansfield still evokes an era of iconographic Hollywood stars and usefully evokes stronger associations of female commodification than acting ability. Mansfield is mentioned several times in *The Atrocity Exhibition* as one of a list of celebrities, with whom Travis becomes increasingly obsessed, along with Dean, Camus and Kennedy, whose presence is signalled in the film by Vaughan's Lincoln.[86]

'Myths of the Near Future'
(further parallel scenes and plot-line echoes)

Sinclair notes in passing the debt that Cronenberg's *Crash* owes to *The Atrocity Exhibition* but other Ballard pieces are relevant too. In *The Kindness of Women*, Ballard's autobiographical sequel to *Empire of the Sun*, we find the clear inspiration for the automotive duelling scenes between Catherine and Vaughan, which do not appear in the novel of *Crash* and which Cronenberg directly appropriates, without apparent acknowledgement. Two of Ballard's personal acquaintances, Sally Mumford and David Hunter, indulge in a game of hide-and-seek ('We pretend to crash into each other').[87] Like Sally, Cronenberg has Catherine drive a small sports car and his depiction of Vaughan's death is explicitly prefigured in *The Kindness of Women* in a chase sequence between Ballard and Sally, where her MG is deliberately rammed and then careers off the road.[88]

In *The Kindness of Women*, there is also a sexual exchange between Sally and Ballard himself, strongly evoking Cronenberg's scene of Catherine and James together in their apartment, during which she describes a future crash scenario and directs the course of his fantasizing: 'Jim, one day we'll be in a crash together. I'd like that…think about it now for me'.[89] Cronenberg reconfigures this scene with Catherine and James and picks up the sense of 'think about it now for me' in the dual sense of James taking ownership of this fantasy instead of Sally and that she finds the notion of him thinking such thoughts arousing.

In 'The Sign of the Stripper' section of the short story 'Zodiac 2000' (1982), Ballard reprises and condenses many of the motifs from *Crash*. The protagonist, Professor Rotblat, becomes drawn into a world of 'hoodlum physicists', by a sinister character called Heller who shows 'frightening violence as he grappled with the young whores in the back of the sports car' with 'assaults as stylised as ballet movements'.[90] They visit 'airport cargo bays' and join a bored audience watching a jaded sex act in a strip club, featuring a woman called Renata. As she leaves the stage, she shows the evidence of male sexual pleasure, semen, to the audience and Ballard instructs us that 'in the codes of Renata's body…waited the possibilities of a benevolent psychopathology'.[91] Although Cronenberg cuts Renata from his version of *Crash*, he transposes the action described here onto the character of Catherine.

Artifice and the crash site

Cronenberg denies us one of the sources of consolation that Jean-Paul Sartre grants his hero in *Nausea* (1938), where Roquentin finds some relief from his sense of life's absurdity in art, particularly music. For Cronenberg, Howard Shore's music is crucial. In *Naked Lunch*, the immediate aftermath of the William Tell routine and Joan's death is accompanied by a sweeping orchestral score, which, although melancholic, could be intended to move the viewer in a conventional fashion to empathize with the characters and Bill in particular. The rarity of this effect in *Naked Lunch*, the vast majority of incidental music being jazz, might suggest that it is at relatively rare moments of insight our feelings are meant to coincide with those of the protagonists, i.e. that there are certain human experiences and emotions that transcend the immediately subjective and reach out to a more metaphysical realm, most obviously the death or near-death of a loved one.

Bernard Herrman's score for *Psycho* (Alfred Hitchcock, 1960), particularly when Marion Crane (Janet Leigh) desperately journeys out of town, unknowingly on the way to the Bates Motel, powerfully evokes the driving rain, the action of the car and the claustrophobic desperation of the heroine. Like Herrman's score here, Howard Shore's main theme in *Crash* uses 4/4 time, an ostinato rhythm and is constructed with the same undulating semitone motifs that deny a sense of resolution at the end of each musical unit. Having studied classical guitar himself for eleven years, Cronenberg would appreciate such devices, particularly in relation to *Crash*, which uses electric guitar for the main theme.[92] Apparently unwittingly, Sinclair senses this aural kinship in describing Shore's use of 'edgy (but minimalist) aural motifs, in the way that Bernard Herrmann used to doctor mood for Hitchcock', and in relation to an earlier film, Beard mentions, 'just as Bernard Herrmann understood *Psycho* better than anybody...as fundamentally a foreclosed and deeply sad work...so Howard Shore understands *Dead Ringers*'.[93]

The mesmerizing fascination of the crash appears in one of Cronenberg's Nabokovian influences. Vaughan-like, Lolita studies 'the photographic results of head-on collisions', and she 'silently stared, with other motorists and their children, at some smashed, blood-bespattered car with a young woman's shoe in the ditch'.[94] In *The Kindness of Women*, in a description of an actual car crash, two real-life acquaintances of Ballard also provide the template for both James' initial accident with Helen and the pile-up sequence in both novel and film version of *Crash*. In Ballard's novel, it is the female victim's legs, rather than her breasts, which are consciously and provocatively exposed but there is the same sense of stylization, the 'self-conscious pose, like dancers arrested in an audience-catching flourish at the end of their performance'.[95] Cronenberg chooses not to make the metaphor quite as obvious as Ballard who describes here a crowd of spectators, some with cine-cameras, to the extent that 'a new kind of street theatre had been born', but instead he regards 'the car as mobile theatre'.[96]

Ballard's gradual approach towards the site of an accident evokes the fictional overtones that Cronenberg uses in his version of the pile-up sequence in *Crash*: 'we moved forward, waved on in a theatrical way by a police patrolman, as if we were film extras late for the day's shooting'.[97] Likewise, Vaughan's stolen snaps of crash victims' injuries that he is so eagerly clutching when he first reaches James, build into the storyboards we see in his workroom in Seagraves' house. The motorway pile-up seems to suggest a film set, rather than a real accident site and not just because of Seagrave's reconstruction of the Mansfield crash. Sinclair describes the film as 'a low-key fashion shoot', and, as James' car slows in the traffic, Vaughan is already craning out of the car for the best shots and, later, as Catherine sits next to an accident victim, she takes on the appearance of a bored extra, smoking and mimicking the movements and gestures of the woman, before being called to take her part in Vaughan's bizarre photo-assignment.[98] In the original novel, Vaughan's status as an actor/director is made more explicit: 'Vaughan was dramatising himself for the benefit of these anonymous passers-by' and 'the frustrated actor was evident in all his impulsive movements.'[99] Cronenberg articulates this by less direct means. In casting Koteas in the role of Vaughan, he uses an actor with an uncanny resemblance to the quintessential Method actor of our times, often associated with an obsessive level of preparation for roles: Robert de Niro.

The notion that the Dean crash reconstruction is a wholly original addition to Ballard's novel of *Crash* is a little misleading. Dean's iconic power to evoke a specific fictional milieu of Hollywood death crash, the destruction of an icon of misunderstood youth and emergent sexuality, permeates much of Ballard's fiction. In *The Kindness of Women*, the young Jim Ballard describes his delight, during his childhood in Shanghai, at seeing 'thrillingly rehearsed accidents' by 'a troupe of American dare-devil drivers'.[100] Years later in London, in 1969, he goes on to describe the spectacle of a demolition derby show, in which 'the advertised highlight of the afternoon was the recreation of a spectacular road accident'.[101] In *The Atrocity Exhibition*, Travers creates a dramatic commentary on six possible versions of 'the imaginary sex death of Che Guevara' including 'auto-deaths'.[102]

The actual crash reconstruction is skipped over in the novel, which jumps to 'twenty minutes later' as the protagonists are driving an injured Seagrave to hospital (moved by Cronenberg to Vaughan's flat).[103] In Ballard's novel, an anonymous announcer converts the test into entertainment by adopting the style of the showman as, through a loudspeaker, he 'jocularly introduced the occupants of the car: "Charlie and Greta, imagine them out for a drive with the kids, Sean and Brigitte..."'.[104] Cronenberg transfers this notion of reconstruction as packaged entertainment by the style of Vaughan as ringmaster and the momentary suspense (at the track and in the film theatre) about whether Seagrave as Turnupseed has actually injured himself or not.

The crash we see involving James and Helen is the *only* genuine crash we see in the whole film. Vaughan aspires towards a particularly spectacular death but it is one of his making, i.e. he is attempting to impose his will through a manipulated fiction to create his own future. It is the very *fictionality* of his life, which is alienating for a cinematic audience (not, as Botting and Wilson assert, due to faults in Koteas' acting). As an obsessive fan/stalker, his credibility is weakened by being so obsessed with the deaths of stars, who themselves were only actors in other people's fictions. He appears to be unable to distinguish between the actors and the parts they played despite the fact that from his own reconstructions he knows that actors are not 'real'. If these reconstructions were not meticulously planned to preserve the drivers' safety, then there would be no need for him to aspire to a final end with a real film star as death would come sooner or later anyway.

Vaughan's claim that his staging of the crash represents 'the ultimate in authenticity' is flawed since clearly this is a reconstruction of an event, not the event itself but, also, because unless Dean was trying to commit suicide, the original action was unintentional, an accident, which cannot ever be re-created because it was unpremeditated. For everyone but those involved in the crash itself, the event only assumes importance as it is re-created and re-performed. Vaughan's 'Was I glib?' sounds closer to a self-conscious and rather pretentious thespian than a figure pursuing a more scientific 'project'.

In the film, the side-on camera position of the James Dean crash shows the cars back up, before racing forward to meet one another, in effect performing a video rewind in real time. Cronenberg extends this idea in a scene, not in Ballard's original novel or the published screenplay, as new and old crash devotees watch a safety video. Transfixed, as the tape is rewound over and over, Helen, in particular, loses track of time and space. When the tape jumps, she mimics its movement suddenly standing and stumbling forward drunkenly, almost crashing into a glass table. The clumsiness of this action, her fumbling with the remote control and her repeated demands to replay 'this tape', all betray a reversion to childish behaviour, where a known narrative is demanded again and again for comfort and security, i.e. a character uses a fiction to subvert chronology.

Progression or Repetition?
(the significance of narrative structure and the denouement)

In the 'Atrophied Preface', ironically placed at the end of the novel, Burroughs claims that 'you can cut into *Naked Lunch* at any intersection point' and 'the pieces can be had in any order being tied up back and forth like an innaresting sex arrangement' (*sic*).[105] Sinclair asserts that the narrative in *Crash* 'has no beginning, no end. It goes on forever, unresolved, unemphatic' and 'what has happened once will happen again, the forward momentum disappears into its own shadow. You are going nowhere. You can enter the dream at any point'.[106] Much criticism of *Crash* has concluded that 'the banality of its narrative drive fails to direct us towards anything other than a disappointing and unresolved denouement', thereby echoing responses to Eliot's *The Waste Land*, that 'it exhibits no progression', and 'the poem ends where it began.'[107] At the close of *Crash*, Cronenberg places his protagonist apparently performing similar actions, so that on the surface little appears to have changed. Bouquet asserts that '*Crash* is thus a film constructed on repetition, but a repetition that is undramatic, non-progressive, serial.'[108]

However, techniques associated with Eliot, such as 'indirection and all forms of emotional reticence, notably those of irony, symbolic association, and antithetic metaphor (catachresis)', could equally apply to Cronenberg's *Crash*.[109] For example, we cut from Helen sitting astride James in an airport car park to Catherine in a similar position with James in their flat, suggesting, if not some causal link, then at least some incorporation of Helen into James' fantasy life (and possibly Catherine's, if the experience is shared).

Equally, repetition also brings us back to de Sade, whose 'obsessive additions, variations, repetitions, permutations' create what Ihab Hassan describes in an ironic echo of Burroughs, 'an algebra of coitus'.[110] Cronenberg's use of incremental repetition can be seen in the opening three scenes. The first scene features impersonal sex between Catherine and an unnamed lover in an aircraft hanger. The second shows James and an unnamed girl but this time the lover is given a function (a 'camera girl', i.e. part of James' public role of making commercial fictions, safety videos), limited dialogue is included and there is an explicit link made with cars. The third scene conveys how the two protagonists compare notes and incorporate their fantasy in their own sexual exchanges. It appears that *jouissance* is available but only in a limited form and only by the anticipation and re-enacting of experience, rather than any spontaneous act itself. Cronenberg himself has explicitly underlined the importance of these scenes: 'the sex scenes are *absolutely* the plot and the character development'.[111]

In *The Last Words of Dutch Schultz*, Darrell Wood feels that 'the rapid juxtaposition of scenes is of crucial importance: significance is communicated by the order of events'.[112] Cronenberg's notion of disconnectedness is conveyed by carefully constructed image composition and structural juxtaposition of sequences rather than cutting within scenes. By choosing to structure the opening of his film in a conscious departure from Ballard's novel with three consecutive sex scenes, Cronenberg in effect negates the erotic by a surfeit of repeated images. Such structuring conveys not just the boredom of the characters themselves with a strong sense of loss and absence, but implicitly also creates in the audience the same longing for 'something else', which is part of the attraction of Vaughan for James and Catherine.

It is tempting to imagine that if Cronenberg follows both Nabokov and Ballard in the same perpetual temporal mode, then there can be no direction or progression in their narratives, but this is not so. Like *Crash*, many of Nabokov's novels have a structure that on first reading appears to be circular, for example, *Ada* has been seen as nothing more than 'a succession of tenuously related tableaux'.[113] However, the underlying form of a Nabokovian narrative is not exactly circular but based on a spiral model. It does *not* end *exactly* where it began.

Pale Fire, described by Cronenberg as 'still one of my favourite novels', ends on an unrhymed line as though interrupted and as L. L. Lee asserts, 'we can only suppose, as Kinbote supposes that the final line would repeat the first line, starting a new spiral. Everything has changed from the first line, but it contains within itself the future, the death of Shade and the death of Kinbote, as well as the suggestion of timelessness'.[114] In *Pnin*, 'the novel has gone, not full circle, but full spiral...Pnin's lecture, is to be repeated but not in the same form' and in the same novel, the painter Lake's theory of colour follows a spiral model: 'the order of the solar spectrum is not a closed circle but a spiral of tints' which at its end does not return to where it began exactly but 'goes on to Cinderella shades transcending human perception'.[115] L. L. Lee refers to the structure of *Lolita*, which includes Nabokov's additional explanatory afterword (added after initial publication) and the fictional John Ray Jnr's Foreword, as 'a spiral that contains within itself its own time, escaping time'.[116] Similarly, *The Gift* 'is built in its own spiral, the beginning is contained in the end but has become different; it is the author's own personal wrestling with time, a victory and a defeat'.[117]

Conclusion
In his plot summary of Ballard's novel, Sinclair talks, apparently unwittingly, of 'the spiral pursuit of Vaughan'.[118] Cronenberg diverges from Ballard and follows the

Russian novelist more closely in creating narrative structures that are also *spiral* in construction as can be seen from the denouement of the film. For Kauffman, 'Catherine and Ballard orchestrate a collision that leaves Catherine without a scratch; she weeps from disappointment'.[119] However, this scenario has been uncannily anticipated both in Sally Mumford's disappointed reaction at not being more seriously injured by her accident in *The Kindness of Women* ('not even a scratch – I feel really cheated'), and at the close of *Lolita*, Humbert explains, 'And while I was waiting for them [the police and the ambulance people] to run up to me on the high slope, I evoked a last mirage of wonder and hopelessness'.[120] These examples articulate a typical tonal feature of Cronenberg: the melancholic epiphany. In the published screenplay of *Crash*, as Catherine lies on the embankment, she is described 'as though she has been crying, and there is wetness at the corner of her eyes'. A mixture of pain at her injuries and frustration at not succeeding in dying, creates a strong sense of melancholy and the comparisons in Cronenberg's screenplay evoke a sensuous, romantic heroine, like John Keats' La Belle Dame Sans Merci as 'she begins to move, stretching her arms behind her head, as though awakening from a deep sleep'.[121] Although a surface reading might suggest that Cronenberg's *Crash* has an episodic procession of apparently interchangeable sex scenes, the denouement, whilst echoing the opening three scenes and clearly signalling itself as a conscious framing device, does not necessarily convey a lack of progression.

If E. M. Forster's answer to 'the everlasting Why?' in *Room with a View* (1908) is 'a Yes – a transitory Yes if you like, but a Yes', then perhaps the same might be said of *Crash*.[122] This affirmation would seem to occur beyond the confines of the film, and the resistance of full narrative closure indicates that Cronenberg's film shares with Eliot's text a sense of movement 'towards some moment which is outside the poem and may never come, which we are still waiting for at the close. It does not so much move towards a solution as make clearer and clearer that a solution is not within our power'.[123]

Ballard's novel does *not* end with a confrontation between James, Catherine and Vaughan. The novel describes a period of increasingly eccentric stalking, culminating in Vaughan nearly running them down in James' car on their own driveway. After this, there is a proleptic leap forward to Vaughan's death ten days later, again in James' car during an attempt to crash into Taylor's limousine. Cronenberg retains the absence of a climactic crash: in neither novel nor film do we actually see Vaughan's demise. Indeed, in the novel, the sense of anticlimax allows Ballard to have James feel that 'increasingly I was convinced that Vaughan was a projection of my own fantasies and obsession'.[124] Even when James and Catherine are in a position to describe the wreckage of Vaughan's crash, Ballard places there instead a rhetorical question about the motivation of spectators: '[d]id they see within them [the deformed vehicles] the models for their own future lives?'[125] Cronenberg however chooses to focus instead on the romantic couple.

Cronenberg's *Crash* ends with James and Catherine moving inexorably towards the crash that will represent their final epiphany. On the surface, it appears that the protagonists here emulate Eliot's characters in 'having no hope, can turn neither to the world nor to God. In possible states of mind, it represents the nadir of despair'.[126] However, unlike Eliot's progression via 'the stairway' of Part III of *Ash Wednesday*, Cronenberg's source of salvation by which his characters might be re-animated, is on decidedly humanistic, rather than Christian terms. The means are similar but the ends are different. The love they begin to make, although elevated in significance from the many couplings that we have seen in the film up to this point, is still directed towards a human rather than an other-worldly object. For Ballard, 'the book and the film end on a note of exultation, of profound satisfaction, of accomplishment'. The characters 'assume a position like Cortez, like a *conquistador* who senses the ocean beyond the mountains'.[127]

The love scene in Catherine and James' apartment (their only fully naked encounter in *Crash*, possibly indicating a more complete honesty in their desire), closely prefigures the scene on the embankment in terms of proxemics and melancholic tone. In the earlier scene, Catherine is in effect verbalizing a *different* fantasy for James and for herself. She does nearly all the talking, often asking questions that are clearly rhetorical. For him, it is the thought of actually sodomizing Vaughan that is exciting and anal intercourse with his wife facing away from him and his eyes, nearly closed, allows him to put Vaughan in place of her. For Catherine, the pleasure she gains is a voyeuristic fantasy of watching her husband with Vaughan and also of receiving more vigorous attention herself now as James is aroused by her teasing incremental fantasy. However, the couple synthesize their experience of Vaughan into their own fantasy life *with* one another, which arguably brings them closer together.

A key similarity is signalled by 'the warm crescendo of orchestral strings', in both scenes, which signifies 'a romantic climax'.[128] The final scene, with Catherine lying twisted on an embankment and James showing concern for her, is arguably the only romantic moment in the film (albeit via a conventional and clichéd Hollywood device), underlining that this is a love, not a sex, scene and that the object of pleasure is a being other than the self. The form of intercourse is still rear-entry but there is not the sense of the other person acting as a form of masturbatory receptacle. After all, it is not only for narrative cohesion that James and Catherine remain together through the course of the film. They are *married* and despite dalliances with others (which they openly tell about and actively involve their partner in developing their own sex life), *they stay together*: a fact surely inimical to a reading of the sex scenes as completely empty and meaningless.

Like *Prufrock*, *Crash* can be read as a love song, indeed the only way in which love can be articulated in a postmodern society and in both texts, the failure of love is marked as tragic, rather than meaningless. Ballard asserts that 'the film is very much a love story – this is one of the few ways left to the late twentieth century to meet itself with deep love and affection – between husband and wife; the story of their rediscovery of their love for each other'.[129] Cronenberg's reading of the ending, accepted by Grunberg, is that 'you don't realise, until the last scene, that these two people are in love with each other and that the whole effort of the film has been for them to find a way, odd though it is, to come back together'.[130]

Cronenberg's description of *Crash* as an 'existential romance' draws on a literary heritage stretching back past Ballard's 'death of affect' and Nabokov's spiral narratives to de Sade who, according to Carter, 'cites the flesh as existential verification in itself, in a rewriting of the Cartesian cogito: "*I fuck, therefore I am*"'.[131] For Timo Airaksinen, 'the finished Sadean world...is like a Mobius strip' and the internal logic of Cronenberg's *Crash* follows the same pattern.[132] At the beginning of the 120 days, the Duc de Blangis tells the women gathered at the Chateau of Silling as dispensable providers of pleasure that they are: 'far beyond the steep mountains whose paths and passages have been obliterated behind you the minute you crossed over them...you are beyond the reach of both your friends and your family: so far as the world is concerned, *you are already dead*.[133] Evoking de Sade's wishes for his own burial in a ditch, 'the victims have been erased from the world and now live, their own ghosts although they are not yet dead, awaiting their death'.[134] The similar self-erasing nature of the narrative in *Crash* evokes Wittgenstein's comments on his philosophical 'propositions': that 'he who understands me finally recognises them as senseless' and 'when he has climbed out through them, on them, over them. (He must, so to speak, throw away the ladder after he has climbed up on it)'.[135]

Notes

1. See *Not a Love Story – A Film About Pornography* (Bonnie Sherr Klein, 1981).
2. Clive Barker, 'The Age of Desire', *Books of Blood*: Volumes 1–3 (London: Sphere Books, 1985), p. 190.
3. Iain Sinclair, *Crash* (London: BFI Modern Classics, 1999), p. 57.
4. Harold Bloom, *The Anxiety of Influence* (Oxford: Oxford University Press, 1973), p. 14.
5. J. G. Ballard in 'A Meeting with J. G. Ballard', Serge Grünberg, *Cahiers du Cinéma* 504 (July-August, 1996), p. 31.
6. Linda S. Kauffman, 'David Cronenberg's Surreal Abjection', in *Bad Girls and Sick Boys: Fantasies in Contemporary Art and Culture* (Berkeley; Los Angeles; London: University of California Press, 1998), p. 149.
7. See J. G. Ballard, *A User's Guide to the Millennium* (London: Harper Collins Publishers, 1996), p. 4.
8. See J. G Ballard cited in Sinclair, op. cit., p. 87 and David Cronenberg's homepage, (http://www.netlink.co.uk/users/zappa/jgb_dc.html), p. 1.
9. Roy Grundmann, 'Plight of the Crash Fest Mummies: David Cronenberg's *Crash*', *Cineaste* 22: 4 (January 1997), p. 24.
10. See Stuart Laing, 'The Fiction is Already There: Writing and Film in Blair's Britain' in Jonathan Bignell (ed.), *Writing and Cinema* (Harlow: Longman, 1999), p. 145 and William Beard, *The Artist as Monster: The Cinema of David Cronenberg* (Toronto: University of Toronto Press, 2001), p. 379.

11. Sinclair, op. cit., p. 85.
12. John Ellis, 'The Literary Adaptation – An Introduction', *Screen* 23:1 (1982), p. 4.
13. Michael Delville, *J. G. Ballard* (Plymouth: Northcote House Publishers Ltd., 1998), p. 34.
14. J. G. Ballard, *Crash* (London: Vintage, 1995), p. 31.
15. Ibid., p. 214.
16. Sinclair, op. cit., p. 21.
17. Ibid., p. 39.
18. Beard, op. cit., p. 395.
19. David Cronenberg, *Crash* (London: Faber and Faber, 1996), p. 12.
20. Ballard, op. cit., p. 162.
21. Bart Testa in 'Crash (and burn)?: Responses to David Cronenberg's Crash', *FSAC/ACEC Newsletter (Association canadienne des études cinématographiques/Film Studies Association of Canada)*, p. 1.
22. Gene Walz in ibid., p. 3 and Sinclair, op. cit., p. 20.
23. Brian McIlroy in 'Crash (and burn)?: Responses to David Cronenberg's Crash', op. cit., p. 2.
24. Fred Botting and Scott Wilson, 'Automatic Lover' in Jackie Stacey (ed.), 'Special Debate: *Crash*', *Screen* 39:2 (summer 1998), p. 187.
25. Ibid., p. 189.
26. Ibid.
27. J. G. Ballard, *Crash* (London: Vintage, 1995), p. 65 and p 73.
28. Sinclair, op. cit., p. 45.
29. Ballard, op. cit., p. 119.
30. Laura Mulvey, cited in Linda Badley, *Film, Horror, and the Body Fantastic* (London: Greenwood Press, 1995), pp. 102-103.
31. Ballard, cited in Sinclair, op. cit., p. 62.
32. Michel Foucault cited in Linda Williams, *Hard Core: Power, Pleasure, and the "The Frenzy of the Visible"* (Berkeley: University of California Press, 1989), p. 2 and *The History of Sexuality, Volume I: An Introduction*, trans. Robert Hurley (Harmondsworth: Penguin Books, 1981), p. 21.
33. J. G. Ballard, op. cit., p. 34.
34. Gilles Deleuze, *Masochism: Coldness and Cruelty* (New York: Zone Books, 1989), p. 18.
35. Stephen Pfohl, 'Seven Mirrors of Sade', in Deepak Narang Sawhney (ed.), *The Divine Sade* (Coventry: Warwick Journal of Philosophy, 1994), p. 29.
36. Marquis de Sade, *120 Days of Sodom* (New York: Grove Press, 1966), p. 271.
37. Nabokov, op. cit., p. 291.
38. Karen Jaehne, 'Double Trouble', *Film Comment* 24:5 (Sept.-Oct. 1988), p. 26.
39. J. G. Ballard, op. cit., p. 35.
40. Pierre Klossowski, *Sade My Neighbour*, trans. Alphonso Lingis (London: Quartet Books, 1992), p. 39.
41. Angela Carter, *The Sadeian Woman: The Ideology of Pornography* (London: Virago, 1978), p. 63.
42. Barker, op. cit., p. 24.
43. Chris Rodley, 'Crash', *Sight and Sound* 6:6 (June 1996), p. 10 and see Barker, op. cit., p. 24.
44. J. G. Ballard, op. cit., p. 7.
45. Ibid., p. 35.
46. Ibid.

47. Barbara Creed, 'The naked crunch: Cronenberg's homoerotic bodies', in Michael Grant (ed.), *The Modern Fantastic: The Films of David Cronenberg* (Trowbridge: Flicks Books, 2000), pp. 96-97.
48. Klossowski, op. cit., pp. 22-23.
49. Marquis de Sade cited in Jane Gallop, *Intersections: A Reading of Sade with Bataille, Blanchot, and Klossowski* (Lincoln, Nebraska; London: University of Nebraska Press, 1981), p. 26.
50. Susie Bright, 'Accidents Will Happen', (http://www.salon.com/march97/interview970321.html), p. 1 and Sinclair, op. cit., p. 122.
51. Testa, op. cit., p. 1.
52. Ibid., p. 2.
53. Steven Marcus, *The Other Victorians* (London: Weidenfeld and Nicolson, 1966), p. 195.
54. Timo Airaksinen, *The Philosophy of the Marquis de Sade* (London: Routledge, 1991), p. 5.
55. Carter, op. cit., p. 24.
56. Gallop, op. cit., p. 2.
57. Ibid., p. 9.
58. Kauffman, op. cit., p. 104 and p. 105.
59. Ibid., p. 114.
60. David Cronenberg, 'Logic, creativity and (critical) misinterpretation: an interview with David Cronenberg', conducted by Xavier Mendik, in Grant (ed.), op. cit., p. 181.
61. Vladimir Nabokov, 'On a Book Entitled *Lolita*', an Afterword to *Lolita* (London: Corgi Books, 1956), p. 330.
62. See Linda Williams, *Hard Core: Power, Pleasure, and the "The Frenzy of the Visible"* (Berkeley: University of California Press, 1989), p. 160.
63. Ibid., p. 132.
64. Ibid., p. 133.
65. Williams, op. cit., p. 123.
66. J. G. Ballard, op. cit., p. 124.
67. Ibid., p. 180.
68. Victor Sage, 'The Gothic, the Body, and the Failed Homeopathy Argument', in Xavier Mendik and Graeme Harper (eds.), *Unruly Pleasures: The Cult Film and its Critics* (Guildford: FAB Press, 2000), p. 152.
69. J. G. Ballard, *The Atrocity Exhibition* (London: Triad/Panther, 1979), p. 85.
70. Delville, op. cit., p. 5 and see Sinclair, op. cit., p. 57.
71. J. G. Ballard, *The Kindness of Women* (London: Grafton, 1992), p. 175.
72. Ibid., p. 176.
73. J. G. Ballard, *Crash* (London: Vintage, 1995), p. 26.
74. Burroughs cited in Mottram, *William Burroughs: The Algebra of Need* (London: Marion Boyars Publishers Ltd, 1977), p. 58.
75. Klossowski, op. cit., p. 30.
76. J. G. Ballard, *The Atrocity Exhibition* (London: Triad/Panther, 1979), pp. 111-112.
77. Sage, op. cit. p. 146.
78. See Gregory Stephenson, *Out of the Night and Into the Dream: A Thematic Study of the Fiction of J. G. Ballard* (London: Greenwood Press, 1991).
79. Ballard, op. cit., p. 125.
80. Ibid., p. 83.
81. Ibid., pp. 83-84.
82. Ibid., p. 84.
83. Ibid.

84. J. G. Ballard, *Crash* (London: Vintage, 1995), p. 130.
85. Sinclair, op. cit., p. 45.
86. J. G. Ballard, *The Atrocity Exhibition* (London: Triad/Panther, 1979), p. 28, 30.
87. J. G. Ballard, *The Kindness of Women* (London: Grafton, 1992), p. 224, 229.
88. Ibid., p. 231.
89. Ibid., p. 225.
90. J. G. Ballard, 'Zodiac 2000' in *Myths of the Near Future* (London: Jonathan Cape, 1982), p. 71.
91. Ibid.
92. See Peter Morris, *A Delicate Balance* (Toronto: ECW Press, 1993), p. 15.
93. See Sinclair, op. cit., p. 45 and William Beard, 'Lost and Gone Forever: Cronenberg's Dead Ringers', in Robert Haas (ed.), Special Issue: David Cronenberg, *Post Script* 15:2 (winter-spring 1996), p. 24.
94. Vladimir Nabokov, *Lolita* (London: Corgi Books, 1961), p. 174 and p. 184.
95. J. G. Ballard, *The Kindness of Women* (London: Grafton, 1992), p. 219.
96. Ibid., p. 220. See also Cronenberg cited in Gavin Smith, op. cit., p. 18.
97. J. G. Ballard, op. cit., p. 219.
98. Sinclair, op. cit., p. 45.
99. J. G. Ballard, *Crash* (London: Vintage, 1995), p. 88.
100. J. G. Ballard, *The Kindness of Women* (London: Grafton, 1992), p. 15.
101. Ibid., p. 233.
102. J. G. Ballard, *The Atrocity Exhibition* (London: Triad/Panther, 1979), p. 98.
103. J. G. Ballard, *Crash* (London: Vintage, 1995), p. 86.
104. Ibid., p. 122.
105. William Burroughs, *Naked Lunch* (London: Paladin, 1992), p. 224 and p. 229.
106. Sinclair, op. cit., p. 45 and p. 82.
107. Marq Smith, 'Wound envy: touching Cronenberg's *Crash*', *Screen* 40:2 (summer 1999), pp. 199-200. See F. R. Leavis, 'The Waste Land', in Hugh Kenner, (ed.), *T. S. Eliot: A Collection of Critical Essays* (Englewood Cliffs: Prentice-Hall Inc., 1962), p. 97.
108. Stéphane Bouquet, 'Sweet movie', *Cahiers du Cinéma* 504 (July-August, 1996), p. 24.
109. George Williamson, *A Reader's Guide to T. S. Eliot: A Poem-by-poem Analysis* (London: Thames and Hudson, 1955), p. 17.
110. Ihab Hassan, *The Dismemberment of Orpheus* (Oxford: Oxford University Press, 1971), p. 44.
111. Cronenberg cited in Chris Rodley, '*Crash*', *Sight & Sound*, 6:6 (June 1996), p. 10.
112. Darrell Wood, *William Burroughs: The Camera Eye* (M.A. dissertation, Modern Literature, UKC, 1988), p. 31.
113. Douglas Fowler, *Reading Nabokov* (Ithaca, New York: Cornell University Press, 1974). p. 191.
114. Richard Porton, 'The Film Director as Philosopher: An Interview with David Cronenberg', *Cineaste* 24:4 (1999), p. 9. See L. L. Lee, *Vladimir Nabokov* (Boston: Twayne's United States Authors Series, 226, 1976), op. cit., p. 140.
115. Ibid., p. 129. See Vladimir Nabokov, *Pnin* (Harmondsworth: Penguin, 1960), p. 80.
116. L. L. Lee, op. cit., p. 123.
117. Ibid., p. 83.
118. Sinclair, op. cit., p. 43.
119. Kauffman, op. cit., p. 184.
120. J. G. Ballard, *The Kindness of Women* (London: Grafton Press, 1992), p. 221. See also Vladimir Nabokov, *Lolita* (London: Corgi Books, 1961), p. 323.
121. Cronenberg cited in Rodley, op. cit., p. 64.

122. E. M. Forster, *Room With a View* (Harmondsworth: Penguin, 1955), p. 32.
123. Helen Gardner, *The Art of T. S. Eliot* (London: Faber & Faber, 1949), op. cit., pp. 87-88.
124. J. G. Ballard, *Crash* (London: Vintage, 1995), p. 220.
125. Ibid., p. 222.
126. Ibid.
127. J. G. Ballard in 'A Meeting with J. G. Ballard', Serge Grünberg, *Cahiers du Cinéma* 504 (July-August, 1996), p. 32.
128. Botting and Wilson, op. cit., p. 191.
129. J. G. Ballard, 'David Cronenberg and J. G. Ballard: Set for Collision' (An edited version of The Guardian lecture at the London Film Festival, 17/03/00), (http://www.indexoncensorship.org/issue397/cronenberg.htm), p. 8.
130. Grünberg, op. cit., pp. 31-32. See also David Cronenberg, Crash: Production Notes, Cronenberg Home Page, (http://www.flf.com/crash/allnotes.htm), p. 5.
131. 'David Cronenberg and J. G. Ballard: Set for Collision' op. cit., p. 7. See also Carter, op. cit., p. 26.
132. Timo Airaksinen, *The Philosophy of the Marquis de Sade* (London: Routledge, 1991), p. 2.
133. Marquis de Sade, cited in Maurice Blanchot, 'Sade', in Marquis de Sade, *Justine, Philosophy in the Bedroom and Other Writings* (Arrow Books, 1991), p. 55.
134. Carter, op. cit., p. 136.
135. Anthony Kenny (ed.), Ludwig Wittgenstein, *A Wittgenstein Reader* (Oxford: Blackwell, 1994) thesis 6.54, p. 31.

CHAPTER FIVE

eXistenZ:
'THOU THE PLAYER OF THE GAME ART GOD'

**'I feel I understand
Existence, or at least a minute part
Of my existence, only through my art.'[1]**

In *eXistenZ* (1999), Cronenberg develops a complex range of stylistic features, often new to his work, to problematize the borderline between the different worlds of game and 'reality'. In so doing, he most closely draws on the work of a man whom he terms 'part of my nervous system's basic repertoire', Vladimir Nabokov.[2] If Nabokov is, as Tim Lucas describes him, Cronenberg's 'literary mentor', this chapter seeks to explore what has been passed from tutor to student.[3] As with the first chapter of this thesis, the texts used here provide analogous stylistic links to the main film discussed, *eXistenZ*, rather than attempting to prove a direct causal connection.

eXistenZ is Cronenberg's first wholly original script since *Videodrome* and a comparison can be made between these two films and Nabokov's *Invitation to a Beheading* (1960) and *Bend Sinister* (1960). Nabokov described his pairing as 'two bookends of grotesque design between which my other volumes tightly huddle', a phrase that might usefully be applied to Cronenberg's brace of films that represent the 1983–1999 period.[4] For Chris Rodley, '*eXistenZ* is *Videodrome*'s inverse twin, in which the interactive self invades cinema', although it is debatable whether there is such a clear-cut division between the two.[5] To exploit a metaphor from *Dead Ringers* (1988), if *Videodrome* (1982) and *eXistenZ* can be seen as twins, it is as Siamese twins, whose separation (by 16 years) has been only partially successful.

For Cronenberg, 'the spark for it' can be traced to an interview he conducted with Salman Rushdie in 1995.[6] The fatwa that was extended to the novelist for several years both horrified and fascinated Cronenberg, who admits that meeting the novelist in hiding at the time 'crystallised things for me', to the extent of having Kiri use the term 'fatwa' in *eXistenZ* to describe the pursuit of Allegra. During the interview, some of Cronenberg's questions about computer games suggest that the premise of *eXistenZ* had already occurred to him and he is using Rushdie as a sounding board: 'do you think there could ever be a computer game that could truly be art?' and 'could a games designer could never be an artist?' Cronenberg concludes that 'I could see that there could be an artist of a games player, a kind of Michael Jordan of the Nintendo'.[7] However, prior to this, in discussing how to visualize Burroughs' *Naked Lunch* (1959) in a way that the viewing public could cope with, Cronenberg had referred to 'the difficulty any audience would have plugging into it', in a metaphor also used by Gilles Deleuze.[8] Even seventeen years before the Bioport technology of *eXistenZ*, there is a search for a signal over the credits of *Videodrome*, as Cronenberg hopes we also will 'plug in'.

Cronenberg and Nabokov share a belief in the importance of the creative act, which takes on an almost religious dimension. John Lyons states that Nabokov's 'narrative method...is the examination of a text (or vision of aesthetic order) by some real or imagined artist who vies with God in disordering a universe'.[9] Before Gas' declaration that 'thou the player of the game art God', Cronenberg uses a number of religious images in the very first scene of *eXistenZ* to suggest the God-like power of the artist, such as the choice of twelve apostle-like volunteers, the pseudo-Biblical diction in Ted's assurance to Dichter that 'everything's provided for' and Levi's warning that 'we have enemies in our own house' as well as the dubbing of Allegra as a 'demoness'. The church hall setting with the audience as an eager congregation looking up (literally and metaphorically) to a single inspirational speaker on a platform above them evokes a prayer meeting, and the security and assassination attempt suggest the attacks on figures like Malcolm X and Martin Luther King, deemed to be threats to the orthodoxy by raising the consciousness of their followers. This is captured in Allegra's dialogue that 'The world of games is in a kind of trance. People are programmed to accept so little but the possibilities are so great'. What she is offering is 'not just a game' but 'an entirely new games system' and it is the system (of belief as well as technology) that characters like Dichter oppose.

Sartre and existentialism
Cronenberg states that 'as a card-carrying existentialist I think all reality is virtual. It's all invented. It's collaborative'.[10] He goes on to say, 'I jokingly said that the movie is existentialist propaganda. I meant it playfully, of course. But I have come to believe that this is the game we are playing'.[11] Nabokov himself asserts that '[w]hat I feel to be the real modern world is the world the artist creates', and suggests that the idea of a stable, objective 'reality' might be comforting but is essentially self-delusive, reflected in his creation of different worlds such as Padukgrad in *Bend Sinister*, Zembla in *Pale Fire* (1962), the America of Lolita's trans-continental odyssey, and the anti-world narrative of Terra and Antiterra in *Ada* (1970).[12]

However, it is not immediately clear what Cronenberg might mean by labelling himself an existentialist. He has stated, 'Do you remember when you found out you wouldn't live forever?...That's the basis of all existentialist thought, which, of course, is an underpinning of the movie. It's not called "eXistenZ" for nothing'.[13] However, it is perhaps only possible to consider isolated elements of existential philosophy as they appear in *eXistenZ* on a case-by-case basis and that in doing so, underline that, despite cloaking himself in the guise of an existentialist, Cronenberg only appropriates those features, which appear dramatically appropriate to him at a specific point in the narrative, rather than attempting a direct and consistent dramatization of a coherent philosophical viewpoint.

In *Nausea* (1938) Sartre portrays the human world through the hero Roquentin and his subjective experience of sickness, contrasting experience via appearances with the world as felt by the imagination. The way in which Cronenberg problematizes boundaries between worlds of illusion and 'non-illusion' is very close to Sartre's notion that 'what defines the imaginary world and also the world of the real is an attitude of consciousness'.[14] Sartre states that 'the real and the imaginary cannot co-exist by their very nature. It is a matter of two types of objects, of feelings and actions that are completely irreducible', and to make sense of Cronenberg's narrative, we too have to decide at any given time, whether we feel we are in a fictional universe or not.[15] This chapter suggests that what Samuel Taylor Coleridge termed 'the willing suspension of disbelief' is stretched to the very limit by both Nabokov and Cronenberg, both of whom require their audience to express a complex denial of the illusory nature of fictional narratives.

Sartre asserts that 'freedom...is characterised by a constantly renewed obligation to remake the self'.[16] Cronenberg articulates the same notion in the circularity of the narrative in *Crash* and the Chinese box structure of *eXistenZ*'s playing with different game worlds. Sartre states that 'one must choose: to live or to tell' and at the end of *Nausea*, Sartre's solution to Roquentin's perception of the essential absurdity of life is the latter, he starts to tell his story.[17] Cronenberg's Bill Lee in *Naked Lunch* (1991) uses writing to 'write his way out' of the depression following Joan's death and at the close of that film proves that he is a writer by writing in front of the border guards of Annexia. In *Crash* (1996), Vaughan and James focus on accident reconstruction (reflected in Vaughan's sketchpad-cum-scrapbook of future projects) and in *eXistenZ* game-playing is the means by which the protagonists overcome what Sartre terms 'contingency', the notion of the universe as chaotic and purposeless. Writing, reconstruction, playing: all of these activities essentially give specific human experiences a form and purpose. This is particularly true of *eXistenZ*, where the apparent chaos that Ted encounters is not real chaos but a dramatization of the learning the rules of a new game. As such, the game provides a very positive alternative to non-gaming life. If you can learn the rules of the game, you progress and survive and despite the occasional surprise in the narrative of supposed friend being unmasked as enemy, like Yourish or Kiri, no one ever suggests there are no rules. Staying 'one step ahead of the game' has the illusion of unpredictability but ultimately that is all it is: an illusion.

Foregrounding the author

During his initial lectures at Cornell, Nabokov would remind students that '[l]iterature does not tell the truth but makes it up'.[18] Most special-effects-driven films, ostensibly dealing with virtual reality, *The Lawnmower Man* (Brett Leonard, 1992) and particularly *The Matrix* (the Wachowski Bros., 1999), are dominated by special effects, which leave the viewer in little doubt as to where they are at any point in the film. In creating alternative worlds that appear to fold back on themselves, Nabokov problematizes the notion of narrativity altogether. *eXistenZ* can be seen as an exploration of the process of conscious artifice methods by which we allow ourselves to be deceived, a process Sartre terms 'bad faith'.

Nabokov rarely tries to draw his reader into a blind identification with his fictional figures but instead draws our attention to their very fictionality. In doing this, it could be said that in a story like 'Spring in Fialta', 'Nabokov weaves a tougher web of illusion, an illusion of *unreality*'.[19] Alfred Appel notes no less than 27 examples of direct address in *Lolita* (1959) and observes that 'to the Elizabethan playgoer or the reader of Cervantes, the work-within-a-work was a convention; to an audience accustomed to nineteenth-century realism, it is fantastic, perplexing, and strangely affecting'.[20] Much of the critical reaction to *eXistenZ* has focused on the confusion of illusion and 'reality', about whether we know we are in a game world or not, culminating in the final 'twist', the revelation that the body of the film is actually inside another game world, tranCendenZ, and that even at the very end we are left echoing the words of the Chinese waiter character: 'Are we still in the game?'

However, this misses the point. This is no sudden shift in the final phase of the film. We *do* know that we are inhabiting a fictional universe if we pay close attention to the range of clues, signalling the fictive quality of our experience throughout the film. Chris Rodley claims that 'although the "reality bleeds" continually signalled throughout the movie are not an original device, they presage a massive narrative haemorrhage at the end'.[21] However, to extend the metaphor, the 'bleeding' is so profuse and internal that there is barely enough to haemorrhage by the close.

Self-referentiality and the use of commentaries, notes and fictional editor's forewords in works like *Lolita* (1959) and particularly *Pale Fire* (1962) all create a sense of life as a process of interwoven interpretation and subjective readings and counter-readings. *Bend Sinister* (1947) refers to fictional events taking place 'by special arrangement with the mind behind the mirror'.[22] The protagonist, Krug, becomes aware of 'a kind of stealthy, abstractly vindictive, groping, tampering movement that had been going on in a dream, or behind a dream, in a tangle of immemorial...machinations'.[23] In *Invitation to a Beheading* (1938), a ludicrously fake acorn falls after Cinncinatus has appealed for help; the spider in the cell turns out to be fake; and the elusive moth, which only Cinncinatus appears to see, are all signs of 'metaleptic transgression, or the blurring of borderlines between the universe of the author and that of the character'.[24] The narrative conceit of *Nausea* is also typically Nabokovian, involving a fictional note as a preface to the main narrative, explaining that it has been constructed from notebooks left by Roquentin, whom we may assume is either mad or dead. Interestingly, Rodley in *Cronenberg on Cronenberg* (1992) includes a parody of the technique with a fictional foreword from a Dr Martyn Steenbeck (alluding to the editing equipment brand name).

A novelization can be seen as the subtext of the film or the text upon which a film could have been based, so that Christopher Priest's novelization of *eXistenZ* (1999) is, in a sense, creating Nabokovian prose. In *Pnin*, the appearance of a 'quiet, lacey-winged little green insect' just as Pnin finds he is to be fired, acts as a reminder of authorial presence, and Nabokov describes the appearance of a moth in *Bend Sinister* as 'an image of Olga's "rosy soul."'[25] For Priest and Nabokov, insects highlight the self-absorbed nature of characters, who fail to be sufficiently self-aware to gain happiness. As Pnin washes up, he drops a nutcracker and hearing the sound of broken glass assumes he has smashed the punchbowl. He puts his hand into the water and cuts it on glass but not from the bowl. However, just before he faces what he assumes will be a loss, 'a quiet, lacey-winged little green insect circled in the glare of a strong naked lamp', and as he plunges his hand into the water, 'a jagger of glass stung him'.[26] Priest uses the same image pattern of the appearance of insects before assassination, death or a major change in the fortunes of the protagonists, reflecting the shared passion of Cronenberg and Nabokov for lepidoptery. The novelization opens with 'Something buzzed and fluttered against Ted Pikul's chest, feeling like a large winged insect', which turns out to be his pink fone. Ted's mind is 'on other things' and 'he swiped at it absently, flapping his fingers with an irritated motion'.[27] The insect motif acts as a symbol of imminent change or loss but more particularly as evidence of authorial presence, which is a key part of the opening sequence of Cronenberg's film.[28]

A useful term here is *mise-en-abîme*. First used by André Gide, it has been defined by Leona Toker as 'a narrative enclave that reproduces the features of the whole work that contains it'.[29] The opening paragraphs of *Laughter in the Dark* (1960) demonstrate this device in terms of plot:

> Once upon a time there lived in Berlin, Germany, a man called Albinus. He was rich, respectable, happy; one day he abandoned his wife for the sake of a youthful mistress; he loved; was not loved; and his life ended in disaster.

> This is the whole of the story and we might have left it at that had there not been profit and pleasure in the telling; and although there is plenty of space on a gravestone to contain, bound in moss, the abridged version of a man's life, detail is always welcome.[30]

The opening scene of *eXistenZ* not only draws upon a basic notion of *mise-en-abîme* but extends it to exploit other typical Nabokovian devices, e.g. 'easily unnoticed precision', 'premature key information', and 'solution to a mystery hidden within its presentation'.[31]

There are fairly clear indications in the *mise-en-scène* that in the very first scene we are in a world suspiciously similar to that of the game eXistenZ. The dominant colour is blue-black, linking the blackboard, posters, the shirts of many audience members as well as that of Levi and Dichter, even Ted's scanning device as part of one kind of aesthetic experience. The fact that Allegra's blue clothing changes in nature, but the colour remains the same once inside the game-within-the-game, strongly suggests a continuity of game levels rather than a sharp dichotomy of 'reality' and 'fiction'. The walls of D'Arcy Nader's storeroom and the grimy steps around the trout farm can be placed within the same colour spectrum as is the background of the motel and Gas' workroom. We should not have to wait until the game starts to dissolve and Allegra becomes aware of new *blue* headgear and armbands to see that the dominant colour of the tranCendenZ game that we have been inhabiting all the time, up to this point, is part of its branding by PilgrImage. By contrast, in the countryside scenes, both within the game itself, such as by the breeding pools at the trout farm and by the roadside as Ted extracts the tooth from Allegra's shoulder (or the bedding and curtains of the motel), the background foliage is an incredibly deep green colour, i.e. a natural colour but its excessive stylization conveys its falseness.

The style of camera placement also weakens divisions between the frame of apparent reality and the game worlds. The initial church hall setting, the motel and the Chinese restaurant all feature extremely low angle shots, even necessitating the inclusion of ceilings in the motel. The use of such high angles (and their opposite in shot/reverse-shot sequences) creates a sense of stylized unease and also a God-like detachment from what we are watching. Particularly in the opening scene, this creates unusual axes of viewpoint, for example, between Allegra by the sandwiches at the door and Levi at the blackboard, connecting the pair stylistically before we see how they are linked through the unfolding narrative. Even in the Chinese restaurant we have an extremely low angle shot of Ted from the point of view of the plate, cut with a more conventional POV from Ted looking down at the unappetizing 'special', which gives the food a life of its own, heightens the sense of stylization and provides the kind of privileged POV increasingly common in computer games.

For Rodley, 'in this bio-degradable, anti-metal world, many of the aesthetic signatures Cronenberg's critics love to disparage – deadpan acting, anonymous-looking locations, lack of "drama" – become virtual virtues'.[32] This however is a little misleading. There is drama but it is couched within the conventions of computer games. At several points in *eXistenZ*, Allegra is on the verge of being killed.

Cinematic time seems to slow down as an attacker with a gun is held in shot for an extended moment. This happens with Dichter in the opening scene, with Gas at the garage and with the gunman on the hillside above the ski chalet. There is the sound of a shot but it does not come from the gun of the assailant, and the attacker falls dead to reveal an unexpected saviour of the protagonists. The mismatch of sound effects ought to make us aware that this is a game-playing motif, not a genuinely dramatic moment evolving from fully rounded characters: Dichter's shooting of Levi, Kiri's of the soldier on the ground and even Ted's subsequent game-death all sound like Bioport being fitted, rather than actual weapons being fired.

Jackson states that Allegra is 'plainly not averse to rescripting herself from a barely articulate wallflower in real life into a devastatingly sexy action babe in eXistenZ life'.[33] However, the obvious point is that it is not she who has 'rescripted' herself but Cronenberg. The change from the ski chalet to the game world is signalled by a shift in Allegra's appearance from relatively flat shoes and shiny trousers, to blue high heels and a blue, short, tight skirt that rides up as she leans back on the crate in the backroom of the game emporium. Jackson's praise reflects an expectation of fictional characters to respond as psychologically motivated, fully rounded individuals. However, Allegra is recast in the guise of a cartoonish, games character for a predominantly male adolescent market, in effect Cronenberg's tongue-in-cheek Lara Croft.

In *Crash*, Cronenberg uses wing-mirror camera placement around the driver and passenger positions to include passenger, car and road in shot simultaneously, (see introduction) as when James is being driven back from the hospital. In *eXistenZ*, he uses similar wide camera positions but in the later film, there is the very conscious use of back projection. Although the urban landscape of Toronto presents a different backdrop to the anonymous countryside of this film, there appears to be no overwhelming technical reason for using back projection. The effect of a suitably dark country road receding into the distance and even Ted's pink 'fone' cued to appear behind the van once Allegra has thrown it out of the window, appears in theory to be that of a classically created Hollywood movie. We are in a moving vehicle. However, its actual effect in a film with relatively complex effects elsewhere like the gas station creature or the trout farm mutant amphibians, is to signal the *fictive* nature of what we are seeing. The driving scenes are suffused with blue (the brand colour of tranCendenZ). In Cronenberg's *Naked Lunch*, the same technique is used to convey the subjective nature of Lee's narrative but here what we are witnessing is another type of video game, a driving simulation.

In *Mary* (1971), Ganin's meeting with Mary does not happen 'because he has not rehearsed it imaginatively'.[34] For Cronenberg, actions can only happen if rehearsed in artistic forms first: sexual possession in *Dead Ringers* ('You haven't had her until I've had her' as Elliot says), marital sex in *Crash* (planned indiscretions are shared and or replayed) and Max's suicide in *Videodrome*. Appel describes how Nabokov 'begins a narrative only to stop and retell the passage differently; halts a scene to "rerun" it on the chapter's screen'.[35] Towards the close of *Lolita*, we have a false trail that is almost immediately retracted: '[t]hen I pulled out my automatic – I *mean*, this is the kind of fool thing a reader might suppose I did. It never even occurred to me to do it'.[36] Forward momentum is also arrested in *eXistenZ* to explain the rules of the game. Nader's trance-like state is caused by a dialogue 'loop' that needs to be repeated like a witch's spell to release him from his state of limbo.

In *Invitation to a Beheading*, Cincinnatus' mother talks of objects known as *nonnons*: 'absolutely absurd objects, shapeless, mottled, pockmarked, knobbly things, like some kinds of fossils' which altered reality to make it seem as if 'everything was restored, everything was fine'.[37] She could have been describing Allegra's game-pod. Like the *nonnons*, these are popular with adults as well as children and involve a similar amelioration of existence in a distortion of 'reality'. Allegra's sense of wilful escapism is stressed by the Umbycord and the fact that she has been unable to sustain any substantial relationships over several years.

'A sign of the times' (special effects in horror and science fiction)
In the gas station segment of *eXistenZ*, the appearance of the fantastical two-headed lizard is preceded by Allegra sensually feeling the wall of the gas station, walking aimlessly across to the pumps, picking up a stone, sniffing the petrol, kicking the dust and turning to throw the stone at the pumps. All these actions, apparently inconsequential in themselves (although a little odd), are concerned with testing the 'reality' of things by how they *feel*. It is only after these undramatic actions have taken place, apparently establishing that we are in a very dull, but very real gas station, that the creature appears. The film *appears* to evoke this effect but only does so if we fail to spot the fictive markers. In the gas station sequence, it could be said that Cronenberg is visualizing a cinematic equivalent of Sartre's scene in *Nausea*, where Roquentin's sense of fascinated repulsion at the feeling of a stone, is one of the catalysts for his apprehension of the absurdity of existence.

In *Invitation to a Beheading*, Cincinnatus resolves that now 'I shall test for myself all the insubstantiality of this world of yours'.[38] Ted and Allegra lead the audience in a similar tactile experiment of the fabric of Cronenberg's universe. Many of the other markers of fictionality are glimpsed only fleetingly, visible after repeated viewings, but the two-headed creature is held for some time in shot and appears again shortly afterwards in a later scene in daylight and to another character, Ted (thereby reducing the credibility of seeing the creature as Allegra's subjective hallucination). Reflecting developments in bio-technology, the mutant amphibian is indeed 'a sign of the times' but, more important, it is a sign of the director. Cronenberg is echoing the sentiments of Nabokov who expressed in interview several times the notion that 'in a first-rate work of fiction the real conflict is not between the characters but between the author and the reader'.[39] This also echoes the views of theorists like Sean Cubitt on the use of special effects: '[i]n the cinema of special effects, the matter of the communication is then not an external referent but the relationship instigated between the film and the viewer.'[40]

Although the appearance of the computer-generated two-headed lizard in *eXistenZ* is not designed for the same visceral shock as the exploding head in *Scanners* (1980) or Jeff Goldblum's metamorphosis in *The Fly* (1986), this special effect still appears for its spectacular qualities, its 'to-be-looked-at-ness'. When Allegra walks slowly towards the creature and appears fascinated by its cuteness of appearance and its guinea pig-style squealing, the film audience is also being encouraged to admire the ingenuity of its creator. Special effects draw attention to themselves when they create phenomena or events not readily found in the world outside the cinema. We do not inhabit any setting long enough in the film to see such creatures or the mutants in the trout farm pools as sympathetic entities but more as directorial signatures like the creatures in George Lucas' barroom scene in *Star Wars* (1977). Moreover, in the case of Cronenberg, this is a *literary* signature as the trout farm scene evokes parallel episodes in Burroughs' work. In *The Western Lands* (1987), the hero, Kim, walks alongside a pool, 'where humanoid newts live', which are 'a shimmering mother-of-pearl colour, with huge limpid grey eyes' through which they now breathe.[41] In *Exterminator!* (1973), the protagonist (a thinly veiled Burroughs surrogate), William Seward, visits 'what appeared to be an abandoned compound or concentration camp', a setting very similar to Cronenberg's trout farm.[42] Outside this camp, Seward comes across a lake, within which 'crablike fish...stirred the surface occasionally releasing bubbles of stagnant swamp smell'.[43] Intrusions by the author can be referred to as '*metalepsis*, a "transgressional" movement from one narrative level to another', and if none of the other 'reality bleeds' are immediately obvious, then we should be under no illusion that after the creature at the gas station, Cronenberg's first completely harmless special effect, we are in a fantastic world, a game world.[44]

In *eXistenZ*, it is this 'texture' of things which creates a 'correlated pattern in the game', signified by the need for characters to *touch* their surroundings. The feel of objects (including one' own body) appears to be key to Cronenberg's notions of reality. Apart from Allegra stroking the garage wall, when Ted enters Kiri's ski chalet, we have a close-up as he digs his fingers into a chair, as if testing its 'reality'. On first entering the game, Ted touches his own face and smells his hand in disbelief. Later in the Chinese restaurant section and almost lost on first viewing, when Ted stands and declares, 'eXistenZ is paused!', he sits back down and places his head on the table, *which is no longer solid*. It has become both the colour and the texture of the bed in the motel, allowing his head to sink into it. Back in the room, he walks around, touching the furniture as he did before, albeit shown in long shot. The 'bleeds' between illusion and 'reality' work *both* ways, into and out of game worlds, problematizing distinctive borders and foregrounding the creative presence behind the narrative. This touches upon the kind of pleasures involved in viewing contemporary horror. The development of fanzines like *Fangoria*, largely devoted to celebrating the monstrous spectacle of the genre and more industry-orientated publications like *Cinefex* (admittedly not exclusively interested in horror), reflect an almost obsessive audience wish both to be amazed but also to know then "how it's done".

Steve Neale's discussion of a key moment in John Carpenter's 1982 film *The Thing* (mentioned in chapter 1) is relevant here. On seeing a severed human head sprout eight legs and waddle out of a door (an image evocative of Odilon Redon's 1891 painting *The Smiling Spider*), a minor character utters the memorable outburst, 'You've got to be fucking kidding!' Neale cites Philip Brophy's article on "horrality" and states that this particular utterance is a sign of, what Brophy terms, a tendency in modern horror to be 'violently self-conscious'.[45] It is worth quoting Neale's remarks at length. He notes that the film

> is aware that the Thing (and the world it inhabits) are cinematic fabrications, the product, in particular, of an up-to-date regime of special effects, it is aware that the powers of this regime have here been stretched to their limit, and it displays both those powers – and that awareness – to the full. It is also a sign of an awareness on the part of spectator (an awareness often marked at this point by laughter): the spectator knows that the Thing is a fiction, a collocation of special effects, and the spectator now knows that the film knows this too.[46]

This complex exchange of knowingness also happens in the gas station sequence in *eXistenZ*, with the creature being Cronenberg's version of Carpenter's 'Thing'. A key difference with the earlier film however is that, for Cronenberg, astonishment is coupled more with curiosity than with disgust. Carpenter's creature is one unknown phenomenon in an otherwise recognizable universe. In the opening of the earlier film, an alien spacecraft careers towards Earth in a fairly clear explanation of where the Thing comes from. In Cronenberg's film, it is not just the presence of one creature, which is unsettling but, as Pikul realizes, the whole existential fabric of the world, which he and Allegra are inhabiting.

In Carpenter's film, we have seen the Thing before all the main characters do, creating both a sense of impending doom and enhancing the status of those characters like McCready who take its threat seriously. In Cronenberg's film, we experience the creature at exactly the same moment as the protagonists. The conceit of the body of the latter film as a computer game is openly introduced from the beginning, so that audiences may logically expect to see some computer-generated imagery. However, at the stage in the film of the lizard's appearance, Allegra's explanation that the creature is a 'Sign of the times', is initially as much as we have to go on as anything else.

If Cronenberg can be thought of as using a 'conceit' in the body of the film, then we might expect some examples of wit. Omar Calabrese's 1992 study of architecture and design, *Neo-Baroque: a Sign of the Times*, may seem some distance from Allegra's description of the forces that produced the lizard. However, the title of this work reflects the fact that the Baroque aesthetic was fascinated by the phenomenon of *trompe d'oeil*, which, as Cubitt points out, 'wants not to trick, but to be discovered in the act of trickery' and to focus attention on 'the spectacle of the image itself.'[47] This element of *trompe d'oeil* comes together in Cronenberg's lizard. The effect is a 'sign of the times' in its reflection of what special effects technology is capable at the time of the film's production and also within the diegesis of the film, mutation is an inevitable by-product of genetic experimentation at places like the trout farm.

Both science-fiction and horror genres demand ground-breaking special effects that have never been seen before, even using what Michele Pierson terms 'gleefully anti-mimetic images.'[48] She goes on to refer to 'a spectatorial relation to its computer-generated special effects that is wondering and even contemplative.'[49] Narrative momentum is arrested, takes become longer than those in the preceding and following scenes and this focus on the effect is intercut with reaction shots of characters looking, which in combination produce a moment of contemplative gazing. Such effects can appear as interruptions of the narrative, a pause during which we admire the ingenuity of the film-maker's craft as we experience what has been termed 'techno-sublime'.[50] Brooks Landon describes this phenomenon as involving 'scenes of seductively awesome technology that present its appeal even in narratives that are broadly critical of the idea of technology'.[51]

In *The Aesthetics of Ambivalence* (1992), Landon makes a link between the aesthetics of science-fiction film from the late 1970s and the style of early film as described by Tom Gunning's theory of early cinema as a 'cinema of attractions'.[52] However, as the detail of Gunning's research shows, despite the audience interest in spectacle and movement in early film, it is too simplistic to see the viewer as passive and merely acted upon, and he describes a highly self-conscious audience who 'remains aware of the act of looking'.[53] In a sense, Allegra acts like a barker in the period discussed by Gunning, describing to Pikul the effect that he is observing, putting his experience of a novelty into some kind of context and allowing for a moment of wonder.

Inherently, both special effects (and commentaries upon them) have an in-built obsolescence. Landon's book, from 1992, predates the expansion of CGI effects in films from the mid-1990s. Through the 1990s, there has also been a further evolutionary impulse to integrate characters with CGI technology (as seen in George Lucas' updating of the Mos Eisley sequence in *Star Wars* (1977) to *Star Wars: A New Hope* (1997), partly to take the technology to a higher level of complexity and partly to integrate technology within the narrative. Wonder has given way to acceptance and possibly even boredom with effects that slow narrative momentum. The amazement shown by Allegra at the appearance of the lizard is, in some measure, incompatible with her role of as a games designer, who is completely immersed in technology. The scene reflects more precisely the nature of a film director who aspires to create a scene of contemplative wonder but cannot quite bring himself to do this uncritically and reflects the highly self-reflexive nature of *eXistenZ* as a whole. In a film about computer gaming, Cronenberg has largely withstood the temptation to indulge in computer-aided effects. The benign two-headed lizard could be said to reflect an explorative and narrative-driven approach to special effects, akin to problem-solving games like *Myst*, where a central attraction for users is the detail and aesthetically pleasing graphics in the landscape and background and is a game with which Cronenberg has shown himself familiar.[54]

It is possible to distinguish between special effects, which are visible, in the sense of clearly designed to be enjoyed as part of a fictional universe and to be consciously marvelled at and those which are invisible, designed to simulate events that occur in the real world but that are difficult or expensive to produce (such as the motion photography used to convey identical twins in *Dead Ringers*). In '*Trucage* and the Film', Christian Metz identifies different kinds of special effects, involving categorization according to a number of factors such as whether the effect is intended to be recognized by the audience or whether it is created during filming or in post-production. Cronenberg's lizard might be termed a 'visible trucage', which requires of the cinematic viewer 'a type of spontaneous sorting out of the visible material of which the text is composed and ascribes only a portion of it to the diegesis'.[55] The lizard is a visible special effect that aspires towards invisibility by having human actors interact with it in the same frame as Allegra pets the creature, an action which includes some camera movement and motion blur. Unlike the overt and dated use of back-projection when Ted and Allegra are in the van together, there is a greater impression given here that actors and effects inhabit the same fictitious universe. However, this is still a refinement of the game-playing process and like Neale's comments on Carpenter's *The Thing*, part of the viewing pleasure is in recognizing special effects as such.

'I only have words to play with'[56]
Language games (the importance of linguistic play)
In the opening (and closing) scene of *eXistenZ*, Cronenberg articulates paradoxical features of language used in a commercial setting. In introducing the game, Levi writes the word 'eXistenZ' on a blackboard at the same time as pronouncing it and emphasizing which letters should be in upper case. What we are being taught by a teacher using a blackboard is a lesson in brand recognition. Without departing from a tightly written script, and using the rhetoric of advertising with carefully weighted repetition, Levi emphasizes the commercialization of language and the commodification of the spiritual. The poverty of imagination and the commercial pressure to always include the manufacturer in the same breath as the product ('eXistenZ by Antenna Research') marks Levi as a games character. Problematically, the host of the tranCendenZ seminar uses exactly the same

phraseology and sales pitch ('Remember it's written like this: capital C, capital Z. transCendenZ. You're going to love it. It's new from PilrImage. Capital P, capital I. And it's coming soon'). The sense of immediacy associated with a film release, the need to establish the brand by precise logo recognition and the imposition of a corporate marketing strategy on the precise wording used in any public event connected with the product, all suggest the de-humanizing effects of working in the game industry or possibly that we are 'still in the game' as the Chinese character hopes at the end.

A little like Hitchcock, Nabokov likes to appear in his own fictions, via alter egos often signalled by anagrams, such as Vivian Darkbloom in *Lolita*, Vivian Bloodmark in *Speak, Memory* (1970) and Blavdak Vinomori in *King, Queen, Knave* (1968). Cronenberg prefers stylistic intrusions than actual personal appearances. He does act as a gynaecologist in *The Fly* but in a dream sequence of Veronica's rather than a 'real' action in the narrative, so that his presence acts as a signal of potential, rather than actual, monstrosity and the decision not to give his character a name leaves his persona in the realm of the fantastic (like the sequence itself, until Veronica wakes and we can place it as a purely uncanny event). Cronenberg's appearance here could be seen as a playful response to Martin Scorsese's description of him as looking 'like a gynaecologist from Beverly Hills' and also echoes Carl Dreyer's observation that 'if one wishes to find an image that portrays the director's action, one must compare him to a midwife'.[57] Such playful intertextuality might be why Cronenberg names one twin Beverly in *Dead Ringers* and the other may allude to Brian de Palma's psychopathic transvestite doctor, Dr Elliot, in *Dressed to Kill* (1980).

Nabokov declares that '[w]hen naming incidental characters...I like to give them some mnemonic handle, a private tag'.[58] Cronenberg claims '[m]y use of names is not exactly the same as Nabokov's because he was a lot more attracted to semantic games'.[59] However, the name Allegra Geller reflects a European (possibly Jewish) sensibility, linking Cronenberg (who had a Jewish upbringing himself) with figures such as Kafka and Dostoevsky. The name Allegra seems almost a blend of Allegro and Viagra, conveying connotations of latent sexual energy, and Geller evokes the magician/illusionist Uri Geller. In form alone, there are similarities between *Bend Sinister*'s 'Paduk' with *eXistenZ*'s 'Pikul': both names have five letters, two syllables, have the same first letter, share three of the same letters and follow a consonant-vowel-consonant-vowel-consonant pattern. By using the name 'Nader', Cronenberg evokes Canadian Ralph Nader, author of *Unsafe at Any Speed* (1965), thereby mocking alarmist statements about violent video driving games like 'Grand Theft Auto' or 'Carmaggedon'. Willem Dafoe's character appears at the pumps to serve Ted and Allegra and is addressed as Gas by Allegra at the same moment that his uniform displays the word 'Gas'. He may not be quite as much a cipher as the Chinese waiter but he is still a game character, who must be addressed by name, who fulfils a limited range of functions and who signals again the presence of the author and the fictive quality of the dramatic universe.

Similar to Levi's blackboard performance, at the door we have the name of the latecomer, Noel Dichter, visible on screen as his ID is scanned but also verbalized by Ted, just in case we have missed the reference (Dichter meaning 'poet' in German). The assassination attempt might then be seen as a rear-guard attempt by the forces of Literature to prevent hi-tech usurpation of modes of creativity, historically dominated by the written word. In the van later, Allegra explains that she knows Ted's name because 'You're labelled'. In a computer game, objects and people are helpfully labelled, i.e. in a visual culture, we know things by *seeing* them.

However, once in the game world, language becomes a crucial part of how successful a player you become. Ted gradually learns the new grammar of the game's language, requiring at times that certain key lines of dialogue or 'loops' be spoken before the game can continue. In the back-room scene in the restaurant sequence, Ted deliberately arrests the flow of the narrative by withholding a series of words. Far from 'rubbing out the word', *eXistenZ* reflects an increasing dominance of the word and, by extension, its creator: the writer. The main plot of the film is predicated around the notion of Allegra's celebrity status with immense earning power and financial interests in what she creates. The Romantic notion of an individual imagination is enshrined, rather than questioned, by her development of the game-pod, of which there is only a single copy, that she nurtures in a cradling action, as if it were her child.

For Anthony Olcott, Nabokov's use of word games make the reader 'acutely aware of the author', such as Humbert drawing attention to the 'rapist' in 'psychothe*rapist*'.[60] In *Lolita*, Nabokov names one of Lolita's classmates 'Aubrey McFate', consciously signalling the presence of the author. The same might be said for Cronenberg's visual puns, jokes and literary allusions as manifestations of his directorial knowingness. In *eXistenZ* (1999), there is a repeated (and lengthy) close-up of the bag holding fast food for Ted and Allegra with the brand name 'Perky Pat's'. It is not only a satire on ubiquitous product placement (which had already been parodied in *Wayne's World* (Penelope Spheeris, 1992) but also, as Cronenberg admits, a 'little homage' to Philip K. Dick. He does attribute the reference to *The Three Stigmata of Palmer Eldritch* (1964), but still offers no explanation as to its purpose.[61] This kind of overt intertextuality constitutes a *literary* product placement rather than a commercial one, an overt in-joke for science-fiction enthusiasts.

Cronenberg uses such fleeting literary allusions elsewhere in earlier work. In *Videodrome* (1982), Barry Convex wrongly attributes to Lorenzo de Medici two statements that underlie the film's concern with vision and seeing: 'the eye is the window of the soul' (Leonardo de Vinci) and 'love comes in at the eye' (W. B. Yeats' 'A Drinking Song'). This may be designed to show the pseudo-religious piety of Spectacular Optical and their knowing appropriation as Cronenberg claims, 'they're misinformed and don't really care...They're very cynical about using whatever suits them'.[62] However, the effect of such allusions is more complex. In relation to

Cronenberg's *Naked Lunch*, Nicholas Zurbrugg notes how that film 'invites the viewer to move from "spot the Bowles", to "spot the Ginsbergian Martin" and "spot the Kerouacian Hank"'.[63] This kind of intertextuality constitutes an in-joke for the Cronenberg *cognescenti*, echoing comments by David Bordwell, whose analysis of art cinema aptly describes Cronenberg's underlying sensibility as manifested in these literary allusions, in which 'the author becomes a formal component, the over-riding intelligence organising the film for our intelligence'. In this process, 'the competent viewer watches the film expecting not order in the narrative but stylistic signatures in the narration', so that 'the initiated catch citations: references to previous films by the director or to works by others'. The result is that the film presents itself as the work of an artist who has created 'a chapter in an *oeuvre*'.[64] By using such literary allusions for the observant few, Danny Peary notes that regular viewers of cult films 'believe they are among the blessed few who have discovered something in particular films that the average moviegoer and critic have missed'.[65] However, Cronenberg's use of such literary 'product placement', is, by its very nature, exclusive and elitist.

For Nabokov, the exact demarcation between game and serious issue is not always completely clear. In 'Terra Incognita' (1931), the narrator witnesses a fight to the death, misguidedly imagining that 'this was all a harmless game, that in a moment they would get up and, when they had caught their breath, would peacefully carry me off'.[66] What appears to be a game turns out to be real, whereas in *Invitation to a Beheading*, what Cincinnatus takes to be real, eventually dissolves into nothing but an existential illusion. Which of these two mutually exclusive options appears in *eXistenZ* remains unclear, even at the end. If we cannot distinguish game world from non-game world, we cannot know if characters genuinely suffer and die. Ted's question to Allegra after she has shot Kiri, 'What if we're not in the game any more?', receives no answer from her, or, indeed, from the coda that follows.

In describing the appeal of early film, George Bluestone ironically highlights a flaw in Cronenberg's conception of computer gaming: 'it was a delight in an illusion resembling reality that first brought customers to the zoetrope, the nickelodeon, and the carnival sideshows. We take no special delight in the sight of a family eating, of a mother feeding her baby. But when precisely these images appeared as illusory images on a screen, they caused a sensation'.[67] It is as though it is enough for Cronenberg to create a world, which is so life-like that telling illusion from the world outside the game is initially difficult.

However, in 1999, rather than 1899, this in itself is not a sufficiently interesting premise around which to base a game or, indeed, a film. The titles of some of the games in Nader's Emporium, such as 'Being Run Over' evoke the kinetic thrills and cultural backlash associated with early films such as *How It Feels To Be Run Over* (Cecil Hepworth, 1900), but the rest of the film fails to deliver this. Cronenberg claims to be 'fascinated by game design', although he admits 'I don't play it myself' and the lack of ambition in the basic premise behind the games would seem to bear this out, highlighted by critics like Tom Shone.[68] Despite Cronenberg's protestations that the film expresses the new freedom and creativity offered by new technologies, *eXistenZ* seems to be grounded in what non-game players *think* computer games are like. Ted is allowed to stumble through the game in a way that most games would punish with immediate extinction.

'Centrifugal' narratives and their effect on closure

The spiral narrative structure that was discussed in the last chapter in relation to *Crash*, moves a stage further in *eXistenZ* to become virtually 'centrifugal'. Events not only fold back on themselves but by the close of the film the protagonists have moved spatially, chronologically or dramatically to a position outside the fictional narrative, which destabilizes the border between film and extra-film 'reality'. In both Nabokov and Cronenberg, this process involves moments of heightened perception within the narrative, that occur at sporadic moments throughout the narrative and become more cataclysmic towards the end of the work, when characters become aware of themselves as characters in a fictional structure of someone else's making and the narrative collapses as the action reaches the 'eye' of the hurricane, the centre of the narrative centrifuge.

In *eXistenZ*, when Nader has left the back room, Allegra comments that he is a 'disappointment' and 'not a very well drawn character'. Self-referentiality begins long before the final scene and signals an eddying narrative, which apparently keeps returning to the same place, i.e. the game returns to the motel room but things are not exactly the same. Ted becomes increasingly fearful that he cannot distinguish one realm of experience from another. In Nabokov's short story 'Torpid Smoke', the narrator breaks out of a listless reverie and on turning on the light, 'he perceived himself...with that utter revulsion he always experienced on coming back to his body out of the languorous mist'.[69] On returning from the game world, Ted is unsettled at being unable to distinguish fully between the world of the game and what he believes to be 'reality'.

As G. M. Hyde stresses in referring to Hermann in *Despair* (1932), 'the end of his fiction is the end of his life', as he tries to become the film star with whom he has unconvincingly identified himself throughout the novel and at the denouement of *Invitation to a Beheading*, Cincinnatus 'suddenly understood that everything had in fact been written already'.[70] In particular, Nabokov's protagonists 'are usually haunted by the ending of the narrative...They are concerned with finding the right way to read the beginning and middle so that the final scene, their own deaths, will seem a logical and just resolution to all that has come before'.[71] Several characters, like Fyodor, Shade and Van Veen survive beyond their death through literary works, and the process of writing is portrayed as analogous to game creation or playing as Nabokovian protagonists write about their own lives as a way of making sense of them.

In *The Gift* (1963), the opening description of a Berlin street is referred to by Fyodor: '[s]ome day...I must use such a scene to start a good, thick old-fashioned novel', and, at the end, he reveals to Zina that he is planning a novel, the novel that we have been reading, 'the gift' of the title.[72] In *Ada*, the text presented to Van on his 97th birthday *is* the text that we have been reading and in *Pale Fire*, Kinbote would like to find himself in Shade's poem in an egocentric expectation of the narrator finding himself at the centre of his own narrative. In Cronenberg's *Naked Lunch* in the coach station scene and in the coda of *eXistenZ*, the narrators discover themselves to be an important part of their own narratives. In Ballard's *Crash*, in finding pictures of his own accident and recovery in Vaughan's scrapbook, James effectively discovers himself in his own narrative. In Cronenberg's *Crash*, the scene between Helen and James, where she is in the middle of recounting her sexual history, is creating a fiction in which he is the latest instalment. Similarly, in *Four Weddings and a Funeral* (Mike Newell, 1994), albeit in the generic area of romantic comedy, Charles (Hugh Grant) finds himself in a sexual narrative as told by Carrie (Andie McDowell), albeit as the penultimate, rather than the most recent, episode.

At the end of Nabokov's novels, he reminds the reader of the protagonist's fictionality. In *Glory* (1972), the hero, Martin, is just 'cancelled' and he disappears from the room mysteriously, prompting his friend, Darwin, to search underneath furniture for him and in *Bend Sinister*, Nabokov explains that Krug, the protagonist, suddenly realizes 'that he and his son and his wife and everybody else are merely my whims and megrims'.[73] The notion that characters (and by extension, the readers too) are merely dreams of their creator, who upon awakening would destroy them, is reflected in comments by Jorge Luis Borges, 'that if the characters of a fictional work can be readers or spectators, we, its readers or spectators, can be fictitious'.[74] Similarly, in Lewis Carroll's *Alice Through the Looking Glass* (1887), one of Nabokov's first choice of literary works to translate, Tweedledum warns Alice not to wake the Red King because '"If that there king was to wake," added Tweedledum, "you'd go out - bang! – just like a candle!"'[75]

Appel describes how Nabokov 'reveals that the characters have "cotton-padded bodies" and are the author's puppets, that all is a fiction; and who widens the "gaps" and "holes" in the narrative until it breaks apart at "the end" when the vectors are removed, the cast of characters is dismissed, and even the fiction fades away'.[76] This is effectively what happens in *eXistenZ* in the coda as characters from the body of the film are discovered to have been game players of tranCendenZ, evoking more modern involuted novels like Jostein Gaarder's *Sophie's World* (1991) or movies like *In the Mouth of Madness* (John Carpenter, 1994), where horror novelist Sutter Cane (Jurgen Prochnow) reveals to John Trent (Sam Neil) that he is only an invention in Sutter's latest novel.

On visiting the set for the bazaar scene in *Naked Lunch*, Serge Grünberg feels that 'suddenly this totally artificial Tangier where the sky is dotted with powerful projectors and where doors only open onto a naked wooden framework, is revealed for what it is – precisely a set, a vast labyrinth, which when seen from a crane resembles a brain in cross section', an example of 'crude Brechtian distanciation'.[77] What is 'naked' is not so much a laying bare of human nature as a revelation of the mechanisms of storytelling. In *eXistenZ*, the coda returns us to the church hall and the main conceit of the film is revealed, although as I have suggested, the fictional nature of the body of the film is signalled throughout. The characters talk of their own feelings about the roles they played. 'Kiri' declares, 'you know, my accent in the game was thick, I could hardly understand myself' and 'Gas' and 'Levi' express their initial reservations about being removed from the narrative so soon but are ultimately content as 'Levi' states, 'I thought the character was boring'.

Rodley asserts that 'as soon as *eXistenZ* is over you feel the need to "play" the film again to understand its rules more fully, certain you must have missed something' and this is undoubtedly true.[78] *eXistenZ* seems designed specifically for consumption on video (particularly given the film's central game-playing conceit) and that the allusive and deceptive nature of the film not only repays repeated viewings but actually requires it. For critics like Joseph Frank, modernist fiction tends to replace causal relationships with word-groups, which relate to one another internally. The meaning of such groups is not clear 'until the entire pattern of internal references can be apprehended as a unity', with the result that 'modernist fiction...cannot be read, but only re-read' because 'a knowledge of the whole is essential to an understanding of any part'.[79] In *Pale Fire*, Shade suggests that 'human fate may be, like the design of a complicated game, apparent only in retrospect', i.e. understanding is only possible via a process of artistic involution.[80]

In *eXistenZ*, Cronenberg, literally, plays with a number of Nabokovian features, including motifs of game-playing, the use of *mise-en-abîme*, the significance of naming, self-consuming narrative structures and the markers of authorial intrusion. He places the figure of the artist at the core of the narrative in a hybrid of Romanticism and literary modernism, suggesting that at the end of the twentieth century, an artist is just as likely to be the creator of video games as the writer of fictional autobiography. Irving Howe suggests that for Nabokov, 'the main question will no longer be the conditions of existence but existence itself', and as a potent expression of the cinematic experience, *eXistenZ* articulates how we wilfully indulge in illusions, dramatizing the Sartrean paradox of how we have more and less freedom than we may think. [81] In the novel that Salman Rushdie went on to write following his interview with Cronenberg, he states '[f]irst to create an illusion, then to show that it is an illusion, then finally to destroy the illusion: this, I began to see was honesty.'[82]

Notes
1. Vladimir Nabokov, *Pale Fire* (London: Weidenfeld & Nicolson, 1962), lines 971–973.
2. David Cronenberg in Richard Porton, 'The Film Director as Philosopher: An Interview with David Cronenberg', *Cineaste* 24:4 (1999), p. 9.

3. Tim Lucas, 'The Image as Virus: The Filming of *Videodrome*', in Piers Handling (ed.), *The Shape of Rage: The Films of David Cronenberg* (Toronto: Academy of Canadian Cinema, 1983; New York: New York Zoetrope Inc., 1983), p. 151.
4. Nabokov cited in ibid., p. 49.
5. Chris Rodley, 'Game Boy', *Sight and Sound* 9:4 (April 1999), p. 8.
6. Rodley, op. cit., p. 9.
7. 'Interview with David Cronenberg', *Shift Magazine* 3.4 (June–July 1995), (http://www.cronenberg.freeserve.co.uk/cr_rushd.html), p. 13.
8. Cronenberg cited in Chris Rodley, *Cronenberg on Cronenberg* (London: Faber & Faber, 1992), p. 161 and 'Interview with David Cronenberg', by Jill McGreal in Wayne Drew (ed.), *David Cronenberg: Dossier 21* (London: British Film Institute, 984), p. 7. See also Gilles Deleuze, 'Letter to a Harsh Critic', in *Negotiations: 1972–1990* (New York; Chichester: Columbia University Press, 1990), p. 8.
9. John O. Lyons, in L. L. Lee, *Vladimir Nabokov* (Boston: Twayne's United States Authors Series, 226, 1976), p. 136.
10. Chris Rodley, 'Game Boy', *Sight and Sound* 9:4 (April 1999), p. 10.
11. Ibid.
12. Vladimir Nabokov, *Strong Opinions* (New York: McGraw-Hill, 1973), p. 112.
13. David Cronenberg, (http://www.splicedonline.com/features/cronenberg/html), p. 8.
14. Ronald Aronson, *Jean-Paul Sartre: Philosophy in the World* (London: Verso, 1980), p. 47.
15. Jean-Paul Sartre cited in ibid., p. 54.
16. Sartre cited in Gregory McCulloch, *Using Sartre: An Analytical Introduction to Early Sartrean Themes* (London; New York: Routledge, 1994), p. 42.
17. Sartre cited in Christina Howells, *Sartre: The Necessity of Freedom* (Cambridge: Cambridge University Press, 1988), p. 50.
18. Alfred Appel Jr, op. cit., p. 347.
19. Barbara Heldt Monter, '*Spring in Fialta*: the choice that mimics chance' in Alfred Appel, Jr and Charles Newman (eds.), *Nabokov: Criticism, Reminiscences, Translations and Tributes* (London: Weidenfield & Nicolson, 1971), p. 133.
20. Alfred Appel Jr, Introduction, *The Annotated Lolita* (New York: McGraw-Hill, 1970), p. *lxi*.
21. Rodley, op. cit., p. 9.
22. Vladimir Nabokov, *Bend Sinister* (London: Weidenfield and Nicolson, 1960), p. 203.
23. Ibid.
24. Leona Toker, Nabokov: *The Mystery of Literary Structures* (Ithaca, New York: Cornell University Press, 1989), Toker, p. 138.
25. Vladimir Nabokov, *Pnin* (Harmondsworth: Penguin, 1960), p. 144. See also Vladimir Nabokov, 'Introduction', *Bend Sinister* (Harmondsworth: Penguin, 1960), p. 17.
26. Vladimir Nabokov, *Pnin* (Harmondsworth: Penguin, 1960), p. 172.
27. Christopher Priest, *eXistenZ* (New York: Harper Entertainment, 1999), p. 1.
28. See Michael Grant, 'Cronenberg and the poetics of time', in Michael Grant (ed.), *The Modern Fantastic: The Films of David Cronenberg* (Trowbridge: Flicks Books, 2000), pp. 128-129.
29. Toker, op. cit., p. 78.
30. Vladimir Nabokov, *Laughter in the Dark* (Harmondsworth: Penguin Books, 1960), p. 5.
31. William W. Rowe, 'The Honesty of Nabokovian Deception', p. 171 in Carl R. Proffer, (ed.), *A Book of Things about Vladimir Nabokov* (Ann Arbor, MI: Ardis Inc., 1974), p. 179.
32. Rodley, op. cit., p. 9.
33. Jackson, op. cit., p. 46.

34. Leona Toker, op. cit., p. 105.
35. Alfred Appel Jr, op. cit., p. *xxxi.*
36. Vladimir Nabokov, *Lolita* (London: Corgi Books, 1961), p. 295.
37. Vladimir Nabokov, *Invitation to a Beheading* (Harmondsworth: Penguin, 1963), p. 123.
38. Vladimir Nabokov, op. cit., p. 63.
39. Dabney Stuart, *Nabokov: The Dimensions of Parody* (Baton Rouge; London: Louisiana State University Press, 1978), p. 89.
40. Sean Cubitt, 'Introduction. Le réel, c'est l'impossible: the sublime time of special effects', *Screen* 40:2 (1999), p. 126.
41. William Burroughs, *The Western Lands* (New York: Viking, 1987), p. 189 and p. 190.
42. William Burroughs, *Exterminator!* (New York: Viking Press, 1973), p. 43.
43. Ibid., p. 44.
44. Toker, op. cit., p. 23.
45. See Philip Brophy, 'Horrality: The Textuality of Contemporary Horror Films', *Screen* 27:1, (January-February 1986), p. 11.
46. Steve Neale, '"You've got to be fucking kidding!": Knowledge, Belief and Judgement in Science Fiction', in Annette Kuhn (ed.), *Alien Zone* (London; New York: Verso, 1990), p. 161.
47. Cubitt, op. cit., p. 127.
48. Michele Pierson, 'CGI effects in Hollywood science-fiction cinema 1989-95: the wonder years,' *Screen* 40:2 (1999), p. 161.
49. Ibid., p. 170.
50. Brooks Landon , *The Aesthetics of Ambivalence*: *Rethinking Science Fiction Film in the Age of Electronic (Re)production* (Westport, CT and London: Greenwood Press, 1992), p. 68.
51. Ibid.
52. See Tom Gunning, 'The cinema of attractions: early film, its spectator and the avant-garde', in Thomas Elsaesser with Adam Barker (eds.), *Early Cinema: Space, Frame, Narrative* (London: British Film Institute, 1990), pp. 56–62.
53. Tom Gunning, 'An Aesthetic of Astonishment: Early Film and the In(Credulous) Spectator', *Art & Text* 34 (1989), p. 40.
54. 'Interview with David Cronenberg', *Shift Magazine* 3.4 (June-July 1995), (http://www.cronenberg.freeserve.co.uk/cr_rushd.html), p. 13.
55. Christian Metz, 'Trucage and the film,' cited in Neale, op. cit., p. 166.
56. Vladimir Nabokov, *Lolita*, op. cit., p. 35.
57. Martin Scorsese, 'Internal Metaphors, External Horror', in Wayne Drew (ed.), op. cit., p. 54. See Carl Dreyer, *Dreyer in Double Reflection*, Translation of Carl Theodor Dreyer's writings *About the Film* (*Om Filmen*), edited and with accompanying commentary and essays by Donald Skoller (New York: E.P. Dutton & Co. Inc., 1973), p. 137.
58. Vladimir Nabokov, *Ada* (Harmondsworth: Penguin, 1970), p. 393.
59. Michel Ciment, `Entretien avec David Cronenberg`, *Positif* 337 (1989), p. 43.
60. Proffer, op. cit., p. 107. See also Vladimir Nabokov, *Lolita* (London: Corgi Books, 1961), p. 115.
61. Porton, op. cit., p.7. In the novelization of *eXistenZ*, the Head of PR at Antennae Research is called Alex *Kindred*, as a knowing reference to Dick's middle name. See Novak, op. cit., p. 2.
62. Cronenberg cited in Tim Lucas, 'The Image as Virus: The Filming of *Videodrome*', in Piers Handling (ed.), op. cit., p. 157.
63. Nicholas Zurbrugg, 'Will Hollywood Never Learn? David Cronenberg's *Naked Lunch*', in Deborah Cartmell and Imelda Whelehan (eds.), *Adaptations: From Text to Screen, Screen to Text* (London; New York: Routledge, 1999), p. 105.

64. David Bordwell, 'The Art Cinema as a Mode of Film Practice', *Film Criticism* 4:1 (fall, 1979), p. 59.
65. Danny Peary, *Cult Movies: The Classics, the Sleepers, the Weird, and the Wonderful* (New York: Dell Publishing, 1981), p. xiii; cited in Ian Conrich, 'An aesthetic sense: Cronenberg and neo-horror film culture', in Grant (ed.), op. cit., p. 42.
66. Vladimir Nabokov, 'Terra Incognita', in *A Russian Beauty and Other Stories* (Harmondsworth: Penguin, 1975), p. 122.
67. George Bluestone, *Novels into Film* (Berkeley: University of California Press, 1968), p. 6.
68. Michael Rowe, 'A New Level of *eXistenZ*', *Fangoria*, 181 (April, 1999), p. 48. See also Tom Shone, 'Talking Nonsense', *The Sunday Times*, (*Culture*) 2 May 1999, p. 7.
69. Vladimir Nabokov, 'Torpid Smoke' in *A Russian Beauty and Other Stories* (London: Weidenfeld and Nicolson, 1973), p. 37.
70. G. M. Hyde, *Vladimir Nabokov: America's Russian Novelist* (London: Marion Boyars, 1977), p. 115. See also Vladimir Nabokov, *Invitation to a Beheading* (Harmondsworth: Penguin, 1963), p. 194.
71. Lucy Maddox, *Nabokov's Novels in English* (Athens, Georgia: University of Georgia Press, 1983), p. 3.
72. Vladimir Nabokov, *The Gift* (London: Weidenfield and Nicolson, 1963), p. 16.
73. Vladimir Nabokov, 'Introduction', *Bend Sinister* (Harmondsworth: Penguin, 1960), p. *xiv*.
74. J. L. Borges, 'Partial magic in the Quixote', in *Labyrinths* (New York: New Direction, 1964), p. 196.
75. Lewis Carroll, *Alice Through the Looking Glass* (Leicester: Galley Press, 1988), p. 81.
76. Alfred Appel Jr, op. cit., p. *xxi*.
77. Serge Grünberg, 'Sur les terres de Cronenberg', *Cahiers du Cinéma* 446 (no. 446 (July-August, 1991), p. 38.
78. Rodley, op. cit., p. 9.
79. Stephen Jan Parker, *Understanding Vladimir Nabokov* (Columbia: University of South Carolina Press, 1987), p. 16.
80. Maddox, op. cit., p. 2.
81. Irving Howe in Ellen Pifer, *Nabokov and the Novel* (Cambridge, Massachusetts: Harvard University Press, 1980), p. 92.
82. Salman Rushdie, *The Ground Beneath Her Feet* (London: Vintage, 2000), pp. 447-448.

CHAPTER SIX

'THE CHILD IN TIME':
TIME AND SPACE IN CRONENBERG'S *SPIDER*

'Time, the human dimension, which makes us everything we are.'[1]
This chapter is entitled 'The Child in Time' for three main reasons. Firstly, not since
The Brood in 1979 has David Cronenberg shown any interest whatsoever in
relationships between parents and children. However, *Spider* (2003), adapted from
the 1990 novel of the same name by Patrick McGrath, more than just features the
actions of a child, it places them at its absolute core. Secondly, of all the films which
he has scripted himself, it is his very first to feature a repeated use of the past tense.
Thirdly, I will be suggesting that Ian McEwan's 1987 novel, rather helpfully entitled
The Child in Time, provides a useful point of comparison for one of the key scenes
in the film version of *Spider*. Cronenberg's work also shows many similarities with
that of Fyodor Dostoevsky: a derelict hero who constructs his own reality,
particularly by writing the denial of a past tense to his characters to explain their
actions and the use of threshold locations as places where crises occur. It is
Dostoevsky's conception of the fantastic dream, however, which is most relevant for
the specific flashback scene, which I shall be discussing in more detail.

Spider is Cronenberg's first film in 25 years to feature a generational relationship.
Admittedly, in his back catalogue there are the geeky Mantle brothers as children
in the brief Prologue of *Dead Ringers* (1988), but Cronenberg chose to remove all
references to their parents from his source material, Bari Wood and Jack
Geasland's 1977 novel *Twins*. There is no sense in which this opening explains their
later character. Indeed, it is the brothers' complete lack of sexual and social
development, which is most striking and disturbing. It might be argued that there
is an implied parental situation in *The Fly* (1986) with the Geena Davis character,
Veronica, falling pregnant to Jeff Goldblum's increasingly insect-like hero, but this
is more a standard horror trope to motivate a sequel than it is part of Brundlefly's
reason for kidnapping her.

For Mikhail Bakhtin, Dostoevsky's characters 'remember from their past only those things which have not ceased to be current for them and which continue to be experienced in the present,' and those writers who have exercised the greatest influence over Cronenberg, including Nabokov and Ballard, focus almost unremittingly on a drive towards the present.[2] Indeed, more than rejecting a sense of the past, from Max Renn's 'New Flesh' in *Videodrome* (1982) to Bill Lee's Interzone adventures in *Naked Lunch* (1991) to Vaughan's 'project' in *Crash*, Cronenberg's films are centrally concerned with embracing a future, in which change is in the hands of the individual. Cronenberg's early film work typically features an absent father figure and initially it may seem as if *Spider* represents a departure from that with Spider's father occupying a prominent on-screen role. However, Bill Clegg dies in the Blitz and since his appearances in the film occur after the kitchen flashback, all the images we have of him are fashioned through the distorting prism of Spider's delusional memory.

In terms of McGrath's novel, the time frame is overtly established as Spider begins his journal in an attempt at ordering his thoughts: 'Today's date: October 17th, 1957'.[3] The memories of his childhood that constitute the flashbacks are drawn from twenty years earlier. Cronenberg's chronology is much more ambiguous. In the film, Spider lives in a landscape of the mind and much of what we see is drawn from the past, either his own or a chronologically vague range of periods. The 'Keep Britain Tidy' poster held lingering in shot in the cafe would date the film around the early 70s. However, Spider revisits the street where he grew up and a young mother, dressed in casual jeans and sweatshirt, pushing a buggy, suddenly emerges from his old house. Nothing else in the film, apart from the opening sequence at the train station, strikes us as contemporary and this eruption of the present seems strangely out of chronological kilter so that we share some of the protagonist's sense of disorientation.

According to Ralph Fiennes, Cronenberg 'wanted a generic London in which we don't quite know where or when we are.'[4] Cronenberg has spoken about this himself, claiming that 'there was also a timeless element which I was conscious of wanting to capture without being coy.'[5] Different, yes; timeless, no. The narrative is moved forward in time from the novel, removing the spectre of post-war poverty in some measure, including 'some structures that would have been there as late as the 1960s.'[6] Cronenberg's decision not to use specific datable props such as cars, which were prepared but ultimately not used, suggests that the hero's existential crisis supercedes notions of a specific period chronology.

In discussing Dostoevsky, Bakhtin states '[t]o orient oneself in the world meant for him to think of all its contents as being simultaneous and to guess at their interrelationships in a single point in time.' This 'leads him to dramatise in space even the inner contradictions and stages of development of a single person, causing the characters to converse with their doubles.'[7] For Cronenberg, the games of sexual substitution between apparently identical twins in *Dead Ringers* is taken a stage further in *Naked Lunch* where Judy Davis plays both Joan Lee and Joan Frost with deliberate blurring of identities between them. In *Spider*, Miranda Richardson takes this fracturing of perception to another degree, playing three characters: Spider's mother (Mrs Cleg) and the two characters that Spider conflates with her – the prostitute,Yvonne and the landlady, Mrs Wilkinson. Hence, although the vision through the kitchen window is a flashback, it is really only a means for the adult Spider to understand the present by conversing with his alter ego as a child.

'Looking Back' (*Total Recall* or *The Memory Wars*?)
In the sequence entitled on the DVD version 'Looking Back', the adult Spider revisits Kitchener Street and the house where he grew up. He creeps round the back of the house and approaches the kitchen window. The camera adopts a subjective POV of someone standing outside the window, looking slightly down. A hand, that we assume is Spider's, enters the shot, lower frame right, reaching forward into an open window and drawing a curtain aside. Revealed inside, like the lifting of a veil of memory, is a flashback to Spider's childhood as he sits at the kitchen table, talking to his mother. The hand that becomes visible is blurred as it invades the focal distance of the shot. Like the opening credit sequence of *Crash* (1996), or any of the transition sequences in *eXistenZ* (1999), Cronenberg is playing here with Derrida's notion of the parergon (see my introduction).

Of course, Cronenberg is not the first to use a flashback in which a hero looks through a window into another time of his or her life. There are precedents in both film and literature. In *Wuthering Heights* (1847), Emily Bronte places the impoverished Heathcliff and Catherine Earnshaw outside the mansion of Thrushcross Grange, owned by the wealthy Hinton family, looking in at a life of affluence from which they appear to be excluded. That is until the pair are caught, Heathcliff chased off and Catherine taken in, only to appear weeks later, transformed into a lady, changed in dress, speech and attitude. In *A Christmas Carol* (1843), Charles Dickens uses the Ghost of Christmas Present to illustrate the errors of Scrooge's ways by looking in on the poor but harmonious life of Bob Cratchit and family as seen through their kitchen window. Orson Welles uses the same stylistic trope, using a forward (and later reverse) tracking shot through a boarding house window in an investigation into the past of his protagonist in *Citizen Kane* (1941). In all three examples here, actions by or upon children are seen to have a formative influence upon them in later life.

In the short story 'The Dream of a Ridiculous Man' (1877), Dostoevsky uses the dream to represent 'the *possibility* of a completely different life', involving 'an *extraordinary situation* which is impossible in normal life' in order 'to test an idea'.[8] Like the visions of psychic Johnny Smith in *The Dead Zone* (1983), the hallucinations of Max Renn in *Videodrome* and Beverly Mantle's dream in *Dead Ringers*, in *Spider*, the hero appears in his own visions but seems powerless to affect what he sees.[9]

Inside the kitchen, the boy is asked by his mother what he is doing. He replies, 'Making something', followed by 'Just for you', and the adult Spider repeats these phrases aloud as he peers through the window. However, the mother then says that 'Food's on the table' to which the adult Spider outside responds, 'Not on the table' *before* the boy speaks. In the first two examples, the adult's action of repetition provides an echo but the third anticipates the dialogue like a prompt to the actors and reactive speech is replaced by a pre-emptive phrase. Interposing himself creates the sense of the adult Spider as a character in the same time frame and as part of an interactive dialogue as well as reflecting the feelings of the audience who cannot, in that split second, see food on the table. Knowledge of what is about to "happen" allows the viewer to interpose himself on his own personal soundtrack, *as if* he were part of the drama he is seeing.

The boy runs outside and as this is the first scene to use this flashback technique, we are not sure what he will find, i.e. whether he will run into the adult Spider out in the yard. This does not happen. The adult Spider is not there, which suggests initially that the two cannot occupy the same shot. However, as the boy walks out of the back gate, he passes the adult Spider, who presses himself against a wall. This last action only makes sense if the adult feels he has to move spacially in order not to be seen or struck by those within the vision, creating the illusion of the existence of both characters, man and boy simultaneously, a logical impossibility. The events in the kitchen are intercut with a pub scene where the boy goes to fetch his errant father. As the boy looks round the bar, he passes the adult Spider sitting at a table with a drink. From standing outside the scene and acting as first chorus, then prompt, the adult has moved within the remembered scene. He occupies his own space like an extra with a prop and has the ability to move but not address the protagonists directly.

Back in the kitchen, the adult Spider moves into the doorway. He is gradually edging into the house as the memory increases in detail. His mother recounts the backstory of her childhood and explains her nickname for him, whilst the boy is having his hair brushed in the foreground and the adult watches from the doorway, i.e. boy and adult are held within the same shot again. There is the noise of the father returning via the back door, causing the boy to scamper away down a corridor into the house. As the boy runs past the adult Spider, now occupying an alcove space beneath the stairs, he palpably *brushes the adult's coat*, making it move. The two worlds, present and past, the now and the memory collide, a further impossibility, and they do so around the figure of the child. The adult Spider seems to suddenly appear ghost-like in different parts of the scene, moving from outside the window to the doorway to the corridor outside and finally to a sitting position on the stairs. In this last position, the camera movement mimics the action of his mother and himself as a boy, moving round him, emphasizing again his occupation of a physical space.

Both the sequences in the pub and the kitchen are reminiscent of Shakespeare's use of Banquo's ghost in the banquet scene in *Macbeth*. The ghostly presence of the adult Spider maintains a spacial integrity within the scene, although he cannot apparently be heard. Banquo can be seen only by his murderer to whom he gestures, while other guests look upon a vacant place at the table. Equally, there is something of the technique of *Randall & Hopkirk (Deceased)* (1969), both the original ITV series and the 2000 BBC remake with Vic Reeves in role of ghost. Neither the ghost of Banquo nor Hopkirk can physically affect the worlds in which they move but both can communicate with one person within the vision.

Ian McEwan's novel *The Child in Time* (1987) is ostensibly about the loss of a three-year-old girl through abduction and the attempt by her parents to come to terms with this in the following years, during which the crime is never solved. The narrative is suffused with the loss of the child and the reconstruction of the protagonist's own childhood as part of the process of understanding this loss. Like Spider, the hero of McEwan's novel (Stephen Lewis) returns to a location in the south-east of England, the scene of a key memory from childhood. Like Spider, he too has a vision of his parents at a moment from the past when there is some tension between his mother and father with the hero an excluded spectator looking on. The vision is also framed by a window and although the exact location is not a kitchen but a pub, it feels very much like a conflation of Cronenberg's kitchen and pub scene. McEwan draws upon the metaphor of film to convey the vision that his character experiences: 'Stephen stood on the edge of a minor road in Kent on a wet day in mid-June, attempting to connect the place and its day with a memory, a dream, a film, a forgotten childhood visit. He wanted a connection which might begin a process of explanation and allay his fear.'[10]

Like Spider, the hero here seems paradoxically included and excluded from the scene. There is an intense lucidity about Stephen's vision and yet he also knows that if he were to step in the path of a car passing the pub, 'he could not be touched.'[11] He feels as if 'he was in another time but he was not overwhelmed. He was a dreamer who knows his dream for what it is and, though fearful, lets it unfold out of curiosity.'[12] The description of McEwan's hero might equally describe Cronenberg's Spider: 'it was a face taut with expectation, as though a spirit, suspended between existence and nothingness, attended a decision, a beckoning or a dismissal.'[13]

The three conditions that Todorov specifies for the fantastic to exist do occur in McEwan's and Cronenberg's flashback scenes, although both are part of a subjective narrative making the status of the vision ambiguous. The hero, though eccentric, is a recognizable part of human society; a sense of hesitation is experienced by a character within the fiction (the protagonist outside a window, fearing he has been be seen); and whilst the viewer may reject allegorical interpretations initially, it becomes increasingly difficult to resist ascribing metaphorical significance to actions such as Spider's murder of his mother. However, as with his dramatizations of *Naked Lunch* and *Crash*, Cronenberg eschews the use of voice-over (present in McGrath's first draft of the screenplay) as a cinematic device, which he finds too intrusive, making the operation of a Todorovian fantastic more problematic.

As Stephen watches the scene unfold, he thinks 'the obvious thing was to enter, buy a drink and take a closer look.'[14] This is what Spider does later in another pub scene, where his pint not only seems to have been partially consumed but he is also busily scribbling down his thoughts in his notebook as he listens to what is going on around him. Ultimately, Spider finds his vision consoling but the reaction of McEwan's protagonist is different. Stephen does not have the option of delusional psychosis and he backs away from the window distraught – 'he had nowhere to go, no moment which could embody him.'[15] It is this search for embodiment, typical of a Cronenberg hero, that leads Spider to retrace the steps of his murder and almost kill again in his threatening presence above the sleeping figure of Mrs Wilkinson, onto whom he has projected the identity of his dead mother.

Cronenberg shows a repeated interest in protagonists in limbo, on thresholds and in impossible states. In *The Dead Zone*, Johnny Smith lives only a half-life that ebbs away with each succeeding vision. In *The Fly*, Seth Brundle is caught between states of being human and fly but is wholly neither. In *Dead Ringers*, the Mantle brothers are neither joined, nor wholly individual. In *Spider*, we are offered two versions of the same event. Spider's mother cannot have been both gassed by the boy and buried out in the allotments after being murdered by her husband. One of these accounts must be untrue. If the boy is the perpetrator as suggested by the final sequence, then everything in the film we have just seen that proceeds from his imagined recreations, i.e. from the kitchen window scene onwards, is cast as unreliable.

Mouldy wallpaper

Other McGrath texts have a number of features in common with *Spider* (book and film). The narrative of *Asylum* (1996) concerns a murderer, Edgar Stark, who denies responsibility for killing his wife. Blame here is shifted onto the victim herself rather than another family member as in *Spider*, but it still focuses on the 'retroactive adjustment of the memory,' to fit in with paranoid delusions.[16] *Asylum* is heavily autobiographical (McGrath's own upbringing within the grounds of Broadmoor Hospital, where his father was Superintendent, is well documented). The novel is predominantly set in mental institutions and focuses on the analyst-patient relationship between Peter Cleave, the ambitious psychoanalyst, and Stella Raphael, the heroine and object of Stark's attention.

Cronenberg has admitted that, before filming, he read *Dr Haggard's Disease* (1993), the novel that McGrath wrote after *Spider*. Like *Spider*, both *Asylum* and *Dr*

Haggard's Disease focus on an obsessional love (albeit romantic rather than maternal) and both dramatize projected guilt. Stark accuses his wife of unproven infidelities as a justification for murdering her and Haggard projects his grief for a lost love onto the son of the object of his affections. Like *Spider*, both novels are constructed as relentlessly first-person narratives with little objective testimony beyond the unreliable figures of Stella Raphael and Dr Edward Haggard. Stella herself is committed after allowing her son to drown and disavowing responsibility and Haggard is an openly addicted morphine addict.

Notably, Haggard retreats to a gothic mansion to suppress his grief at a lost love and experiences the delusion that the cracked plasterwork on some walls is actually moving:

> I caught the movement out of the corner of my eye, and bending to inspect the wall discovered to my utter astonishment that the lines of the cracking formed distinct patterns, distinct *figures* – rich and organic clusters of motifs, I mean leaves and tendrils of the vine, in extended scrolls and spirals, and here and there bizarre figures, festoons of fruit, skulls, masks, snakes, and the longer I gazed into the wall, following the intertwining, convoluted lines of the pattern, and identifying newer and stranger grotesques half-hidden in its frenzied sweeps and swirls, the greater became my feeling of unease and excitement – the cracks in the plaster were no mere accidents of time but *the product of conscious design*.[17]

Here we have the overt and unacknowledged inspiration for the credit sequence in Cronenberg's film of *Spider*. Cronenberg notes, 'there's something really important in the tone of the film, in its physical texture. It's a kind of mouldy wallpaper and very British, for which I feel a great fascination...Don't ask me why.'[18] In the book, grief is projected onto the environment to produce a moment of expressionist nightmare. In Cronenberg's film, the opening credit sequence with its shots of stained paint and stonework encourages the viewer to look closely and find meaning in the Rorschach-style images with the fading to black between each one creating the sense of a series of psychoanalytical tests.

The novel *Spider* in some ways is an unusual choice for Cronenberg in that McGrath's own background places him within a tradition of psychoanalytical treatment which Cronenberg is at pains to deny. The inclusion of a past tense for his hero, not only includes flashbacks to when he was a boy but also in the cafe, when he looks at a poster of rolling green fields, we cut to a scene of him at the Institution. However, there is nothing in these brief scenes, as Spider is working outside in a bland Tellytubby-like landscape, to suggest either that he is in any way being treated or that he has been "cured". The joke made by the Head of this place that he is unlikely to repeat his crime because he only has one mother is no more true than any other crime of murder. His period of incarceration is just that and having "done his time", he is released with little in the way of what might be termed support mechanisms, other than the halfway house as a roof over his head. Indeed, this might be seen as just another institution as the only other inmate whom he befriends, Terrence, feels unable to step out and leave the apparent shelter this provides from the world. The jigsaw which Spider is given to do features a seagull, an image which appears to play little part in his life and his successful placing of a missing piece shows a control over a created reality not available to him in his everyday experience. Terrence's comment that the piece 'could go nowhere else' also applies to inmates of this place. He is ultimately given his liberty because he does not appear violent and because the object of his murderous intent is dead, *not* because he has been brought to any recognition or understanding of what he's done. That takes place *after* his release, not before.

Spider's collection of personal objects develops from a small tin as a boy to a sock hidden down the front of his trousers in the Institution to the battered suitcase that he carries to the halfway house. The action of retrieving the sock from down the front of his trousers is repeated several times, almost parodying attempts via cod psychology to explain the acquisition of these objects as an act of pseudo-sexual sublimation. The adult Spider's photograph of his mother, which we see him inspect whilst in the Institution, is part of his constructed self. We see him overtly manipulate the image, covering up one side and then the other, imposing his mother's face on the body of a topless model. Such private collections of items, whether functional or only for aesthetic contemplation, assume a spiritual function. In J. G. Ballard's *Concrete Island* (1974), in the shelter where the crash survivor Maitland is kept by derelicts Proctor and Jane Sheppard, there is a wooden table, upon which 'a number of metal objects were arranged in a circle like ornaments on an altar. All had been taken from motor-car bodies – a wing mirror, strips of chromium window trim, pieces of broken headlamp'.[19] In Ballard's short story 'News from the Sun' (1982), Slade, a disturbed patient, constructs 'psychosexual shrines to the strange gods inside his head'. All but one are cleared away by Dr Franklin who keeps the contents of one drawer intact and 'laid out like a corpse on its bier of surgical cotton'.[20] These are part of what Louis de Bernières terms 'the private museums that each of us carries in our heads', and in his use of the instruments, Cronenberg is dramatizing the cinematic equivalent of the deviant psychopathology in Ballard personal shrines.[21]

'I was also thinking of Kafka and Dostoevsky'[22]

For Bakhtin, in Dostoevsky's *Crime and Punishment* (1865), 'The threshold, the foyer, the corridor, the landing, the stair, its steps, doors which open onto stairs...[t]hat is the space in this novel.'[23] These are the locations of crises for characters perpetually in some kind of limbo state. In *A History of Violence*, Cronenberg repeatedly frames his hero Tom in a doorway at the foot of the stairs, particularly after despatching the killers from his past in view of his wife and son, demonstrating to them the true nature of his identity as a killer himself. In McGrath's *Spider*, the protagonist finds himself unable to cross the bridge over the canal, but following Dostoevsky, Cronenberg transposes this key symbol of transition to doorways, where he repeatedly places his hero.

Spider's arrival at the halfway house, itself an image of a threshold state, is filmed in a standard shot-reverse/shot sequence at the doorway. However, the use of extreme low angles in combination with the only use of CGI in the film conveys, not visceral but existential, horror as the gasworks opposite appears to loom over him. The sequence is reminiscent of the distorted hotel building in F. W. Murnau's *Der Letzte Mann* (1924) that appears to be bearing down upon the broken doorkeeper mentally broken from losing his job.

In connection with threshold locations, Cronenberg uses the stylistic trope of a forward tracking shot, whilst occupying Spider's subjective POV, approaching where a crisis occurs. As Spider explores his sparse room, he comes to the window only to be met again by the imposing figure of the gasworks. The same camera movement is used as Spider approaches his parents rowing in the kitchen, framed against the darkness of the corridor from where he is watching them. The forward tracking shot that leads into the flashback through the kitchen window does not herald a bravura experiment in deep focus photography as in *Kane*, and Cronenberg's camera moves slowly towards, but not through, the window. The forward tracking shot is also used most obviously in the opening sequence as more than just an echo of the Lumière Brothers' *The Arrival of a Train at La Ciotat Station* (1895). Falcon refers to this opening as constituting the only objective shot in the film but this is not strictly true.[24] At the station, itself a clear symbol of transitional states, we are unsure if the camera is moving forwards or just that people are flooding past a static position. After a few seconds, it becomes clear that both are moving so that as we enter the fictional world of the film, we are not sure who is important and who is not, the camera finally coming to rest on the adult Spider disembarking very slowly and setting down his case with great care.

Further examples of threshold positioning occur around the allotment. Spider emerges from a series of aqueduct arches that frame him emphatically like a creature emerging from a bolt-hole. The setting acts as a catalyst for a flashback in which Spider's mother (according to her son's account) stands in the doorway of the shed, transfixed by the sight of her husband having sex with Yvonne. This threshold is where she is struck in the face with a spade and it is where both visions of his mother, Madonna and Whore, collide, resulting in the death of one and the distortion of the other. One of the most striking examples of Cronenberg's use of thresholds occurs when Bill steals the keys of the halfway house. A shot from the POV of the sofa in the day room sees Spider descending the stairs in the right hand of the frame and on the left we see further into the depth of the building as an open door shows the office of Mrs Wilkinson, who is sitting with her back to us. A dividing wall creates a split-screen effect in the middle of the shot here and the two halves of the screen are also framed by two separate doorways, almost as if characters are placed in adjacent boxes. Similarly, in *A History of Violence*, when a breathless Tom arrives home to defend his family only to discover there is no apparent threat, the frame is divided by adjacent doorways. On the right is the son, alarmed at cracks appearing in the façade of his newly heroic father, and on the left are the wife and daughter, equally unsure if they know who Tom is anymore.

In the final section of *Spider*, we see the boy Spider link the gas tap in the kitchen to his bedroom by an elaborate web of pulleys and levers, so that he can kill the woman whom he thinks has usurped the position of his mother when she returns drunk from the pub. This allows Cronenberg to craft several shots in which the frame is dissected and bisected by lines of string, motivated within the scene. This is evocative of the car wash scene in *Crash*, where the whirring electric windows and roof of a Lincoln convertible gradually close up to form the equivalent of an iris focusing attention on the sexual exchange taking place within the car as well as adding depth to the shot. Here, the extreme high angle shots in Spider's bedroom of the boy on the bed looking up at the webs stretching across the room work in a similar way to shots of Chris Ecclestone as Derrick Bentley in Peter Medak's *Let Him Have It* (1991), creating a 'spider's eye view', as it were, of an insecure protagonist.

The final action in connection with his parents happens over the threshold of their front door as the lifeless body of his mother is carried out by his distraught father, clarifying the truth which most viewers will have long since suspected – 'You've done your mum in.' When the adult Spider revisits Kitchener Street and finds the The Dog and Beggar pub, where his father used to drink, a close-up of his feet emphasizes how he cannot step over the kerb. Something is preventing him from crossing this boundary. By the close of the film, we know what this is. The act of murder itself is perpetrated using doorways to guide the string from the gas tap in the kitchen to his bedroom. The boy carefully and slowly steps back from the curb and stands against the wall, prefiguring the style and location of the adult Spider's movements in his visionary flashbacks in the kitchen and the allotment. Past and present fuse as we cut to the adult Spider occupying the same space where the boy was, apparently looking down at the scene of his mother's corpse. The sequences with Spider both as a boy and later as an adult edging away from a kerb place him firmly as a character on a threshold, in terms of his sanity, the acceptability of his actions in a conventional society and his recognition of what he has done.

Crime and Punishment ('What have you done?')

Cronenberg's *Spider* shares several similarities with Dostoevsky's *Crime and Punishment*, which also features a character creeping within a house in order to steal keys from a woman; in the novel after murdering her, in the film prior to an implied murder. Both feature a blunt object as murder weapon: the back of Raskolnikov's hatchet and Spider's hammer. Both narratives portray the consequences of premeditated murder of a woman and both examine the operation of guilt, one in terms of confession and redemption, the other in suppression and projection onto others. Both heroes hold their weapons above recumbent female victims and peer closely at them, one before attacking, one after.

Ralph Fiennes' interpretation of the pause at the last minute seems to suggest consideration of how to do the act rather than whether it should be done at all. The scene is slightly reminiscent of Roman Polanski's version of *Macbeth* (1970) where the sleeping King Duncan is approached by the protagonist intent on murder. There is a similar pause before the sleeping victim and, like Cronenberg's film, Polanski has his victim wake (ambiguous in Shakespeare's text). However, Polanski's victim is killed whereas Mrs Wilkinson is spared to deliver the repeated question, not relating to what Spider was about to do but his troubled past, 'What have you done?'

In *The Body in Pain* (1985), Elaine Scarry strives to distinguish between a weapon, a tool and an artefact. For her, 'what differentiates them is not the object itself but the surface on which they fall', i.e. whether it is a sentient or non-sentient surface.[25] She explains that 'there are certain instruments (such as those in medicine and dentistry) that we call tools even though they enter human tissue; but it should be noticed that this identification is learned and even after this, it requires a conscious mental act to hold steady the perception...of the object as a tool'.[26] It is this 'conscious mental act', which both Spider and the Mantle twins are unable to sustain. Scarry's discussion postulates first a child below a raised knife, then a lamb, then a block of wood as a shift from weapon to tool at the second stage and by the third stage 'wounding' has become 'making'.[27] This is what happens in the final scene of *Dead Ringers*, as Beverly appears not to see his brother as a fully sentient being but like the cadaver of the early dissection scene and in *Spider*, where the hero appears to be considering making a sculpture of a living woman. Cronenberg asserts that 'some of my male characters like the Mantles are not reacting to the female body with disgust, but with real curiosity', and that this curiosity creates a simple dilemma: 'how do you deal with women? Well, you know, like anything else, you cut her open and see how she works. Well, medically that's very sound, but emotionally it doesn't work at all'.[28]

The specific motif of a white, middle-aged, male, scientist/artist leaning over the body of a prostrate woman (sleeping, drugged or dead) either about to or in the process of dissecting her is a recurrent image in Cronenberg's work. The Roswell-like autopsy in *The Brood*, the opening sequence in *Shivers* (1976) where Hobbes tries to neutralize his virus, the operating theatre sequence in *Rabid* (1977) twice reprised in *Dead Ringers* and Spider holding a hammer and chisel above the sleeping form of his Landlady all focus on *the female (or feminized) body on the slab*. In *Dead Ringers*, when Beverly complains that the women look 'normal' from the outside but on the inside they are 'all wrong', he is articulating the notion of a fragile border between legal/criminal, male/female and places the male in the position of suggesting corrective surgery for a perceived imperfection in the female body. This could be extended to *Crash*, where James Ballard leans over the recumbent Gabrielle and searches her body for new points of entry. It is a further example of an existential remapping of the female body by opening it up to see how it works or how it might work differently, according to a male inquisitor.

Elaine Showalter traces the motif in a *fin-de-siècle* painting of a doctor performing an autopsy on a drowned prostitute. She features two of the best-known examples by J. H. Hasselhorst and Barbara Kruger.[29] Kruger's painting features an elderly surgeon holding the recently removed heart of a female dissection subject and is dated 1988, the same year as *Dead Ringers* was released. Showalter also cites Ludmilla Jordanova's work on the relationship between science and sexuality, including *fin-de-siècle* sculptures portraying Nature as a female body that must be uncovered by a male inquirer, such as Barrias's 1895 work *La nature se devoilant devant la science* (Nature Unveiling Herself Before Science).[30] Seeking to explain the relative lack of dissection of *male* bodies, Showalter asserts that 'men do not think of themselves as cases to be opened up. Instead, they open up a woman as a substitute for self-knowledge...The criminal slashes with his knife. The scientist and doctor open the woman up with the scalpel.'[31] Cronenberg appears to place himself as the inheritor of this tradition of nineteenth-century male 'dissectors': 'I am being this clinician, this surgeon, and trying to examine the nature of sexuality. I'm doing it by creating characters I then dissect with my cinematic scalpels.'[32]

Notes From Underground
'The Sensitives': The (literary) derelict as hero

Spider is only the latest in a long line of Cronenberg's derelict heroes: from the telepath Cameron Vale in *Scanners* (1980), literally first seen underground as a shambling down-and-out, to Max Renn in *Videodrome*, who finds himself on a rusting, condemned ship, to Rose in *Rabid*, whose body is unceremoniously dumped in a garbage truck at the close of the film. Cronenberg's own first on-screen appearance is as a derelict himself: 'Man in Bin #82' in *Shivers*. Cronenberg uses male underground protagonists, who create their own paranoid reality very much in the mould of writers like Dostoevsky. An early project about a group of unhappy telepaths, which eventually became *Scanners*, was termed 'The Sensitives', and this is a recurrent element of the Cronenbergian hero. Like the hero of *Notes From Underground* (1864) who is a 'a hypersensitive individual,' he is too responsive to the world around him, such that he cannot exert his will upon events but appears as a noirish figure, at the mercy of forces beyond his control.[33] Dostoevsky's hero recounts things he almost did, such as starting a fight, and Cronenberg's Spider could be described in the same way: he almost speaks coherently, he almost returns to the Dog and Beggar and he almost kills Mrs Wilkinson.[34] His only significant, completed action is the murder of his mother. A typical hero of both Nabokov and Dostoevsky is solipsistic to the point where he cannot distinguish between himself and the world around him and Nabokov's explanation for the inspiration for *Lolita* (1959) of the ape in the Jardin des Plantes in Paris, which produced a drawing lauded as the first by an animal but which actually only featured the bars of his own cage, might indeed describe a typical Cronenberg hero.[35]

Cronenberg's visualization of the boarding house evokes a typically Dostoevskian scene of shabbiness. Floorboards are bare, paint is peeling from the walls, and furniture is sparse and rickety. Spider's search for a hiding place for his journal motivates a closer look at the fabric of his room. Under the paper lining of his chest of drawers is rejected as too obvious and even the prying up of a floorboard has to be subsequently covered up by a frayed piece of carpet. An imposing close-up of the gasworks is the immediate view out of his only window. He is a derelict amongst other derelicts, forced to eat at spare, long tables, evocative of the Cathode Ray Mission in *Videodrome*. Even the cafe where he goes is shabby, the food hidden by a veil and the window covered by a faded curtain.

An interesting part of this conception of "the underground man" is revealed by Cronenberg's repeated use of certain actors. The quintessential Cronenbergian leading man is Jeremy Irons, the only actor whom he has cast twice as his protagonist in *Dead Ringers* and *M Butterfly* (1993). Indeed, had Cronenberg chosen to use a real set of identical twins to play the Mantle brothers in *Dead Ringers*, he would not have been able to cast Irons at all here. Even the most cursory look at Irons' other film work – *The Mission* (Roland Joffe, 1984), *The French Lieutenant's Woman* (Karel Reisz, 1981), *Waterland* (Stephen Gyllenhaal, 1992), *Betrayal* (David Jones, 1983), *Kafka* (Steven Soderbergh, 1991) and *Lolita* (Adrian Lyne, 1996) – might suggest that he too specializes in solipsistic, literary heroes. His television work, particularly for the BBC, extends from *Brideshead Revisited* (1982) to a dramatized reading of Dostoevsky's *The Dream* (1990) and Heathcote Williams's apocalyptic poem *Autogeddon* (1991), the latter repeated to coincide with the release of Cronenberg's *Crash* in 1996. Typically his work is infused with an on-screen persona that is literary, slightly effete and European in cultural sensibility.

However, perhaps less obvious than Jeremy Irons, are other certain figures who reoccur in roles that are smaller, but no less important. Although Stephen Lack was rather lifeless as the lead in *Scanners* (1980), Cronenberg used him again as Wollek the sculptor in *Dead Ringers*. Les Carlson appears in *Videodrome* (Barry Convex) and the lead in the short film *Camera* (2000). Particularly notable though is Robert Silverman. He appears as cancer patient and sculptor Ben Pierce in *Scanners* (originally the central character in early drafts of Cronenberg's screenplay), as go-between/pimp Hans in *Naked Lunch*, as patient Jan Hartog in *The Brood* and as store owner/games character Darcy Nader in *eXistenZ*. In each case he is a minor character, but the choice to repeatedly cast him emphasizes the key type he represents: creepy, effeminate, artistic. Cronenberg discusses directing an episode of *Friday the 13th: The Series*, entitled 'Faith Healer' (1988), in which he worked with Silverman: '[h]e played a man with a fatal, consumptive disease and there was something almost palpably tragic in his eyes, in his manner. I really believed this guy was dying,' also a key feature of Carlson's melancholic expression in *Camera*.[36] Cronenberg admits Silverman has found it hard to get film work: 'He's a strange presence...He's so convincing and scary, so *sad*.'[37]

192 | DAVID CRONENBERG: AUTHOR OR FILM-MAKER?

Suicide is also clearly an important phenomenon to both Cronenberg and Dostoevsky. The Russian novelist's works contain 22 successful suicide attempts, seven in *The Diary of a Writer* (1876) alone. By comparison, *Videodrome*, *The Fly*, and *M Butterfly* all end with the explicit suicide of the protagonist. *Dead Ringers* closes with a victim complicit in his death (Beverly Mantle) and a waiting for death akin to suicide (his brother Elliot). *Rabid* (1976), *Scanners* and *The Dead Zone* close with an action that will inevitably lead to death (wilfully exposing oneself to a victim of a killer disease, a battle to the death with a telepath brother and attempting to assassinate a presidential candidate respectively), and *Crash* ends with an unsuccessful joint suicide but the promise of further attempts in the Ballards' mantra 'Maybe the next one.' *eXistenZ* ends with the death of the "viewer" as Pikul and Allegra shoot into the camera, echoing Edwin S. Porter's close-up at the end of *The Great Train Robbery* (1903).

In *The Possessed* (1871), Kirillov's argument for suicide involves the attaining of a God-like state, evoking *Videodrome*'s notions of transcendent 'New Flesh' via self-destruction: 'Now man is not yet what he will be. There will be a new man, happy and proud. For whom it will be the same to live or not to live...Everyone who wants the supreme freedom must dare to kill himself...He who dares to kill himself is God.'[38] According to N. N. Shneidman, 'suicide is seldom committed out of reflection. It frequently happens that one event, often unimportant in itself, is just enough to precipitate the unconsciously borne rancour and all the boredom which had been held in suspension for a long time.'[39] In *Videodrome*, Max may appear to live, as Nickki Brand puts it, in a state of overstimulation but his seedy down-market pornography is indicative of a strong sense of ennui long before he meets her and is exposed to the Videodrome Signal, typified by the sales meeting where he lounges distractedly like a small child.

Asylum and *Dr Haggard's Disease* both end with the suicide of the protagonist. McGrath's *Spider* ends with an increasingly mad Spider contemplating going up to the attic with some rope and implying he will hang himself soon. However, unlike many of his previous films, Cronenberg chooses not to close his narrative with suicide, attempted or successful, instead focusing on the collection of rope and string from a building site so as to recreate in his room the intricate webs from the ceilings at which he gazed up as a boy and used to kill his mother. Cronenberg frequently alters source texts to direct his narrative towards extinction but interestingly where such suggestions exist already (in McGrath's novel), he avoids this. Like a typical Dostoevsky novel, McGrath's *Spider* ends with a note of fatigue as if the narrator has no more energy or inclination to continue. Cronenberg, however, does not close either with suicide or with boredom but with a return to beginnings. A spiral structure positions the adult Spider in what appears to be exactly the same car that took him away as a child many years before, being returned apparently to the same institution but with a slightly clearer sense of what he has done.

Diary of a Madman ('Spider, c'est moi')[40]

Cronenberg is happy to use an allusion to Flaubert's *Madame Bovary* (1857) as part of his speech about his work, particularly when speaking to French journalists and repeatedly in interviews he underlines his personal and professional affinity with the character of Spider: 'I can easily see myself becoming Spider...I could see myself walking the streets muttering to myself and what I was saying would have meaning for me but for nobody else.'[41] He claims that 'it wasn't until I was editing the movie that I thought, my God, this is the archetype of an artist...writing passionately and obsessively and with great attention to detail in a language that's incomprehensible to anybody else and maybe even to himself.'[42] This, however, has been central to Cronenberg's conception of his art and his own role within it for many years now. He has consistently portrayed the artist according to quintessential Romantic tenets: a writer, misunderstood, unappreciated by his own time and culture, uses a personal form of language to express his (and it always has been a "his") unique view of the world. It is not the possession of telepathic powers, which sets the hero apart from his fellows post-*Scanners* but the isolation of an artist, compelled to write and yet unable to find a language in which to express himself to others. It is a philosophy that he articulated over a decade earlier in *Naked Lunch* and which draws heavily on Nabokov: 'Nabokov's narrators are passionate annotators of reality...they keep diaries and notebooks and collect scraps of information to use in making their notes in the margin of the real.'[43] In *The Gift*, the dying poet Chernychevski perceives that 'if I have lived, I have lived only in the margin of a book I have never been able to read.'[44]

Like Vaughan with his scrapbook in *Crash* and Lee with his typewriter in *Naked Lunch*, Spider has his coded journal, which he keeps carefully hidden. All of them view writing as a secretive, and by implication, subversive act. Lee in *Naked Lunch*, claims to have stopped writing at age 10 as it was 'too dangerous'. Cronenberg asserts that 'I think that imagination and creativity are completely natural and also, under certain circumstances, quite dangerous'. However, there is a key problem here for Cronenberg. He is drawn to the subversion of writing but his art form, cinema, is just not possible to produce in isolation and requires an audience. The hero of *Notes From Underground* states that 'I'm writing this just for myself' but whatever his protestations of such a sensibility, Cronenberg cannot do this.[45] Whereas Burroughs develops this idea of imaginative creation as potential threat to suggest a potential breakdown of western dualistic structures of thought, Cronenberg uses it as a position from which to privilege notions of the author. His examples of the dangers of imagination draw upon individual writers: 'look what happened to Salman Rushdie' or the concept of political dissidence: 'Romanians had to register their typewriters as dangerous weapons!'[46]

Twenty years before the release of *Spider*, Cronenberg was already visualizing himself as part of a long line of literary derelicts: 'All of the fabled American artists became derelicts...Walt Whitman, Melville. Maybe me, someday.'[47] The identification that Cronenberg makes with his heroes is particularly focused on their creative processes and more particularly, as writers. He describes the spartan conditions under which he wrote *Videodrome* in an isolated rented room, strongly evoking his realization of Lee in *Naked Lunch*: 'I just had a chair, a table, a typewriter.'[48] Cronenberg claims that 'even though we don't look alike' (a rather contentious statement), "Jimmy Woods" presence on the screen began to feel like a projection of me.'[49] Tim Lucas refers to 'one obligatory moment in which the hero dons glasses and adopts the mannerisms of the man calling the shots,' and certainly there are similarities between Max and Cronenberg himself from a certain physical similarity (highlighted when Max tries on a pair of glasses from Spectacular Optical) and in terms of role, they are both purveyors of visual images.[50] This might be extended to film producer James Ballard, who begins to create his own fantasies under the tutelage of Vaughan in *Crash*, Ted Pikul, who affects the direction of his game in *eXistenZ* or Spider at the kitchen window, who peoples a scene with remembered dialogue.

Cronenberg permitted shots of himself directing the boys in the opening sequence of *Dead Ringers*, like his posing with William Burroughs and Peter Weller as Lee during the promotion of *Naked Lunch*).[51] He readily admits that 'the kids in *Dead Ringers* are partly modelled after me. I did wear glasses as a kid, I was interested in Science and I was precocious... I completely identify with those two little monsters'.[52] He claims too that 'the only reason I played the gynaecologist in *The Fly* was because Geena Davis begged me to. She didn't want a stranger between her legs, and felt more comfortable with me there'.[53] Cronenberg is almost encouraging elisions to be made between the creator and his creations, and the need to step into his own fictions as if to underline those aspects of the plot most important to him personally make claims of disinterested even-handedness hard to sustain. This could be part of a perverse game which he plays with critics, although this kind of identification does problematize attempts to distance himself from the attitudes of his fictional characters, if they appear misogynistic.

A more direct source of inspiration for the Cronenberg's realization of Spider may have been Don DeLillo's novel *The Body Artist* (2001). Here the heroine, Lauren Hartke, discovers a shambling derelict wandering in her house and names him Mr Tuttle due to his mostly incoherent mumblings, which appear to be snatches of some interior monologue and whose physical appearance, most notably trousers of uneven length resembles Ralph Fiennes's portrayal of Spider. In DeLillo's book, this character appears to the heroine on a lonely isolated island, much like the self-imposed retreat of McGrath himself, who lived in a shack on the Queen Charlotte Islands in British Columbia in the late 1970s.

The last word

Dostoevsky is also interested in the use of so-called "loopholes." Bakhtin defines the term thus: '[a] loophole is the retention for oneself of the possibility to alter the final, ultimate sense of one's word' and '[a]ccording to its sense, the word with a loophole must be the last word, and it presents itself as such, but in fact it is only the next-to-last word, and is followed by only a conditional, not a final, period.'[54] This privileges the writer as the conventional Romantic focus of heightened plane of perception but also problematizes nature of language and writing. The significance of the "loophole" notion here is that the meaning of any text can be altered according to context. In a sense, it seems possible to reduce many Cronenberg films to a single question from within the fiction: 'Who is this?' (*Dead Ringers*), 'Have you come?' (*Crash*), 'Are we still in the game?' (*eXistenZ*) and 'What have you done?' (*Spider*). However all these questions contain a multitude of potential meanings depending on which part is emphasized. In *Spider*, Mrs Wilkinson's question is put twice, the first stresses the 'have you', the second emphasizes the 'what' slightly more, balancing a focus on the deed and the perpetrator.

In talking about a Dostoevskian hero, Malcolm Jones is also describing a Cronenbergian one, who 'takes refuge from the torments of a lop-sided intersubjectivity in a world of intertextuality, of dream, of fantasy, of fiction, of philosophising, a world in which a consciousness of the power of the "written" over the already-experienced and the still-to-be-experienced leads him to put his trust increasingly, though with "loopholes" as Bakhtin would put it, in "writing" rather than immediate spoken dialogue.'[55] Cronenberg converts McGrath's conception of Spider's articulate paranoia into the mumbling incoherence of Fiennes's verbal delivery and the unreliability of a narrator is further dramatized by denying the viewer clear fictive markers. As in *Videodrome*'s infamous stomach-slit scene, *Naked Lunch*'s parrot cage scene and any shift in and out of the game world in *eXistenZ*, there are no wobbly screen effects to signal a shift in time or space. In *Spider*, Cronenberg provides his hero with a past tense, not to explain his character but to problematize it still further. Memory is portrayed as a construct of the individual, not a reliable source of objective evidence. As for Dostoevsky, Bakhtin describes how he unsettles his reader 'by means of an almost imperceptible transformation, to push the images and manifestations of everyday reality to the limits of the fantastic.'[56] In the first flashback sequence in *Spider*, the half-consumed pint and the action of the boy brushing the adult's coat, show Cronenberg using similar means to convey the dream-like nature of reality and the apparent reality of dreams in the minds of his heroes, as part of an ongoing exploration of the impossible.

Notes
1. Martin Amis, *Time's Arrow* (London: Penguin Books, 1991), p. 76.
2. Mikhail Bakhtin, *Problems of Dostoevsky's Poetics*, trans. R. W. Ratsel (Manchester: Ardis, 1973), p. 24.
3. Patrick McGrath, *Spider* (London: Penguin Books, 1992), p. 13.
4. See Nick James, 'The Right Trousers', Interview with Ralph Fiennes, *Sight and Sound* 13:1 (January 2003), p. 15.

5. See Kevin Jackson, 'Odd Man Out', *Sight & Sound* 13:1 (January 2003), p. 12.
6. Ibid., p. 13.
7. Bakhtin, op.cit., p. 23.
8. Ibid., p. 122.
9. In Volume III of *A History of Sexuality*, Michel Foucault describes how Artemidorus asserts that in dreams of sexual relations between brothers, 'the dreamer is always present in his own dream', and 'he does so as the leading actor'. See Michel Foucault, *The History of Sexuality, Volume III: The Care of the Self*, trans. Robert Hurley (Harmondsworth: Penguin Books, 1988), p. 26.
10. Ian McEwan, *The Child in Time* (London: Jonathan Cape, 1987), p. 57.
11. Ibid.
12. Ibid., p. 58.
13. Ibid., p. 59.
14. Ibid.
15. Ibid., p. 60.
16. Patrick McGrath, *Asylum* (London: Penguin, 1996), p. 43.
17. Patrick McGrath, *Dr Haggard`s Disease* (London: Vintage, 1993), p. 36.
18. See Serge Grünberg, 'Spider c'est moi,' *Cahiers du Cinéma*, no. 568 (May 2002), p. 21.
19. J. G. Ballard, *Concrete Island* (London: Jonathan Cape, 1974), p. 76.
20. See J. G. Ballard, 'News from the Sun' in *Myths of the Near Future* (London: Jonathan Cape, 1982), p. 85.
21. Louis de Bernières, *Captain Corelli's Mandolin* (London: Vintage, 1998), p. 34.
22. See Jackson, op.cit., p. 12.
23. Bakhtin, op.cit., p. 144.
24. Richard Falcon, 'Spider', *Sight and Sound* 13:1 (January 2003), p. 52.
25. Elaine Scarry, *The Body in Pain: The Making and Unmaking of the World* (New York; Oxford: Oxford University Press, 1985), p. 173.
26. Ibid., p. 174.
27. Ibid.
28. See 'Logic, creativity and (critical) misinterpretation: an interview with David Cronenberg', conducted by Xavier Mendik in Michael Grant (ed.), *The Modern Fantastic: The Films of David Cronenberg* (Trowbridge: Flicks Books, 2000), p. 176. See also Cronenberg cited in Stephanie Bunbury, 'David Cronenberg Doubles Up', *Cinema Papers* 71 (Jan. 1989), p. 24.
29. Elaine Showalter, *Sexual Anarchy: Gender and Culture at the Fin de Siécle* (London: Virago, 1992), pp. 132-133. See also Michael Fried's *Realism, Writing, Disfiguration* (Chicago: London: The University of Chicago, 1987). Fried's extended analysis of Thomas Eakins's *The Gross Clinic* (1875) has several similarities with Cronenberg's surgery scenes. There is a male doctor standing over his patient, an unflinching focus on the wound, the presence of an audience to the procedure, the artist himself is in the picture (like Cronenberg in *The Fly*), and Fried persistently links painting with the act of writing.
30. Showalter, ibid., pp. 145-146.
31. Ibid., p. 134.
32. See Chris Rodley, *Cronenberg on Cronenberg* (London: Faber and Faber, 1992), p. 152.
33. N. N. Shneidman, *Dostoevsky and Suicide* (Oaksville, Ontario; London: Mosaic Press, 1984), p. 33.
34. Fyodor Dostoevsky, *Notes From Underground*, (New York: Signet Classics, 1961; originally published in 1865), p. 129.
35. See Alfred Appel Jr and Charles Newman (eds.), *Nabokov: Criticism, Reminiscences, Translations and Tributes* (London: Weidenfield & Nicolson, 1971), p. 21.

36. See Tim Lucas, 'Ideadrome: David Cronenberg from *Shivers* to *Dead Ringers*', *Video Watchdog* 36 (1996), p. 27.
37. Ibid., p. 28.
38. Fyodor Dostoevsky, *The Possessed* (1871), p. 133.
39. See Shneidman, op. cit., p. 16.
40. See Serge Grünberg, op. cit., pp. 16–22.
41. See Jackson, op. cit., p. 15.
42. Ibid., p. 12.
43. Lucy Maddox, *Nabokov's Novels in English* (Athens, Georgia: University of Georgia Press, 1983), p. 9.
44. Vladimir Nabokov, *The Gift* (London: Weidenfeld and Nicolson, 1963), p. 323.
45. Fyodor Dostoevsky, *Notes From Underground* and *The Double*, translated with an introduction by Jessie Coulson, (Harmondsworth: Penguin Books, 1972), p. 122.
46. See Rodley, op. cit., p. 169.
47. Cronenberg cited in 'The Image as Virus: The Filming of *Videodrome*', by Tim Lucas in Piers Handling (ed.), *The Shape of Rage: The Films of David Cronenberg* (Toronto: Academy of Canadian Cinema, 1983; New York: New York Zoetrope Inc., 1983), p. 155.
48. See Rodley, op. cit., p. 94.
49. Ibid., p 95.
50. Tim Lucas, op. cit., p. 37.
51. See Rodley, op. cit., p. 9 and p. 156.
52. Cronenberg cited in ibid., p. 8.
53. Cronenberg cited in ibid., p. 152.
54. See Bakhtin, op.cit., p. 195 and p. 196.
55. Malcolm Jones, *Dostoevsky After Bakhtin: Readings in Dostoevsky's Fantastic Realism* (Cambridge; New York: Cambridge University Press, 1990), p. 62.
56. See Bakhtin, op. cit., p. 85.

CONCLUSION

'The interesting thing for me is that the cinema has always been fed by literature, hugely, right from its inception, and writing is still a crucial part of filmmaking whether it's a novel or not'.[1]

'You'll see liquified eyeballs, you'll see blistering of the skin, you'll see dazzling changes of colour, maggots, you'll even see corpses bursting open.'[2]

It seems to remain a commonplace expectation that a Cronenberg film delivers the kinds of visceral thrills evoked in Radcliff Vaughan's description above of the discipline of pathology from Patrick McGrath's *Dr Haggard's Disease* (1993). However, since 1982, this has just *not* been the case. Cronenberg has spent the last 25 years making films that may feature brief selected images that disturb and horrify (the dream sequences in *Dead Ringers* or the parrot cage scene in *Naked Lunch*, for instance) but these are not necessarily horror films per se. In *The Novel and the Cinema* (1975), Geoffrey Wagner proposes three types of adaptation: transposition, commentary and analogy. 'Transposition' is whereby 'a novel is given directly on the screen with a minimum of apparent interference;' 'commentary' is where source material is 'either purposely or inadvertently altered in some respect;' and 'analogy' is 'a fairly considerable departure for the sake of making another work of art'.[3] This study has found that, although Cronenberg's apparent intention (and claimed achievement) is in articulating films that express Wagner's third category, 'analogy', what we find more often is the second group, 'commentary', reflecting a literary bond, which he seems unable to break.

Given Cronenberg's literary analysis of his own work, Jill McGreal declares that Martin Scorsese's remark 'that Cronenberg doesn't understand his own films seems extraordinary' and 'ill-judged'.[4] Cronenberg's perception of Brett Easton Ellis' *American Psycho* (1991) as a satire of 1980s Wall Street corporate culture when reviewers dismissed it as a pornographic snuff novel, leads Linda Kauffman to observe that 'it is an interesting moment in culture when the filmmakers are better readers than the literary critics'.[5] However, Cronenberg continually resists openly acknowledging the debt that he owes either to literature or film, constantly craving the status of the original artist, the auteur, whose works can be attributed to his vision alone. One of the main findings of this study is the number and range of Cronenberg's unacknowledged 'borrowings' particularly from J. G. Ballard, William Burroughs and pervasive, possibly unconscious, influences from Vladimir Nabokov. These are not restricted to adaptations of specific works but pervade Cronenberg's entire *oeuvre*, so that his films not only reward, but at times demand, wider cultural, particularly literary, knowledge. In comparing staple horror narratives, what he terms 'the-man-in-the-basement-with-the-knife' stories with what David Breskin terms 'an existential, philosophical horror', Cronenberg uses a literary metaphor: 'we know the difference between Elmore Leonard and Saul Bellow'.[6] It is the literary status of the latter that he appears to crave.

Chapter 1 argued that *Videodrome* (1982) articulates an aesthetic that blends literary expressions of masochism with an exploration of Foucault-influenced notions of spectacle and an embracing of potential extensions of the notion of the body, an aesthetic that finds an 'objective co-relative' in Clive Barker's *Books of Blood* (1984–1986). The destabilizing effect of Max Renn's subjective narrative in *Videodrome*, as in Ted and Allegra's adventures in *eXistenZ* (1999), makes any firm points of identification problematic, undermining attempts to see *Videodrome* as a parody of McLuhan or Debord. The interweaving of technology and humanity that McLuhan warns about, Cronenberg and Barker celebrate in their view of sexuality as culturally derived and as subjective as Max's narrative. If a director makes desire visible, the end product is pornography; if he or she makes pain visible, then it results in horror. What makes Cronenberg's work interesting but problematic is that he shows pain in desire and desire in pain, creating a new hybrid of existential horror that takes an understanding, derived from literature, of how the sexual philosophy of de Sade and Masoch is interwoven, not mutually exclusive.

There is a consistency in the personal or literary sexual personae of the authors upon whom Cronenberg draws most frequently for inspiration. From Burroughs' overt homosexuality to Barker and Ellis' 'coming out' in the 1990s to the fictional exploration by Ballard of various psychopathologies and Nabokov of paedophilia and nympholepsy, there is the continual question, as phrased by Judith Halberstam: 'What is allowed to be fucking?'[7] In 1965, what Leslie Fiedler intended as a dire warning of the moral laxity into which he felt the youth of the time was slipping, describing Burroughs *Naked Lunch* (1959) as 'a nightmare anticipation...of post-Humanist sexuality', describes what Cronenberg seems to portray as evolutionary, inevitable and to be welcomed.[8]

Cronenberg's method for superseding his literary precursors is to deny their influence, a process that he repeats so frequently in interviews that he appears to believe this. He asserts that *Dead Ringers* (1988) 'was not based on a novel...it's really an original script', despite the presence of numerous similarities at the level of narrative, thematic focus and imagery.[9] Chapter 2 underlined the considerable, and unacknowledged, debt that Cronenberg owes to Bari Wood and Jack Geasland's source novel, *Twins* (1977), which extends from key dramatic incidents such as Beverly's inability to speak on the phone to clear precursors for the gynaecological tools and the talismanic Mantle Retractor. A comparison with other texts featuring doubles, like Angela Carter's *Wise Children* (1992), underscores the uncanny nature of the Mantle twins, while the theatricality of texts like Margaret Attwood's *The Handmaid's Tale* (1987) provides a parallel for the patriarchal medical establishment's casting of the pregnant woman's role as performative. The twins in Bruce Chatwin's *On the Black Hill* (1983), like Cronenberg's Mantle brothers, explore Wittgenstein's notion that pain can be said to be shared when it is the same pain, and in Rose Tremain's *Restoration* (1989), the protagonists, both doctors, displace their feelings for one another into their vocation, symbolized by unorthodox medical tools.

Chapter 3 explored how Cronenberg's *Naked Lunch* (1991) 'heterosexualizes' a gay narrative and appropriates a wide range of Burroughsian themes, motifs and images. In writing about poetic influence, Harold Bloom uses the term '*clinamen*' to describe when 'a poet swerves away from his precursor', and when Ted Pikul claims in *eXistenZ* that he has 'a phobia about my body being penetrated', he is reflecting a consistent swerving away in Cronenberg's films from homosexual source texts both in *Crash* and particularly *Naked Lunch*.[10] In discussing a range of texts that express what she calls 'homosocial desire', Eve Sedgwick describes how women can be used as the 'conduit of a relationship' with a man, in the sense of writers who use women as a means to look at men.[11] This is also found in Cronenberg's aesthetic. In *Crash* (1996), Catherine Ballard facilitates a bond between James and Vaughan, and in *Naked Lunch*, Joan Frost allows Lee to disavow his own homosexual inclinations in the parrot cage hallucination. In these latter two films in particular, Cronenberg's heroes exemplify Judith Butler's observation that 'heterosexuality is always in the process of imitating and approximating its own phantasmatic idealisation of itself- *and failing*'.[12]

Cronenberg welcomes descriptions of his films that class them as examples of '*tessera*', which Bloom describes as work which '"completes" his precursor' and certainly J. G. Ballard's positive response to the film version of *Crash* has allowed that particular film to be viewed in this way.[13] However, it would seem that Cronenberg's ambition exceeds even this level of kudos. His comments on his own script of *Naked Lunch* casts his writing as '*apophrades*', defined by Bloom as when a work 'makes it seem to us, not as though the precursor were writing it, but as though the later poet himself had written the precursor's characteristic work'.[14] Cronenberg claims that in achieving a sense of fusion with his literary inspiration that he 'almost felt for a moment, "Well, if Burroughs dies, I'll write his next book"'.[15]

In Cronenberg's *Naked Lunch*, the fact that Hank and Martin have to make Lee aware that he has written something of substance implies that the greatest creative acts come unbidden. For Serge Grünberg, 'if he (Lee) was conscious of himself as a writer, he would be petrified! So he makes himself hallucinate a world in which he is a secret agent, forced to participate in a vast conspiracy; it is in this context that he writes his reports for his masters...And at the end of the film, he will always deny having written a book called *Naked Lunch*'.[16] However, as William Beard notes, 'repression does not work, and attempts to escape it, from sexual relationships to heroic existential exploration, lead only to the discovery of things inside the self which cannot be borne'.[17] Bloom's literal translation of the term '*apophrades*' is 'the return of the dead' and Cronenberg's attempted denial of a homosexual subtext is fused with a literary denial that, like Burroughs, what he is trying to be is a writer, and it is Cronenberg's more general failure to be both a writer, and specifically the reincarnation of William Burroughs, that 'cannot be borne'. [18]

Chapter 4 stressed the debt that Cronenberg owes to the novel of *Crash* and a wide range of Ballardian texts, particularly *The Atrocity Exhibition* (1969), from which he appropriates dialogue, episodes, images and even imports whole chunks of prose into his script, without acknowledgement in any related interviews. It is the existential freedom that Cronenberg sees as inherently involved in any creative act, which partly leads to the adoption of a perpetual present in all his narratives examined in this study. This also blends with his exploration of moments of pain and sadness, such as Catherine on the embankment in *Crash* and Lee in marketplace in *Naked Lunch*, because Cronenberg's conception of pain is suffused with existential annihilation. As Elaine Scarry notes, 'the most crucial fact about pain is *its presentness*'.[19] The effect of this perpetual present in films like *Crash* is also found in Nabokov's *Lolita* (1959): 'what we are given is theme and variations, and denied any sense of cumulation or growth. We get experience of the order of a child's memories, experience deprived of temporal dimension'.[20] This chronological limbo also evokes Ballard in more recent works like *Cocaine Nights* (1998), where the fictional recreational playground of Estrella de Mar dramatizes 'the timelessness of a world beyond boredom, with no past, no future and a diminishing present'.[21] For Nabokov, 'the only alternative to perversity...is banality', but for Cronenberg, the issue is not one of alternatives but of fusion, creating the dominant mode of *Naked Lunch* and *Crash*: banal perversity.[22]

The drive towards a narrative structure that appears repetitive and circular but is actually *spiral* in form is another bond between Cronenberg and Nabokov. Chapter 5 considered Cronenberg's selective reading of Sartrean existentialism in *eXistenZ*, blended with a range of stylistic features closely associated with Nabokov, particularly a predilection for game-playing conceits, and self-conscious references within the narrative to its own workings, including signs of authorial intrusion. Like Nabokov's novels, Cronenberg's films focus not so much on the relation between one character to another but between the 'author' and the 'reader'. The effect of this for both Nabokov and Cronenberg is not only to 'assert the fictionality of a text, but also serve to unmask overworked clichés, literary conventions, and conditioned reader responses'.[23]

Nabokov and Cronenberg also share a drive towards erasure so that a film like *Crash* 'seems to fold back on itself'.[24] Like Roquentin's ambiguous embracing of art at the close of Sartre's *Nausea* (1938), the ambiguous ending of *eXistenZ* and the circularity of *Crash*'s closing mantra of 'Maybe the next one...' portray art as solving the problems of life only in terms of standing outside it, providing a temporary release from its difficulties but ultimately evading, rather than resolving, its inherent paradoxes. Cronenberg's ambiguous codas suggest an agreement with Sartre's declaration that 'no man who undertakes a work of literature or philosophy ever finishes'.[25] Like *Wes Craven's New Nightmare* (Wes Craven, 1994), Cronenberg's *Naked Lunch* and *eXistenZ* show the writing of the script at the same time as embodying its expression, which, in the previous chapter, I termed a 'centrifugal' structure – that eddies towards a nodal point.

However, Cronenberg's relation to de Sade's position of final erasure, is more contradictory. Jane Gallop cites de Sade's will in full, which does not end with annihilation but a reference to 'the small number of those who did try to love me up to the last moment'.[26] As she notes, 'one cannot deny *autrui* (other people) and then make exceptions for a few close friends', undercutting a pose of apparent nihilism.[27] The tension that exists in de Sade's work between an apparent embracing of negativity and the desire to be read (he was distraught at the loss of one of his books in prison) is reflected in the book and film of *Crash*, which appear to reject much of the morality of the world, but both Ballard and Cronenberg still want their work to be available and experienced by the public.[28]

Cronenberg's films and interviews betray a desire for visibility and appreciation, which undercuts any attempt to see his works as rebellious or cataclysmic. What is perhaps surprising in studying Cronenberg is not that he rejects the fairly simplistic view of critics like Robin Wood, who have labelled him as reactionary, but that he should appear to need the approval of humanist critics at all. In discussing the commercial failure of *Videodrome*, Cronenberg either naturally thinks in literary parallels or pretentiously aligns himself with established writers of the literary canon: 'when I studied American literature, it really struck me how all the great American writers of the eighteenth, nineteenth, and twentieth century died in despair. Whitman, Melville, Hawthorne, Poe'.[29] He refers to the Romantic cliché of a starving artist, unloved and unappreciated by his contemporaries, giving Kafka as an example of an artist who only received a widespread readership after his death.[30]

In both *Naked Lunch* and *Crash*, Cronenberg makes a linear and heterosexual film, from literary material that is fragmented in nature and homosexual in orientation. He is not attempting changes in form like Burroughs' cut-up experiments but subverts expectations *within* film forms, partly by adopting features from unexpected generic areas, such as the opening of *Crash* from pornographic narratives, but more substantially from his interpretation of previous literary texts. This can be as obvious as the allusion to Philip K. Dick's 'Perky Pat' in *eXistenZ* or the borrowing of scenes almost wholesale from Ballard, such as the hanger scene in *Crash* originally in *The Kindness of Women* (1991) or the parrot cage scene in Cronenberg's *Naked Lunch* which appropriates imagery directly from Burroughs' *Queer* (1985) and *The Western Lands* (1987).

Burroughs *follows through* with his wish to 'rub out the word' but for all his admiration for Burroughs, Cronenberg cannot bring himself to produce a film about nothing.[31] Brion Gysin describes the book he produced with Burroughs, *The Third Mind* (1978) as 'the negation of the book as such – or at least the representation of that negation'.[32] However, Cronenberg cannot negate the book without erasing the author, which is something he cannot bring himself to do when there is such a strong contrary impulse in his work to valorize, privilege and make visible what he would ideally wish to be, the writer. In *Exterminator!* (1979) Burroughs acknowledges the difficulty of severing the link between writers and their material, words: 'how many of you can forget you were ever...a writer, leave everything you ever thought and did and said behind and walk right out of the film'.[33] Although at the end of *eXistenZ*, Cronenberg adopts the Nabokovian motif of cancelling his characters and problematizing the nature of his medium, in other films, notably *Naked Lunch*, he seems unwilling or unable to forget his literary aspirations. It is striking quite how often Cronenberg answers the first question in interviews about his latest film with a reference to literature, as if he represents de Quincey's notion of the human brain as a palimpsest, unable to erase all previous experience – here of a literary variety. Perhaps though this should not be seen in a negative sense. Like Borges' character Menard, it could be said that he '(perhaps without wanting to) has enriched, by means of a new technique, the halting and rudimentary art of reading: this new technique is that of the deliberate anachronism' (think of the removal of contemporary time markers in *Crash* and *eXistenZ*) 'and the erroneous attribution' (reflected in the misappropriation of poetry in *Videodrome*).[34]

Nabokov, Ballard and Burroughs all share one overarching link with Cronenberg. In *Pnin* (1960), Joan Clements refers to an unnamed author (possibly Nabokov) who is trying 'practically in all his novels...to express the fantastic recurrence of certain situations'.[35] Iain Sinclair asserts that for Ballard, 'all the texts (short stories, novels, reviews, essays) are part of one project', and similarly Barry Miles describes how Burroughs' 'desire continually to update his books' is in keeping with Burroughs' statement that his work 'constitutes one long book'.[36] In 1983 Cronenberg asserts, 'I actually think that is the way the world works, that we are in fact fumbling around in the dark. Nobody's in control. There is only the appearance of control...'[37] Seventeen years later, this is echoed by Ted Pikul in *eXistenZ*: 'We're both stumbling around together in this unformed world whose rules and objectives are largely unknown, seemingly indecipherable or even possibly non-existent'. In rejecting the notion that repetition is concomitant with a poverty of imagination, Cronenberg declares 'but what about the Goldberg Variations? In music, the idea of variations on the theme is very well understood'.[38] This study has found that beneath apparently empty repetition lies a serious-minded attempt by Cronenberg to show what he sees as an inherent tendency in language to evacuate meaning and erase itself.

However, this endeavour is fatally flawed by Cronenberg's inability to believe in the death of the author. The allusive and determinedly literary quality of his films evoke David Bordwell's attempts to define the art film genre, in which 'a body of work linked by an authorial signature encourages viewers to read each film as a chapter of an oeuvre'.[39] On being asked whether 'all of your movies together are like a biography', Cronenberg replied, 'well, they should be. They're almost like chapters in an ongoing book'.[40] Ultimately, 'Cronenberg is revealed, at last, as the very paradigm of the author: the man who produces books without having to write them'.[41]

Notes

1. David Cronenberg and J. G. Ballard: Set for Collision', (http://www.indexon censorship.org/issue397/cronenberg.htm), p. 3.
2. Patrick McGrath, *Dr Haggard's Disease* (New York: Vintage, 1993), p. 65.
3. Geoffrey Wagner, *The Novel and the Cinema* (Rutherford, NJ: Farleigh Dickinson Press, 1975), p. 222; cited in Brian McFarlane, *Novel to Film: An Introduction to the Theory of Adaptation* (Oxford: Oxford University Press, 1996), p. 10 and p. 226.
4. Jill McGreal, 'Body Work', A Review of Chris Rodley's *Cronenberg on Cronenberg*, *Sight & Sound* 2: 1 (London: BFI, May 1992), p. 40.
5. Linda Kauffman, 'David Cronenberg's Surreal Abjection', in *Bad Girls and Sick Boys: Fantasies in Contemporary Art and Culture* (Berkeley; Los Angeles; London: University of California Press, 1998), p. 249. Her comments are repeated verbatim in her review/article 'American Psycho', *Film Quarterly*, vol. 54, no. 2 (winter 2000-2001), pp. 42.
6. David Cronenberg cited in David Breskin, *Inner Views: Filmmakers in Conversation* (London; Boston: Faber & Faber, 1992), p. 220.
7. Judith Halberstam and Ira Livingston (eds.), 'Introduction', *Posthuman Bodies* (Bloomington: Indiana University Press, 1995), p. 12.
8. Leslie Fiedler, 'The New Mutants', Partisan Review 32 (1965), p. 517.
9. Rowe, Michael. 'A New Level of *eXistenZ*', Fangoria 181 (April, 1999), p. 74.
10. Harold Bloom, *The Anxiety of Influence* (New York, Guildford; Oxford: Oxford University Press, 1973), p. 14.
11. Eve Kosofsky Sedgwick, *Between Men: English Literature and Male Homosocial Desire* (New York: Columbia University Press, 1985), p. 26.
12. Judith Butler, 'Imitation and Gender Insubordination', in Diana Fuss (ed.), *Inside/out: Lesbian Theories, Gay Theories* (New York; London: Routledge, 1991), p. 21.
13. Bloom, op. cit., p. 14.
14. Ibid., p. 16.
15. Chris Rodley (ed.), *Cronenberg on Cronenberg* (London: Faber and Faber, 1992), p. 162.
16. Serge Grünberg, 'Sur les terres de Cronenberg', *Cahiers du Cinéma* 446 (July/August, 1991), p. 38 [in French].

17. William Beard, "Insect Poetics: Cronenberg's *Naked Lunch*", *Canadien Revue of Comparative Literature/Revue Canadienne de Littérature Comparée* 23:3 (September 1996), p. 846.
18. Bloom, op. cit., p. 15.
19. Elaine Scarry, *The Body in Pain: The Making and Unmaking of the World* (New York; Oxford: Oxford University Press, 1985), p. 9.
20. William Cooper, 'Despair', *The Listener*, 11 August, 1966; cited in Norman Page (ed.), *Nabokov: The Critical Heritage* (London: Routledge & Kegan Paul, 1982), p. 196.
21. J. G. Ballard, *Cocaine Nights* (Counterpoint Press, 1998), pp. 34-35.
22. P. N. Furbank, *Encounter*, January 1965, 84, 86; cited in Page, op. cit., p. 164.
23. Stephen Jan Parker, *Understanding Vladimir Nabokov* (Columbia: University of South Carolina Press, 1987), p. 17.
24. Michael Grant, 'That Guy's Gotta See Us!', unpublished response to Marq Smith, 'Wound envy: touching Cronenberg's *Crash*', *Screen* 40:2 (summer 1999), pp. 193–202, p. 5.
25. Ibid., p. 19.
26. Marquis de Sade cited in Jane Gallop, *Intersections: A Reading of Sade with Bataille, Blanchot, and Klossowski* (Lincoln, Nebraska; London: University of Nebraska Press, 1981), p. 13.
27. Ibid., p. 14.
28. See Annette Kuhn, '*Crash* and film censorship in the UK', *Screen* 40:4 (winter, 1999), pp. 446–450.
29. David Cronenberg in Chris Rodley (ed.), op. cit., p. 103.
30. David Cronenberg cited in David Breskin, op. cit., p. 229.
31. Brion Gysin cited in Mottram, op. cit., p. 195.
32. Brion Gysin in William S. Burroughs and Brion Gysin, *The Third Mind* (London: Viking Press, 1978), p. 18.
33. William Burroughs, *Exterminator!* (London: Calder, 1984) cited in Eric Mottram, *William Burroughs: The Algebra of Need* (London: Marion Boyars Publications Ltd, 1977), p. 222.
34. See Jorges Luis Borges, "Pierre Menard, Author of the *Quixote*", in *Labyrinths: Selected Stories and Other Writings* (New York: New Directions, 1964, p. 71.
35. Vladimir Nabokov, *Pnin* (New York; Harmondsworth: Penguin Books, 1960), p. 134.
36. See Iain Sinclair, *Crash* (London: BFI Modern Classics, 1999), p. 49 and Barry Miles, *William Burroughs: El Hombre Invisible* (London: Virgin Books, 1992), p. 96. See 'The Last European Interview', with Philippe Mikriammos, *Review of Contemporary Fiction* 4:1 (spring 1984), pp. 12–18; cited in Hibbard (ed.), *Conversations with William S. Burroughs* (Jackson: University Press of Mississippi, 1999), p. 82.
37. David Cronenberg, 'The Interview', an interview with David Cronenberg conducted by William Beard and Piers Handling in Piers Handling (ed.), *The Shape of Rage: The Films of David Cronenberg*, (Toronto: Academy of Canadian Cinema, 1983; New York: New York Zoetrope Inc., 1983), p. 187.
38. 'Interview with Cronenberg', (http://www.flf.com/crash/cmp/cronenberg-interview.html), p. 1.
39. David Bordwell, *Narration in the Fiction Film* (New York; London: Routledge, 1985), p. 211.
40. David Cronenberg, (http://www.splicedonline.com/features/cronenberg/html), p. 9.
41. Iain Sinclair, op. cit., p. 20.